TAYLORED CITIZENSHIP

TAYLORED CITIZENSHIP

State Institutions and Subjectivity

Char Roone Miller

Westport, Connecticut
London

Library of Congress Cataloging-in-Publication Data

Miller, Char Roone.
    Taylored citizenship : state institutions and subjectivity / Char Roone Miller.
    p. cm.
    Includes bibliographical references and index.
    ISBN 0-275-97223-2 (alk. paper)
    1. Consensus (Social sciences)—United States—History—20th century.
2. Citizenship—United States—History—20th century. 3. Political socialization—
United States—History—20th century. I. Title.
JC328.2.M55 2002
306.2'0973—dc21   2001021174

British Library Cataloguing in Publication Data is available.

Copyright © 2002 by Char Roone Miller

All rights reserved. No portion of this book may be
reproduced, by any process or technique, without the
express written consent of the publisher.

Library of Congress Catalog Card Number: 2001021174
ISBN: 0-275-97223-2

First published in 2002

Praeger Publishers, 88 Post Road West, Westport, CT 06881
An imprint of Greenwood Publishing Group, Inc.
www.praeger.com

Printed in the United States of America

The paper used in this book complies with the
Permanent Paper Standard issued by the National
Information Standards Organization (Z39.48-1984).

10 9 8 7 6 5 4 3 2 1

Every reasonable effort has been made to trace the owners of copyright materials in this book, but in some instances this has proven impossible. The author and publisher will be glad to receive information leading to more complete acknowledgments in subsequent printings of the book and in the meantime extend their apologies for any omissions.

For My Family

Many people deserve thanks upon the completion of this project. I would specifically like to mention Matt Crenson, Dick Flathman, Bill Connolly, Sue Hemberger, J. Woodford Howard, Kirstie McClure, J.G.A. Pocock, Dorothy Ross, Ron Walters, David Bernell, Margaret Brassil, Douglas Dow, John Forren, Doug Harris, Anthony Lang, Dale Miller, Louvena Miller, Darrell Leslie, Jo Leslie, and Jana Leslie-Miller. Thank you.

Contents

I.	**Introduction**	1
1.	National Institutions and Citizenship	3
II.	**Basic Training: The Military and the Construction of American Subjectivity**	27
2.	"Pick Up a Pig and Walk": The U.S. Military's Early Adoption of Systems of Management	29
3.	"The Ultimate Strength of the Army": Managerial Bureaucracy in a Nation at War	43
4.	Tests and Nuts: Testing and the Organization of Citizens	61
5.	A "Different Breed of Cat": Military Intelligence and Intellect Militant	81
III.	**Harmonious Curriculums: Education and the Nation-State**	97
6.	Industrial Subjects: Education and Efficiency	99
7.	Expansive Perceptions: Pluralism and American Education	113
8.	"Harness the Potential": World War II and the Organization of Education	131

9. "Trying to Get Hold of the Mental Process": Education, Mental Hygiene, and Individualism 151

IV. Conclusion 167

10. Discipline and Citizen 169

Bibliography 179

Index 203

Part I

Introduction

Chapter 1

National Institutions and Citizenship

> When "morals decay" those men emerge whom one calls tyrants: they are the precursors and as it were the precocious harbingers of *individuals*. Only a little while later this fruit of fruits hangs yellow and mellow from the tree of a people—and the tree existed only for the sake of these fruits.
> —Friedrich Nietzsche, *The Gay Science*,
> Preface for the second edition

Government, it is often said, rests on the consent of the governed. This book examines an establishment and maintenance of American consent in the twentieth century. Government, in this usage, means more than state institutions, and is intended to suggest the rules and powers that are generally accepted by the governed, as well as the ways that state institutions create consent.[1] *Taylored Citizenship* examines the roles state institutions played in the creation of the governed's consent to bureaucratic powers of government; specifically, the part discipline played in creating consent, control, and notions of individualism.

"One might well," Max Weber wrote, "define the concept of nation in the following way: a nation is a community of sentiment which would adequately manifest itself in a state of its own; hence, a nation is a community which normally tends to produce a state of its own."[2] In addition, one might well add, this state normally tends to produce a nation and citizen of its own—

not, of course, with complete success. State institutions attempt to construct how citizens understand their proper roles in society and how they think of themselves. *Taylored Citizenship* explores the roles of military service and public education in constructing consent for bureaucratic authority and examines the contributions to American political subjectivity made by state institutions.

An examination of the ways state institutions construct nationalism and citizenship has never been more consequential than today, when we have an awareness of both the dangers of national identities and the dangers of the loss of national identities. We know and fear the extreme powers nation-states wield to make people fight, die, kill, work, and inflict harm or order upon others. We have also witnessed televised terrors from Bosnia-Herzegovina, a possible consequence of the loss of a national identity in favor of alternative ethnic identities. At the same time, class identities could usefully check the power of international capitalism, which wreaks its own terrors in the sweatshops of Saipan, San Juan, and Los Angeles, and whose pollutants reek with no respect to national boundaries. Significant stakes rise in negotiating nationalism's territory.

More modestly, recent American elections have turned on questions of the proper roles of government and the proper extent of state power, often revealing surprising rifts in thought about nations and states. Republicans (and Democrats) argue strenuously that the state has become too large and intrusive while nationalism has become too weak; in effect, reducing the power of state institutions even as they increase an intellectual dependence on the nation. They attempt to reduce the size of welfare institutions, yet complain of the attention that "multiculturalists" pay to non-national identities and denigrate many cross-border identities. The relationship between identity and the state demands much closer examination by political scientists.

In order to examine the roles some state institutions played in constructing citizenship and nationalism during the twentieth century, this book explores two important institutions of the state—the military and schools—with a focus on the roles these institutions performed in organizing the political imaginations of the populace during World War II. This historical moment exemplifies the application of social organization associated with industry and bureaucracy to the nation, in a large-scale attempt to reorganize the nation for the productive power necessary to win the war. Examining these two "branches" of government highlights powers of the state directly related to constructions of consent, legitimacy, and political identity, particularly the powers and authorities associated with scientific management or Taylorism. Focusing on these elements of state power, furthermore, allows for a recontextualization of the powers of government (i.e., this study emphasizes the state's roles in management, administration, and consolidation of social knowledge). This focus helps expose elements in our own contemporary acceptance of state power, specifically the acceptance of bureaucratically and nationally given goals and valuations of personal behavior, action, and thought.

In this analysis, I argue three claims. First, the early twentieth century witnessed the growth of a government with distinctive demands for consent. Older political and religious authority weakened or transformed in comparison with new forms of industrial authority.[3] This new government relied on forms of power and coercion developed during industrialization, mostly arranged to order workers within bureaucratic authority.

Both military service and public education consolidated bureaucratic authority. That is, they worked to ensure the continued legitimacy of, to use Max Weber's phrase, bureaucratic domination.[4] Domination in Weber's usage was integrally related to the establishment and maintenance of administrative authority. "Every domination both expresses itself and functions through administration. Every administration, on the other hand, needs domination, because it is always necessary that some powers of command be in the hands of somebody."[5] Both branches relied on increased administrative power and reciprocally consolidated administrative power. The growth of the state's involvement (and non-state involvement) in administrative domination stands as a challenge to overly simple notions of democracy. Such extensive authority and power confounds the possibilities of citizens and subjects having control over their own lives. Weber also recognized the changes in the meaning of democracy necessary to establish administrative domination. "As soon as mass administration is involved, the meaning of democracy changes so radically that it no longer makes sense for the sociologist to ascribe to the term the same meaning as in the case discussed so far."[6] Within the new systems of mass administration, democracy acquired new meanings that accommodated the powers of domination manufactured by the bureaucratic systems of domination, whether of business, industry, or state. This book explores democracy's accommodations with the hopeful assumption that making domination more apparent opens it up to greater scrutiny and criticism, disrupts settled formulations of citizenship and politics, and suggests alternative formulations that could enrich and enliven political life.

Second, these state institutions helped to centralize the political imaginations of individuals and groups within the nation-state, thus, in effect, assimilating alternative political communities within the forces of nationalism. However, this assimilation did not necessarily destroy differences, but rather, it was often an assimilation in which the state became the recognizer of difference.

The military, for example, attempted to defer and perhaps annihilate alternative communities of value and recognition in favor of a national identity through discipline, rigorous regimentation, and ritual. This, in effect, produced a subjectivity with few alternatives, and one more inclined to accept the valuations of the state's military system. Systems of education, alternatively, did not destroy earlier non-state identities so much as turn them into elements of a national identity in a manner modeled on industrial divisions of labor. Education during World War II validated alternative communities and identities through their different contributions to the nation-state.

Third, I argue that this particular tightening of national and administrative authority did not have solely repressive and restrictive consequences. This authority produced new forms of resistance and, more significantly, important possibilities for human freedom and autonomy. For example, the military deconstructed many notions of race, family, community, ethnicity, and religion in its attempt to build better soldiers. By disentangling the subjectivity of so many (male) citizens from earlier forms of home and community, the military nationalized a social alienation that accommodated new possibilities for individualism and difference. Citizens to a much less degree had to submit to the rules and demands of non-state identities and communities.

The application of Taylorism, furthermore, through government and industry, standardized bodies, behavior, and beliefs to the point in which individualism had to be radically reimagined; perhaps in this way the state served as a precocious harbinger of individuals. The individualism produced as the fruit of this tree was more self-sufficient than ever before and more unpredictable. The self became more mysterious and less orderly. If this individualism is to have much weight, it must be the precursor of a self transformed in terms of demands for recognition. The need for recognition, particularly as experienced from the nation, poses one of the most salient problems for studies of citizenship. Which is more politically efficacious: strong identification and demand for recognition from the nation, or subjectivity with little need for national recognition and weaker identification? (To put the question starkly.) I argue that, while not without liability, the deconstruction of national identity and national goals offers quite important possibilities for human freedom that must be explored. These possibilities enable conceptions of belonging (greatly weakened, no doubt) that are more lively in addressing administrative power and possibly non-national power. While in some ways strengthened by the discipline of state institutions, the process of identification was also changed in ways that enhanced individualism.

Deconstruction of national identity also makes identification a more conscious act with more possibilities, although this is a prospect not without risks. If citizens are less connected to imagined communities, such as the nation, and in less need of outside recognition, citizens possibly lose political strength against such powerful institutions as multinational corporations.[7] J.G.A. Pocock, for example, worries that

when a world of persons, actions, and things becomes a world of persons, actions, and linguistic or electronic constructs that have no authors, it clearly becomes much easier for the things—grown much more powerful because they are no longer real—to multiply and take charge, controlling, and determining persons and actions that no longer control, determine, or even produce them.[8]

There is resignation in Pocock's account, but there is also nostalgia for firmer connections between subjects and their state—connections somewhat more beyond the choice or consent of the citizen. This firmer connection grounds the meaning of citizenship; that is, it imagines a firmer ground to stand on but also grounds it by making it less mobile. I argue that the disentanglements and denaturalizations enacted on the citizen by the institutions of the state during the twentieth century could make citizenship a concept more able to deal with the political questions of the postmodern age, including the exploitation of non-Americans by American companies, environmental destruction of non-American land by Americans, and what Hannah Arendt has called the defining political question of this century—the political position of refugees and the stateless. These are questions that probe at the boundaries of imagined communities and suggest the value in multiple and less fitted identities.

In furthering such an examination, this book applies the attention of recent citizenship and nationalism studies to studies of institutions. Contemporary studies of citizenship have focused on the creation within the citizen of notions of legitimacy and identity. This has typically meant the explanation of textual productions of legitimacy and identity. For example, Priscilla Wald examines the "national narratives of identity [that] seek to harness the anxiety surrounding questions of personhood." For Wald, these national narratives fail to fit individuals and produce a sense of estrangement that reveals the meanings of citizenship.[9] Wald's attention to narrative forms is widely shared by recent studies of citizenship and follows the attention of Benedict Anderson and Walter Benjamin in focusing upon the roles of books, movies, and even landscapes in allowing people to imagine communities. Anderson's attention to novels, newspapers, and songs occurs within shifting interpretations of Marx, specifically in the post-Benjamin attempt to conceive of an intellectual material society and the constitutive material of consciousness.[10]

In a studied avoidance of positioning the economic structure as the determinative factor of society, Benjamin replaced the Marxist focus on the materialist means of production with an attention to intellectual artifacts as the product of the means of artistic production. But unlike much of the work that relies on him, Benjamin also suggested the textual aspects of all parts of life, possibly including state institutions. "Every expression of human mental life can be understood as a kind of language, and this understanding, in the manner of a true method, everywhere raises new questions," he wrote in "On Language as Such and on the Language of Man."[11] State institutions also express human mental life, and certainly pose new questions, and can be examined as constitutive elements of the mental landscape without giving them determinative power.

Recent institutional studies explore institutional actions and actors but ignore some of the intellectual consequences of these institutions, such as the role state institutions play in the creation of citizens' ideas of legitimate authority. Concerning state institutions, Theda Skocpol wrote,

> The structure of those organizations, their place within the state apparatus as a whole, and their linkages to class forces and to politically mobilized groups in society are all important issues for the analysis of states in revolutionary situations, actual or potential. Such an analytic focus seems certain to prove more fruitful than any focus primarily or exclusively upon political legitimation.[12]

But political legitimation for states in and out of revolutionary situations is a concern and a product of state action.

With this focus, Skocpol distinguishes her approach from some elements of Weber, particularly Weber's interest in legitimacy.[13] "Yet not only does an organizational, realist perspective on the state entail differences from Marxist approaches, it also contrasts with non-Marxist approaches that treat the *legitimacy* of political authorities as an important explanatory concept."[14] This reluctance to examine questions of legitimacy and consent is based on the fact that many states remain in power with large majorities substantially dissatisfied; at the time of the publication of *States and Social Revolutions*, South Africa was the perfect example. If the state retains control of major systems of coercion, police, and military, it simply does not matter, according to Skocpol, that they may be unpopular. While states do remain in power through the monopolization, or at least domination, of violent force there are other, more stable ways to maintain a state. To remove consent from examination is to avoid the very significant question of the ways that the state maintains itself through construction of its citizens.

This examination of the roles of state institutions in constructing elements of citizenship views the rituals and disciplines of these institutions as a way to examine some of the compelling aspects of Michel Foucault's studies of institutions. By focusing on the role of Frederick Winslow Taylor's theories of management, the role of institutional discipline in producing political consciousness can be more fully examined. Taylor's theories exploited a wide social acceptance of administrative authority and promoted specific methods of power. Taylor's methods also supply an insightful position from which to observe the construction by the state of elements of citizenship that played an important role in the maintenance of state legitimacy in the late twentieth century; not, of course, the only position. There are many possible positions from which to examine the trends and transformations of the twentieth century that could aid the examiner in affirming a more powerful individualism or alternative communities. This study of the influence of methods of management on conceptions of citizenship allows for a political engagement with elements of the twentieth century that apparently had highly socializing and controlling consequences, and allows an exploration of the ways that these changes could also offer possibilities for individualism and political action.

Discipline incubates in war. "The discipline of the army," Max Weber wrote, "gives birth to all discipline."[15] In elaboration of Weber's claim, I argue in Chapters 2–5 that the military's systems of administration and discipline in World War II trained citizens into subjectivities of obedience to those in hierarchical and bureaucratic positions of authority (by way of exploring the intellectual connection between powers of the nation-state and industrial capital).[16] This was an obedience predicated on the reduced power of earlier governors—local communities, family ties, ethnic ties, and sexual orders—and the transformation of earlier ways of relating to those governors.[17] Furthermore, bureaucratic structures of the military aided in the reconstruction of individual subjectivity, harmonizing conceptions of the individual in society to the American system of industrial nationalism, even as the American political consciousness became attuned to bureaucratic authority, also opening powerful individualist and relativist possibilities. "Discipline 'makes' individuals," claimed Foucault: "it is the specific technique of a power that regards individuals both as objects and as instruments of its exercise."[18] Perhaps Foucault is correct, and discipline produces individualist possibilities; perhaps, as Nietzsche suggested, Caesar understands the rights of the individual, advocates the individual, and even abets individual morality.

The military's adoption of business discipline involved three significant factors. First, military discipline removed recruits from existing communities of meaning and belonging, including, race, ethnicity, religion, and region. Removing people from earlier imagined communities freed them from other governors but made them more dependent on the nation-state for rules governing their lives.

Second, military discipline contributed to a distinctive understanding of order. It solidified a social organization, understood as a collection of different types of people performing roles they were differently suited to perform.[19] This bureaucratization relied on and contributed to the belief in a world ordered according to employable skills. During World War I, differences were widely believed to be liabilities to national identity. However, during World War II, differences became elements of a national system that worked together for the nation in a model borrowed from models of industrial divisions of labor.[20] Those well suited to move pig iron would eventually find their proper place hauling pig iron, while those suited to the scientific study of the movement of pig iron would find their place doing that. This faith camouflaged the politics of bureaucratic capitalism behind the artificial naturalism of work and order but, remarkably, it also contributed a level of relativism to the different identities and actions that people performed. That is, a myriad of differences became equally necessary if the United States and its industries were to function.

Finally, the soil the military tilled possibly became more fertile for a drastic individualism. Given the power of bureaucracy and the nation-state to order and value lives and differences this may seem overly optimistic, but perhaps the possibility of individualism and mobility suggested by the military's power to separate men from previous communities opened into a greater diversity. Perhaps Foucault's claim for the role of discipline in creating individuals can be understood by examining the U.S. military in World War II. In this way the military midwifed a possible decay in discipline. The military's attention to the detailed movements of the body also made the facts of that body less individual and more standardized. The false, slow, and useless movements that the military (and Taylorism) tried to erase further removed soldiers' feelings of individualism in the performance of a task, thereby making the action more of a performance and less of an action of the self. This alienation from one's own individual action opened up a secret, hidden self, scarcely elaborated in action and capable of possessing unseen motivations and desires. In essence, it introduced a self with a greater distance from the demands for recognition and harmony.

Military discipline does reveal large general social changes—perhaps too well—but typically it is understood to be a short-term program. Education displayed many of the same general tendencies. For example, in 1931, Charles Merriam predicted that instantaneous methods of national and international indoctrination were, like basic training, short-term, emergency, measures; long-term social stability would be built, he claimed, on education, particularly education in the social sciences.

The more frantic and impatient system of instantaneous indoctrination will perhaps be reserved for special and critical situations akin to military conscription in times of war; and the more comprehensive and mature systems of training in social science, based on the fundamentals of physical and mental health, will take their place. It is to be expected that provincial or propagandist history, heavy civic indoctrination, and traditional symbolism will decline in amount and importance as the more systematic and scientific systems of instruction in social science appear in the schools, and with competent directing personnel, begin to make themselves felt in the educational system of various states of the world.[21]

Indeed, as education systems became more systematic, scientific, and state-managed, they became some of the state's most powerful institutions; admittedly, in the United States, an institution remarkably diverse in institutional terms but with significant harmony in national objectives. Part III of this book primarily examines the influence American systems of education had on notions of individualism, pluralism, and authority before and during World War II.

Chapter 6 considers the influence of Taylorite scientific management on education—an influence that contributed to popular conceptions of individualism and authority. Chapter 7 examines the promotion of national unity through the alignment of racial and other differences. Chapter 8 examines the orientation of education to achieve national and industrial goals. This role included the use of school buildings for registration and, more fundamentally, the construction of a system of value deferment that placed the nation securely in the role of valuer and legitimizer. After this examination of the power that the war exerted to nationalize the goals of education, Chapter 9 explores the educator's reach to the desires of students to learn, concluding with education's contribution to a new understanding of subjectivity.

Debates over the roles of education in social control, socialization, and democracy have centered around four approaches. First, setting the stage for much of the recent debate over education, conservative critics have argued that education has failed in teaching values to students. Attempts, they maintain, at making education more democratic have only succeeded in opening the mind too much, exposing it to a dangerous relativism. As part of the Reagan-Bush Conservative front, these critics defended the privileges of the students at the best institutions to study the so-called great books, concurrently asserting the value of the increasing economic specialization of the majority of students whose training should be directed toward placing them in the workforce.[22] Second, many liberals in response to the claims of these conservatives have asserted the democratic promise of equal education. They routinely praise the role of the state in furthering a standardized education for all American children and adults, or bemoan the fact that the equalization of education has not done all that it should to democratize the United States. Third, a much smaller group of scholars has critiqued education as a branch of state power. Accounts, often reliant on Marxist descriptions of state power, have suggested that education is a mechanism for the maintenance of capitalism.[23] Fourth, recent critics of education suggest that all of these approaches miss the conflicted nature of education, downplaying, on the one hand, the disciplinary aspects of education and the awareness that education makes political subjects that are obedient to forms of capitalism, while on the other hand ignoring the room for maneuver within systems of education.[24]

This project has a great deal in common with the latter group, particularly in its attention to the conflicted aspects of education as forms of state power and institutions of subjectivity construction. While it critically engages with the roles of education in producing subjectivity closely attuned to the needs and demands of authoritative capitalism and nationalism, it also explores the elements of educational institutions that contributed to new notions of freedom and autonomy. It is this dialectical movement that offers the most valuable parts of this book, suggesting elements of individualism and self-development that need greater exploration, even as it critiques and exposes some of the coercive elements of education.

World War II increased the already substantial pressures on education to function efficiently and more significantly to create efficient workers. This attempt to step-up the productive power of schools did so in the interest of the nation. Taylorite methods figured prominently in this attempt in several ways: through the organization of education, the production of efficient students, and the application of elements of Taylorite standardization to the intellectual order of students.

Some of the more influential education programs applied to students also consolidated the recognition power of the nation. "Intercultural" education taught children the importance of racial, ethnic, and religious differences pulling together for America, strengthening the demand for the recognition of differences and consolidating that recognition in the nation-state. National efficiency, order, and organization served as goals for a well-organized system of education.

Education did more than simply construct good subjects; in some ways, it nourished new possibilities for the subjectivity of citizens. The disciplines applied to students in classrooms, particularly the attempts to construct desires for education within students, abetted a reformulation of individualism that made the individual more mysterious and more radically distinct from others.

SOCIAL DISCIPLINE

Social discipline in World War II consisted of powers of organization, information, and modification. Elements behind the military's consolidation of these powers can be seen in the powerful influence of theories of industrial management. The military in World War II extensively elaborated on the powers of scientific management, including: (1) consolidation of decision-making power within administrative bureaucracies, (2) the collection of data for the management of work and production, and (3) the organization of group consciousness in such a way so as to organize difference around common interests or, more succinctly, powers of organization, information, and modification.

The elements of power and authority symbolized by the name of Frederick Taylor include the shift of decision-making and work-organizing power from the workers who performed the tasks to a class of managers. This shift substantially removed the knowledge of production from the workers. Managers broke up the task of production into many different elements, usually into the simplest steps possible, making the workers who performed these tasks more easily replaceable. Taylorite consultants consolidated the power of managers through the use of scientific studies of the time it took workers to perform particular steps, giving managers clear time guidelines for determining production schedules. Taylor claimed, in his most significant personal contribution to theories of social management, that by dealing with workers individually, managers could slowly change worker's consciousness of their interests.[25] Workers would eventually, Taylor argued, begin to believe that their interests were the same as the managers—the fastest, most *efficient* production possible.

The military greatly extended the power of bureaucratic authority and organization. It taught people who came within its system the authority of bureaucratic hierarchy at a moment when this system of authority was not as firmly settled as it would be later.[26] Granted, there were other teachers of this significant twentieth-century lesson, but the military brought to bear an exceptionally powerful pedagogy.

One tool in particular came of age during World War II: information. The military began extensive testing of recruits. The physical capacities and talents of recruits were opened to far-reaching scrutiny. Significantly, the mental capacities and abilities of recruits also became the focus of scientific scrutiny. One of the most important aspects of the industrial process was to place people into the job for which they were physically best suited. Basic training disciplined bodies, while sorting, modifying, controlling, and, in part, disciplining the mind.

Importantly, the military categorized and organized physical "skills" and productive attributes of the recruit's "body," and also began attitude studies and attitude modification. It was not enough to control the physical bodies of subjects; the subjects' intellectual order also had to be assured. In fact, control of the physical body functioned to adjust the subject's intellectual order. The military engaged in the physical and mental modification of troops. Physical discipline helped the attitudinal modification but did not ensure it. The military began elaborate studies of the intellectual status of recruits and institutional systems of attitude and belief modification. The military's attention to the thoughts and feelings of personnel contributed both to the construction of the idea of a social body and to the construction of an individualism mysteriously veiled by language and even thought.

Beginning with an examination of the background of the military's appropriation of Taylor's theories of management, Part II examines three elements of Taylorism within military institutions. These three elements are often described as the three theorems of Taylorism.[27] Chapter 2 sets the necessary background, Chapter 3 examines the expansion of military bureaucracy, and Chapter 4 examines the production of information, particularly information gathered during induction, that was to guide administrators. Finally, Chapter 5 surveys the extensive work that the military's adoption of Taylor's methods did to modify the social world for many male Americans.

SCIENTIFIC MANAGEMENT

The adoption of the methods of management associated with Frederick Taylor in military and educational institutions contributed greatly to the consolidation of the willingness of citizens to accept the rule of managers. The state utilized elements and understandings from the managerial movements prominent in early-twentieth-century business. Specifically, government moved more substantially into the business of knowledge consolidation, social organization, research, and modification of interests, a transformation that turned the citizen increasingly into an object of management. These four distinct elements of early-twentieth-century management were most clearly elaborated by Taylor, a particularly insightful explicator of social ideas concerning industrial government and management. "More than any other single person," wrote William Akin, "Taylor provided the conceptual framework for the rationalization of work in the twentieth century."[28] Anson Rabinback wrote, more accurately, that "the significance of Taylorism cannot simply be judged by the number of firms that explicitly adopted his methods." Taylorism may not have been overtly adopted by a large number of firms, but Taylor did bring together into one theory diverse elements almost universally adopted by industry. "Taylor's real importance lay in the creation of the first management-oriented industrial ideology and in his ability to synthesize and promote in a coherent framework the broad changes that were already taking place piecemeal in various industries."[29] Taylor was not solely responsible for the changes that drastically altered American political culture, but he did bring together in one place a consistent account of those changes.

The outline of Taylor's biography is fairly well known.[30] Born into a middle-class family from the outskirts of Philadelphia, he was the youngest of eleven children.[31] At sixteen he was sent to Phillips Exeter Academy, in preparation for Harvard University.[32] After passing his Harvard entrance examinations he suffered from eyestrain, which precluded his attendance there. On the advice of eye doctors, he went to work instead for a small machine shop in Philadelphia, where he learned the trades of patternmaker and machinist, after which he took a position at the Midvale Steel Works in 1878. It was here that he eventually became foreman of the machine shop, with expert knowledge of the ways of the work floor. He promptly set out to destroy those ways, particularly the "soldiering" of labor. That is, Taylor knew that workers tended to do much less work than they could really produce and he wanted to increase their productive capacity. Workers resisted, but after three years Taylor seems to have succeeded in raising production through constant managerial pressure. His next decade at Midvale was spent in careful, scientific study of these problems (production and worker resentment). He wanted to increase output without having to drive the workers.

Taylor worked out a system of managerial authority that shifted production knowledge from the workers to the managers. His system broke up production into very small and highly regulated steps, and required that workers obey the instructions of managers concerning these very specific steps. Taylor determined these steps through careful scientific observations and comparisons of the pace at which various workers completed tasks. Taylor structured his system of management so that workers were increasingly atomized, or separated from others with similar relationships to the means of production, and given highly detailed work instructions. Workers became parts of a larger machine. This atomization was organized according to the perspective of the managers. Workers were taught that their interests were the same as the managers and the owners. This interest was the interest of efficiency and the increased productivity that resulted from it. The industrial drive toward individualism and the particularization of parts and steps meshed with other industrial elements that contributed to individualization, including the division of life into different avenues or spheres, particularly the division between work and leisure.[33]

In spite of achieving the presidency of the American Society of Mechanical Engineers in 1906, Taylor's work was still rarely known outside of the community of industrial engineers until Louis Brandeis tapped his ideas to help in the Interstate Commerce Commission (I.C.C.) hearings concerning railroad rates.[34] In 1910, Brandeis used Taylor's theories of management to argue before the I.C.C. that wage increases did not necessitate increases in railroad rates. He argued that properly administered railroads, that is, those governed according to the principles of Taylor, did not need to raise rates to increase wages. The Eastern Rate Case, as it came to be known, stimulated a great deal of interest in notions of efficiency in the following years. Taylor himself was amazed at Brandeis's ability to orchestrate a national campaign that inadvertently promoted "scientific management." "Waking up a whole country . . . I have rarely seen a new movement started with such great momentum as you have given this one," Taylor wrote to Brandeis.[35]

Brandeis, who invented the term "scientific management," wrote to Felix Frankfurter on February 27, 1911, about his work with the I.C.C., expressing his belief that scientific management exemplified the future of social order.[36]

The Commission did, I think, quite as much as they could, and rather more than I thought they would with the efficiency argument. They accepted the fundamental principles that improvements in economy and management were possible, and that they must be made before the need would be recognized. Scientific management will follow that inevitably, as President Willard's remarks have already indicated.[37]

Brandeis referred to Daniel Willard, president of the Baltimore and Ohio Railroad, who declared in response to the I.C.C. decision against granting the railroads a rate increase, "As I see it, there is only one thing for us to do—to put into effect the Brandeis greater efficiency system."[38]

In his 1947 foreword to the collected works of Taylor, Person claimed that this new technique of managing involved two major elements.

First, discovery by experiment of the best way of performing and the proper time for every operation and every component unit of an operation in the light of the state of the art, the best material, tool, machine, manipulation of tool or machine, and the best flow of work and sequence of unit operations. Second, a new division of labor as between management and workers: the assignment to management of the responsibility for discovering the best ways of performing units of operations, and the further responsibility of planning operations and actually making available at the proper time and place, and in the proper quantity, the materials, tools, instructions and other facilities required by the workers.[39]

Responsibility in this case greatly increased the power of managers at the workers' expense. Managers took over the control of the planning of work, which removed a great deal of control, as Taylor planned, from the actual workers.

Person outlined a third important aspect of Taylor's method: the change in consciousness. "The most stirring part of Taylor's testimony before the House committee," he claimed, "is that section in which he develops the thought that true Scientific Management requires a mental revolution on the parts of management and of workers."[40] This intellectual revolution would bring the perspective of management to the workers and, in this way, workers would begin to understand their interest as the same as management. "Therefore, true Scientific Management calls for a unifying point of view and a unity of interests and of efforts seldom present in a particular establishment," Person concluded. This brings many responsibilities and powers to management. "And especially must management be skilled in aiding workers to understand the purpose and meaning of Scientific Management and in maintaining their confidence in the purpose and in the management."[41]

Taylor's attempt to create new ways of thinking and acting was one of his most significant contributions to the growing science of management, and best exemplifies some of the processes by which institutions constructed citizenship. Taylor designed his system to produce the understanding and desire to be a good worker according to the needs of management. This mental revolution was not isolated to the shop floor, but extended into all realms of life. The proper arrangement of work would create the proper citizen. "The writer's observation, however, would lead him to the conclusion that most men tend to become more instead of less thrifty when they receive the proper increase for an extra hard day's work." Taylor told a Congressional Committee questioner who was concerned that increased wages would make workers less frugal. "They live rather better, begin to save money, become more sober, and work more steadily. And this certainly forms one of the strongest reasons for advocating this type of management."[42] Scientific management promised a mental revolution in the relationship of worker/manager, citizen/government, and individual/community. "Taylor's development of a science of management," claims William Akin, "moved logically from the microcosm of work, to the organization of the factory, and beyond to society."[43] Scientific management, like much of the progressive movement, promised to create within citizens the desire to behave.

Taylor's productive subject was also a remarkably sober subject. "A careful inquiry into the condition of these men when away from work developed the fact that out of the whole gang only two were said to be drinking men.

... The fact is that a steady drinker would find it almost impossible to keep up with the pace which was set, so that they were practically all sober."[44] The discipline of scientific management constructed a citizen with particular habits, tastes, consents, and character. "There are, however, two kinds of fitness to be considered," claimed Richard Feiss, manager of the Clothcraft Shops of The Joseph & Feiss Co., speaking to the Society to Promote the Science of Management,

provided a person is suited for industry at all; one is fitness for the position; the other is fitness for the organization. Of these the latter is by far the more important. Fitness for the organization is chiefly a question of character. . . . It is essential, therefore, that every member of the organization have a character sufficiently developed or capable of development to be in harmony with the character of the organization.[45]

Taylor, reported Frank Copley, "continued to stand for something definite; something that varied as it was adapted to particular cases, but *always involved a mental revolution of employer and employee toward their work and toward each other.*"[46]

In applying these theories to government work, Taylor wrote, in a piece published posthumously in the Taylor Society's *Bulletin*, "Government efficiency will never be brought about until the prevailing mental attitude of government employes [sic] has been radically changed; and the great problem is how this great change is to be brought about." Government employees would mentally have to learn to accept the new managerial powers consolidated under Taylorism. "It is not a question of producing physical changes, but rather of working a great mental revolution in large numbers of men, and any such change demands time, and a large amount of time.[47] Taylor and his disciples considered a mental revolution necessary in the application of new methods of management that would eventually apply to the world of work and the state of politics. Feiss reminded his listeners: "that Scientific Management is a solution of the industrial problem involving all the ethics of human relationship was recognized by no one so well as by the Father of Scientific Management himself . . . and his well known words that the 'Product of a factory is not materials, but men.' "[48]

Morris Cooke, a student of Taylor, attempted explicitly to apply Taylor's methods to the institutions of the state.[49] "Notwithstanding much that might be cited to the contrary," he wrote during World War I, "our great national desire is to be efficient in both government and industry."[50] He applied his interpretation of Taylor's methods to a wide range of positions within public works institutions and projects, including during his tenure as Philadelphia's Director of Public Works and Administrator of the Rural Electrification Administration.[51] Upon graduating from Lehigh University in 1895, Cooke worked as a machinist's apprentice and a journeyman mechanic. Afterward he began work in various aspects of publishing, first as a partner in a printing business, then as a salesman for a lithographing firm, and finally as an assistant general manager for the Booklover Library. It was in this final position that Cooke first encountered Taylor in 1903. Taylor was so impressed with Cooke's application of the methods of scientific management to the publishing business that he employed Cooke to assist in his reorganization of the American Society of Mechanical Engineers. Reportedly, Cooke's work contributed to a reduction by half of the cost of distributing the society's annual report.[52]

"The principles of scientific management," Cooke confided, "are the same whether considered in their application to an industry or to a governmental unit."[53] And Cooke believed it was very important to begin to apply those principles to government, including the division of work into scientifically studied steps, the selection and training of employees, the standardization of work in a way that brings together the science and the well-disciplined employee, and the revision of the relationship between management and employee. This revision of the relationship, and more significantly, the intellectual understanding of the relationship between management and workers, was one of the most significant aspects involved in Cooke's application of Taylor's methods to state institutions. "Cooperation of government, employee and employer to carry responsibility for the uninterrupted flow of production and income implies, as we have tried to show in this book, far-reaching changes in attitudes and organization," he claimed in a book written with Philip Murray, a close associate of John L. Lewis and vice president of the Congress of Industrial Organizations (CIO).[54]

Cooke's account assumed the eventual domination within state institutions of the sort of social understandings created in business concerning authority and power. As he wrote when director of the Philadelphia Department of Public Works (a position that he received after Taylor recommended him to the new mayor, Rudolph Blankenburg, a position which Taylor himself turned down): "The evolution of business organization is from the unsystematized through the systematized to the scientific. Governmental work—federal, state and municipal—is still almost exclusively in the unsystematized stage."[55] The evolution of government work would be greatly aided by the adoption of Taylor's methods, Cooke believed.[56]

Taylor's work principally at Midvale, Bethlehem and at two or three other places has resulted in giving birth to what appears to some of us to be the greatest single force operating in the industrial world today. The same result can be brought about in municipal administration. What the problem needs is intensive study and intensive development at a few points with proper publicity.[57]

The application of Taylor's methods took time. In 1915, Cooke reminded readers concerning the application of scientific management to state institutions that "nothing has been so sufficiently studied as to have reached even an approximately scientific standard. All that can be said is that we have started on the long road."[58] Taylor, he reminded readers, took twenty-six years to study the cutting of metal; the study of political society would take at least that long. In 1940, Cooke and CIO vice president Philip Murray suggested that methods of scientific management offered a light at the end of the impending tunnel:

This book is published at a period of world-wide disillusionment. In one field after another the devastating conclusion has been reached that former ways of doing things have been the wrong ones, with results sometimes worse than futile. Certainly no one viewing the American industrial scene dispassionately can avoid the conclusion that there is a better way. This book it is believed points in that direction.[59]

Cooke and Murray's interest in the increased participation of union representatives in matters of management was a distinctive element in the scientific management work of the 1940s and contributed to the promotion of the humanization of management, labor and government in the creation of "a more rational and efficient economy."[60]

Much of the debate surrounding the adoption of Taylor's methods disappeared after the 1920s, but the method continued. In this case, the disappearance of the debate reveals a widespread acceptance of much of the power and authority that Taylorism had constructed. The pressures of World War II, in fact, drove the more extensive adoption of much of the method of scientific management and in a way that more powerfully connected the demands of the nation-state with the powers of industrial management.

The military, the focus of Part II, offers a particularly useful avenue to study the consolidation of administrative domination. The military tore soldiers from earlier communities and associations, focusing their attentions on the state and centralizing their desires for recognition on bureaucracy and the state. This organization of authority within bureaucracy was one of the extensive labors accomplished by the military. By disassociating people from earlier communities of opinion and recognition, the military contributed to the creation of experiences of independence and individualism that acted initially to consolidate bureaucratic authority but also contained possible challenges to that authority. During the induction of the 16 million troops for World War II, the military conducted one of the first extensive studies of personnel focused upon beliefs, values, and opinions. The military consolidated social knowledge needed for the modification of opinion, which was a major preoccupation of military officials.

Education, the focus of Part III, through systems of discipline not unlike the military's—regimentation, order of location, time schedules, and authoritative hierarchy—instilled a sense of bureaucratic legitimacy and the value of work in the interest of the nation. This part focuses on the state's creation, in part, of the connections between citizenship and subjectivity.

Education served a large role in constructing the social roles of the citizen, teaching people their relationships toward others, and teaching conceptions of individual responsibility through performance and reward. It also instituted the acceptance of professional social controls by teaching people to obey professionals and those in higher bureaucratic positions. Students were not only taught that the state is the location of political action and identification, but they were educated to respect social organization in the style of Taylor's efficiency theory. Education also created possible doubts concerning its goals and the goals of bureaucratic relationships in general.

By looking at these different applications of state power together, I can present a more detailed picture of the organizations of state power and citizenship during the vital years of the 1930s and 1940s, a period when the Great Depression and World War II challenged and stressed formulations of national and non-national identities. Focusing on World War II allows me to examine more fully American society at a moment that greatly influenced the second half of the twentieth century.

These two institutions reveal significant contributions to the construction of American citizenship—layers, if you will, upon which current ideas of the meanings and proper practices of citizenship are partially built. It is these layers that contributed to the construction of current assumptions of the meanings and possibilities of citizenship. This book is, in part, an attempt to study a somewhat neglected feature of American politics—citizenship—and to explore with historical specificity the powers that citizenship legitimated and ignored. It is my hope that, by excavating the creation of our own assumptions of citizenship, we can begin to subject those assumptions to a critical historical examination that could enliven political discourse and political action.

One of the most powerful attributes of the politics of the twentieth century has been the organization of political identity into the nation-state in a much more potent and pervasive way than ever before. Granted, the nation-state has been a significant identification and set of institutions since the mid-seventeenth century; yet, in many ways, the twentieth century combines the broadly general powers of national identification with new institutions and forms of social organization, which extended the state's already extensive power to centralize and professionalize. This book digs into the layered sediment of American political culture and excavates buried possibilities of citizenship, exploring the potentialities of increased meanings and arenas for politics. Perhaps the political power of other communities, including the power to recognize a wider array of social differences as valuable, could become more commonplace.

Other communities make possible the recognition of many more differences as valuable. This is an important concern for anyone interested in maintaining diversity and pluralism in the world. Furthermore, this could also lead to questions concerning the necessity of recognition and, perhaps, produce clues that lead to a more radical individualism in which people are more able to determine for themselves what sorts of actions and attentions are valuable to them. Questions of identity could then lead to fresh forms of community, as well as an anticipation of the future and the mellow fruit of individualism.

NOTES

1. Cognates for "citizen" such as "civil" suggest the aspects of "citizenship" that extend beyond the equation of citizenship with the relationship between an individual and the state—meanings that suggest behaviors and beliefs. George Armstrong Kelly explained: "in the wake of the Scottish political economists, Hegel and Marx, the term civil has been used specifically to indicate the commercial or bourgeois society that launched the Industrial Revolution—a society of 'contract,' or economic connections, embedded in, or perhaps dominating, but in some significant way exclusive from, the state. Indeed, the word *civil*, first used as emphatically distinct from *ecclesiastical* in the seventeenth century, became a kind of counterpoint to *political* in the nineteenth, until relieved of this burden by the extension of the word *social* (connected with the rise of sociology)." George Armstrong Kelly, "Who Needs a Theory of Citizenship?" in *Theorizing Citizenship*, ed. Ronald Beiner (Albany: State University of New York Press, 1995), 89.

2. Max Weber, "The Nation," in *From Max Weber: Essays in Sociology*, trans. and ed. H.H. Gerth and C. Wright Mills (London: Routledge & Kegan Paul, 1948), 179.

3. See William Graebner, *The Engineering of Consent: Democracy and Authority in Twentieth-Century America* (Madison: University of Wisconsin Press, 1987).

4. In *Wirtschaft und Gesellschaft*, Weber explained that the term "domination" could broadly describe power and authority of seemingly consensual relationships. "Domination in the broader sense can be produced not only by the exchange relationships of the market but also by those of "society"; such phenomena may range all the way from the "drawing room lion" to the patented *arbiter elegantiarum* of imperial Rome or the courts of love of the ladies of Provence. Indeed, such situations of domination can be found also outside the sphere of private markets and relationships. Even without any formal power of command an 'empire state' or, more correctly, those individuals who are the decisive ones within it either through authority or through the market, can exercise a far-reaching and occasionally even a despotic hegemony." He decided, however, to limit his usage of domination to "authoritarian power of command." Max Weber, *Economy and Society*, Vol. II, ed. Guenther Roth and Claus Wittich (Berkeley: University of California Press, 1978), 945–46.

5. Weber, *Economy and Society*, Vol. II, 948.

6. Ibid., 951.

7. I borrow the term "imagined communities" from Benedict Anderson. He applies the term to nations in a way that highlights the creative aspects of such an imagining. I apply this formulation to other communities, as Anderson suggests, "all

communities larger than primordial villages of face-to-face contact (an perhaps even these) are imagined." Benedict Anderson, *Imagined Communities*, 2nd rev. ed. (New York: Verso, 1993), 6.

8. J.G.A. Pocock, "The Ideal of Citizenship Since Classical Times," *Queens Quarterly* 99, 1 (Spring 1992): 54–55, in *Theorizing Citizenship*, ed. Ronald Beiner (Albany: State University of New York Press, 1995), 51–52.

9. Priscilla Wald, *Constituting Americans* (Durham, N.C.: Duke University Press, 1995), 10.

10. See particularly Walter Benjamin, "Paris, Capital of the Nineteenth Century," 142–62; and "The Author as Producer," 220–38, in *Reflections* (New York: Schocken Books, 1978), and the justly famous "The Work of Art in the Age of Mechanical Reproduction," 217–52, in *Illuminations* (New York: Schocken Books, 1968).

11. Walter Benjamin, "On Language as Such and on the Language of Man," in *Reflections* (New York: Schocken Books, 1978), 314.

12. Theda Skocpol, *States and Social Revolutions* (New York: Cambridge University Press, 1979), 32.

13. In other contexts Skocpol has admitted similarities to Weberian approaches but stressed a significant difference in that "new institutionalists" consider questions of legitimacy unimportant. Ibid., 304 n.4.

14. Ibid., 31.

15. Max Weber, "Legitimacy, Politics and the State," in *Legitimacy and the State*, ed. William Connolly (New York: New York University Press, 1984), 58.

16. This could possibly contribute to a critique of Michael Walzer's claim that different spheres of human activity direct their own distributions of power. I argue, in effect, that these spheres, particularly government and industry, are closely related in their assumptions of authoritative power. I would argue, furthermore, that within and between what might be called spheres are avenues of contestation over the power of various authorities that should be explored and their contingencies revealed. Michael Walzer, *Spheres of Justice: A Defense of Pluralism and Equality* (New York: Basic Books, 1983), 6.

17. There has been much ink spilled in debates over the role of warfare in the consolidation of national discipline. Charles Tilly has argued that the ability to wage war was central to the dominance of the nation-state over other social organizations. See Charles Tilly, *Coercion, Capital and European States* (Cambridge: Basil Blackwell, 1990), 30. Recent critiques of Tilly have accused him of putting the military cart before the national horse. That is, he argues that the idea of the nation developed because leaders found it to be the most productive means of waging war. This argument fails to account for other variables that contributed to the development of the nation and most seriously fails to adequately consider the possibility that the demands of nationalism produced an original need for warfare. See Hendrik Spruyt, *The Sovereign State and Its Competitors* (Princeton, N.J.: Princeton University Press, 1994). Gilles Deleuze and Felix Guattari make a more challenging claim that "theses on the origin of the State are always tautological. At times, exogenous factors, tied to war and the war machine, are invoked; at times endogenous factors, thought to engender private property, money, etc.; and at times specific factors, thought to determine the formations of public functions. . . . *Everything is not of the state precisely because there have been states always and everywhere.* Not only does

writing presuppose the State, but so do speech and language. The self-sufficiency, autarky, independence, preexistence of primitive communities, is an ethnological dream: not that these communities necessarily depend on states, but they coexist with them in a complex network." Gilles Deleuze and Felix Guattari, *A Thousand Plateaus: Capitalism and Schizophrenia* (Minneapolis: University of Minnesota Press, 1987), 427–30. Perhaps even Hegel meant something similar when he suggested, in a dismissal of social contract theories, that "primitive conditions can indeed be found, but they are marked by brute passions and acts of violence. Crude as they are, they are at the same time connected with social institutions which, to use the common expression, restrain freedom." G.W.F. Hegel, *Reason in History* (New York: Macmillan, 1953), 54. Maybe Weber's statement of discipline includes within its meaning a sense of war as chaos, in this way linking the birth of discipline to the birth of chaos, and suggesting something similar to Deleuze and Guattari.

18. Michel Foucault, *Discipline and Punish* (New York: Vintage Books, 1979), 170.

19. This formulation echoed earlier formulations, particularly that of Plato. "We have laid down, as a universal principle, that everyone ought to perform the one function in the community for which his nature best suited him." Plato, *The Republic*, trans. Francis Cornford (New York: Oxford University Press, 1945), 127. Plato's attempt to discover the content of justice *qua* justice concluded that justice was the correct positioning within a community (city). In many ways the extensive adoption of the methods of Taylor could be understood as the utilization of many elements in Platonic thought. It was, like Plato's work, an attempt to articulate a source of authority distinct from either physical force (Homer) or social equality (Socrates).

20. Victoria De Grazia compares adoption by civic society of methods of management from business in the United States to the attempt, in Italy, for the state to enact these methods. "Whereas in the United States, corporate rationalization itself produced a sort of ripple effect through the surrounding community, and then swept American society as a whole with a wave of capitalist modernity, in Italy, the fascist regime, under pressure from big business and impelled by its own desire to discipline its capacity to cope with the complexities of a technological society, proposed the creation of the essential supports for industrial reorganization from the top down." Victoria De Grazia, *The Culture of Consent* (Cambridge: Cambridge University Press, 1981), 13.

21. Charles E. Merriam, *The Making of Citizens* (Chicago: University of Chicago Press, 1931; reprint, New York: Teachers College Press, 1966), 395.

22. See William Bennett, *American Education: Making Work* (Washington, D.C.: U.S. Department of Education, 1988); Allan Bloom, *The Closing of the American Mind* (New York: Simon and Schuster, 1987).

23. Louis Althusser powerfully suggested the importance of education as a set of institutions to maintain capitalism and nationalism. "Nevertheless, in this concert, one ideological State apparatus certainly has the dominant role, although hardly anyone lends an ear to its music: it is so silent! This is the School." Louis Althusser, "Ideology and Ideological State Apparatuses," in *Lenin and Philosophy*, trans. Ben Brewster (New York: Monthly Review Press, 1971), 155.

24. Michael Apple, a wholehearted proponent of this ambivalent approach, has described his work: "It positively refuses, as well, to see people as puppets whose strings are pulled by forces out of their control and of which they supposedly have

little understanding. My operative concept throughout the book is a key word—*contradiction*. Things are both 'yes' and 'no' at the same time." Michael W. Apple, *Education and Power* (New York: Routledge, 1995), xix.

25. "As one of the elements incident to this great gain in output, each workman has been systematically trained to his highest state of efficiency, and has been taught to do a higher class of work than he was able to do under the old types of management; and at the same time he has acquired a friendly mental attitude toward his employers and his whole working conditions, whereas before a considerable part of his time was spent in criticism, suspicious watchfulness, and sometimes in open warfare. The direct gain to all of those working under the system is without doubt the most important single element in the whole problem." Frederick Winslow Taylor, *Shop Management*, in *Scientific Management* (New York: Frederick Taylor, 1911; reprint, New York: Harper & Row, 1947), 143–44.

26. George Lipsitz argues that during the first half of the twentieth century, workers were more concerned with issues of control over work production than they were with wages. He further claims that management was able to seriously deflate these concerns through the use of pension funds, which tied workers more securely into the maintenance of high outputs for themselves and their posterity. In other words, workers were more inclined to assert alternative authorities in the workplace. See "'Damn Foolishness': The Fight for Control at the Point of Production," in *Rainbow at Midnight: Labor and Culture in the 1940s* (Urbana: University of Illinois Press, 1994), 230. John Braeman's review of New Deal literature presents some dissent to this argument. John Braeman, "The New Deal and the 'Broker State': A Review of the Recent Scholarly Literature," *Business History Review* 46, 4 (Winter 1972): 409.

27. In 1929, the Taylor Society claimed that research, standardization, and control through standards were the three themes of Taylor's work. I generally organize material according to this division, except that I also explore the growth of administrative power and underscore Taylor's interest in intellectual management. See Taylor Society, *Scientific Management in American Industry*, ed. H.S. Person (New York: Harper & Brothers, 1929), xvii.

28. William E. Akin, *Technology and the American Dream: The Technocrat Movement, 1900–1941* (Berkeley: University of California Press, 1977), 9.

29. Anson Rabinback, *The Human Motor: Energy, Fatigue, and the Origins of Modernity* (Berkeley: University of California Press, 1990), 240.

30. For a brief autobiography see Taylor's open letter to Morris Cooke, "Personal History: Some Interesting Facts and Comments About His Early Training and Later Pastimes, by the Founder of Scientific Management, A Personal Letter," *Bulletin of the Taylor Society* 2, 5 (December 1916: 5–7.

31. Frank Barkley Copley, *Frederick W. Taylor, Father of Scientific Management*, Vol. I (London: Routledge/Thoemmes Press, 1993), 32.

32. Ibid., 3.

33. Robert Weibe, *Self-Rule: A Cultural History of American Democracy* (Chicago: University of Chicago Press, 1995), 185–86.

34. Copley, *Frederick W. Taylor*, Vol. II, 5–6.

35. Taylor to Louis Brandeis, January 9, 1911, Taylor Papers, File 98J, in Daniel Nelson, *Frederick W. Taylor and the Rise of Scientific Management* (Madison: University of Wisconsin Press, 1980), 175.

36. David Levy, "Brandeis and the Progressive Movement," in *Brandeis and America*, ed. Nelson Dawson (Lexington: University Press of Kentucky, 1989), 108.

37. Louis Brandeis, *"Half Brother, Half Son": The Letters of Louis D. Brandeis to Felix Frankfurter*, ed. Melvin I. Urofsky and David W. Levy (Norman: University of Oklahoma Press, 1991), 17.

38. Ibid., 18.

39. Harlow Person, Foreword to Frederick Winslow Taylor, *Scientific Management* (New York: Harper & Row, 1947), x–xi.

40. Ibid., xiii.

41. Ibid., xiv–xv.

42. Taylor, *Shop Management*, 27.

43. Akin, *Technology and the American Dream*, 9.

44. Taylor, *Shop Management*, 56. Repeated virtually verbatim in Frederick Winslow Taylor, *The Principles of Scientific Management*, in *Scientific Management* (New York: Frederick Taylor, 1911; reprint, New York: Harper & Row, 1947), 71–72.

45. Richard Feiss, "Personal Relationship as a Basis of Scientific Management," paper read before the Society to Promote the Science of Management, Philadelphia, Pa., October 23, 1915, printed in *Bulletin of the Society to Promote the Science of Management* 1, 6 (November 1915): 8.

46. Copley, *Frederick W. Taylor*, Vol. II, 389.

47. Frederick Winslow Taylor, "Government Efficiency," *Bulletin of the Taylor Society* 2, 5 (December 1916): 9.

48. Feiss, "Personal Relationships," 15.

49. Samuel Haber, *Efficiency and Uplift: Scientific Management in the Progressive Era, 1890–1920* (Chicago: University of Chicago Press, 1964), 109.

50. Morris Llewellyn Cooke, "Who Is Boss in Your Shop? Individual vs. Group Leadership, and Their Relation to Consent and the Ideals of Democracy," *Bulletin of the Taylor Society* 3, 4 (August 1917): 3.

51. He also served at various times as Chairman of the Storage Committee of the War Industries Board, a Trustee of the Power Authority of the State of New York, Director of the Giant Power Survey of Pennsylvania, and Chairman of the Mississippi Valley and Great Plains Committees.

52. Copley, *Frederick W. Taylor*, Vol. II, 246.

53. Morris Llewellyn Cooke, "Scientific Management of the Public Business," *American Political Science Review* 9 (August 1915): 494.

54. Morris Llewellyn Cooke and Philip Murray, *Organized Labor and Production* (New York: Harper & Brothers, 1940), 247.

55. Cooke, "Scientific Management of the Public Business," 488.

56. Cooke worked to empower administrators to make decisions that had been the purview of committees. Administrators, he believed, would adjudicate the problem not in terms of personal preference but in the light of facts. "It is only saying that a board of directors cannot intelligently vote on the details of a wage scale or the selling prices for a line of goods. These are questions to be determined by the administrative officials after a study of the facts" (Cooke, "Scientific Management of the Public Business," 489). City managers were the great hope of social engineers. Cooke believed that the growth in the use and acceptance of city managers would increase the realm of questions removed from politics and debate and placed under the power of

facts. "An appointive city manager holding office during good conduct and satisfactory service seems to still further build up the territory over which facts rather than votes and individual opinion determine action" (ibid.). It was in this position that Cooke incurred the wrath of many of the engineers and specialists of the city by complaining of their connections to business interests. Morris Llewellyn Cooke, "Some Factors in Municipal Engineering," *Mechanical Engineering* 37 (February 1915): 82; Copley, *Frederick W. Taylor*, Vol. II, 396; and Carroll Pursell, *The Machine in America: A Social History of Technology* (Baltimore: Johns Hopkins University Press, 1995), 215.

57. Cooke, "Scientific Management of the Public Business," 493.

58. Ibid., 495.

59. Morris Llewellyn Cooke and Philip Murray, *Organized Labor and Production* (New York: Harper & Brothers Publishers, 1940), 6.

60. Milton Derber, *The American Idea of Industrial Democracy, 1865–1965* (Chicago: University of Illinois Press, 1970), 348, 371.

Part II

Basic Training: The Military and the Construction of American Subjectivity

Chapter 2

"Pick Up a Pig and Walk": The U.S. Military's Early Adoption of Systems of Management

> One thinks with a watch in one's hand, even as one eats one's midday meal while reading the latest news of the stock market; one lives as if one always "might miss out on something." . . . Just as all forms are visibly perishing by the haste of the workers, the feeling for form itself, the ear and the eye for the melody of movements are also perishing. . . . Virtue has come to consist of doing something in less time than someone else.
> —Friedrich Nietzsche, *The Gay Science*,
> Book 4, section 329

Frederick Taylor's system of scientific management placed power in the hands of managers to organize, plan, and order. This power facilitated transformations in the interactions between business and government, in which government accepted beliefs and practices worked out in business were applied to government. The government's adoption of these methods lent them greater acceptability and contributed to the state's growing role as a manager over citizens. The role of the citizen, furthermore, increasingly emphasized the citizen's role as the object of state management over the citizen's role as the legitimizer of government. The nationalization of efficiency brought about in this period consolidated the control of managers over employees and citizens. Managers promoted corporate power in which the goals of the owners of the corporation became more clearly than ever before the goals of the workers. Efficient work appeared in the interest of the nation and therefore in the interest of all nationals—the virtue necessary for the republic became doing work in less time than someone else.

This chapter examines the pre–World War II influence of systems of bureaucratic authority and organization on the U.S. military. The military adopted elements of Taylorism (and new methods of management more generally) as they became widely influential throughout American culture. This affected the way that some citizens interacted with their state, added new powers to the state, and influenced widespread social patterns of consent and authority. Furthermore, state adoption gave legitimacy and recognition to methods of administration. Daniel Nelson, in his meticulous study of the rise of scientific management, suggests that the rise of Taylor's system of organization was "closely associated with the emergence of the late-nineteenth-century armaments industry, particularly the reorientation of the eastern steel manufacturers."[1] "For it would be the war," Guy Alchon contends of World War I, "with its labor shortages and mounting costs, that popularized scientific management and encouraged explicit formulations of its relation to employment."[2] The adoption within the military and military suppliers of the methods of scientific management transformed Taylorism into a national and international movement, while the emergence of industry based on war reflected a national authority increasingly established on managerial power.

The first major appropriation of Taylor's theories by the U.S. military or by industry associated with military production occurred during the Spanish-American War. Bethlehem Steel hired Taylor to establish a piece rate system in one machine shop. Taylor's reformist zeal extended to the reorganization of work space, development of a planning department, the adoption of more extensive testing, standardized adjustments for lathes and, significantly, the reintroduction of task work where workers were paid for the number of tasks completed, not by the number of hours worked.[3] Bethlehem Steel's attempt to meet the military's demand for pig iron during the Spanish-American War enabled Taylor to reform work organization—particularly, the implementation of task work.

One of the first pieces of work undertaken by us, when the writer started to introduce scientific management into the Bethlehem Steel Company, was to handle pig iron on task work. The opening of the Spanish War found some 80,000 tons of pig iron placed in small piles in an open field adjoining the works. . . . With the opening of the Spanish War the price of pig iron rose, and this large accumulation of iron was sold. This gave us a good opportunity to show the workmen, as well as the owners and managers of the works, on a fairly large scale the advantages of task work over the old-fashioned day work and piece work, in doing a very elementary class of work.[4]

Task work put every worker on an individually contracted basis and made them directly accountable to management. Under a task work system, management controlled the steps workers took to complete a project. For example, In *Principles of Scientific Management,* Taylor recorded a conversation with the first man chosen to do work studies, Henry Knolle. Taylor fictionalized much of this account, including changing Henry Knolle's name to Schmidt, but the passage conveys the amount of control over citizens increasingly dreamt of by managers.

Well, if you are a high-priced man, you will do exactly as this man tells you tomorrow, from morning till night. When he tells you to pick up a pig and walk, you pick it up and you walk, and when he tells you to sit down and rest, you sit down. You do that right straight through the day. And what's more, no back talk. Now a high-priced man does just what he's told to do, and no back talk. Do you understand that? When this man tells you to walk, you walk; when he tells you to sit down, you sit down, and you don't talk back at him. Now you come on to work here to-morrow morning and I'll know before night whether you are really a high-priced man or not.[5]

Task work, as promoted by Taylor and many others, required that the manager controlled the worker's most particular movements. Accurate information derived from studies of work, managers discovered, aided in control. It stemmed resistance to managerial authority and disciplined workers into habits of performance. Managers needed to know exactly how much work a good worker should be able to perform in order to judge the worker's success. They also needed to know the best way to order the workers to perform. Speed and organization studies attempted to discover information necessary for managers to increase workers' production more easily. Of all the elements of scientific management promoted by Taylor and introduced into military armaments and suppliers, time studies generated the most extensive resistance.

Navy Constructor Holden A. Evans, the first Naval officer to explicitly implement scientific management, began with preliminary organization changes at Norfolk Navy Yard, such as arranging the order in which jobs were completed. Admiral Washington Capps, head of the construction bureau, noticed the efficacy of Evans's changes and transferred him to the Mare Island yard near San Francisco. With the admiral's encouragement, by 1908, Evans turned the Mare Island facility into one of the first scientifically managed government facilities.[6] Evans proposed time studies and, more generally, scientific studies of all factors of production.

Often times the manager and superintendent must *guess* when they should *know.* Give these same men the facts that are given by accurate costs—give them an accurate record of what is taking place in the plant, as shown by a proper cost system—and they can apply their judgement to much better effort. Knowledge then takes the place of guesswork.[7]

When Evans first arrived at Mare Island, he implemented a new cost management system, a centralized tool grinding department, and he reorganized store rooms. Evans also set up a centralized control department and planning office, all elements of reform advocated by Taylor. These elements typically caused little concern among workers. The House Committee that investigated various systems of shop management in 1912 correctly captured the general acceptance:

It appears to your committee that no one can seriously object, and as a matter of fact no one has objected to any system which so standardizes and systematizes the work to be preformed that a greater amount of production is secured with the same expenditure of labor. Employer and employee alike and the public generally are interested in securing the largest amount and the best quality of product that can possibly be secured by the amount of labor expended. All men have a material interest in the accomplishment of that end.[8]

"All men," according to the committee, accepted many elements of Taylorite reorganization. What they did not tolerate were time tests. Time testing allowed management to commandeer knowledge that workers used to control their world. Workers resisted giving up information because it gave managers a tool to drive work and because they believed time tests degraded free citizens.

By late 1907, Evans began to conduct time studies and to use the task and bonus system to increase production. "It can be stated, however, that every operation was studied in an effort to determine the best way of doing the work and the best machines and the best men or class of men for accomplishing the work."[9] Scalers and caulkers accepted the changes advanced by Evans, but when he announced his plans to the boiler shop the foreman and workers resisted, perhaps because the boilermakers knew that the reforms the caulkers had allowed made it possible for the naval yard "to employ but a small number of men, and these are the very best of their class."[10] In order to persuade the boilermakers, Evans and his assistant, F.W. Becker, decided to proceed at a slower pace even than usual, in this instance only attempting one job. They organized the work for the retubing of three water-tube boilers so that each step followed in logical progression a plan created by management. "The operations were so arranged that *the work* shoved the men," Evans recounted, "each operation had to keep ahead of the operation behind and if this was not the case it immediately showed up."[11] The noticeable reduction in time and money that Evans and Becker demonstrated aided in the widespread adoption of "scientific" methods throughout the Mare Island facility, even among the boilermakers.

In November 1908, Evans suggested a plan to the Navy for organizing navy yards as private factories run by a single manager with the power to introduce other elements of scientific management. This was suggested in order to address what Evans believed to be one of the significant liabilities of government work: "The many restrictions in a Government shop do not give the head of department the freedom of action so essential to the highest measure of success."[12] Independently, but concurrently, Admiral Caspar F. Goodrich, commander of the New York Navy Yard and an old friend of Taylor's, suggested a similar plan to strengthen managerial control of naval yards. Goodrich had already persuaded the Navy to establish a commission for the creation of tool steel standards. The commission's initial action was to solicit the counsel of Taylor. In the New York Navy Yard, Goodrich began much like Evans, altering the machine shop's layout and launching a planning department.[13]

President Theodore Roosevelt's Secretary of the Navy, Truman Newberry, approved of the independent plans submitted by Evans and Goodrich and began in 1909 to implement them. Line officers quickly opposed the plans, not because of any theoretical dispute with Taylorism, but because the proposed plans threatened their usual shore leave and disrupted the balance of power between land and staff officers.[14] Their opposition eventually prompted the removal of many aspects of the program from the New York Navy Yard and Mare Island. The Secretary of the Navy appointed by the new Taft administration, George von L. Meyer, even denied Taylor's offer to pay Evans's salary for a year so that he could further study Taylor's methods in Philadelphia.[15] In 1911, however, Taylor protested to President Taft in person. Taft's secretary, Charles D. Norton, persuaded the president to contact Navy Secretary Meyer. After the president's encouragement, Meyer quickly became more receptive to the application of Taylor's theories. He even invited Taylor to attend battleship exercises off the Virginia coast and returned the favor by visiting Taylor in Philadelphia, where he listened to Taylor lecture and toured two shops organized by Taylor.[16] Evans was eventually placed in Norfolk and charged with making the Norfolk facility exemplify the utility of the Taylor system. Again the line officers protested and Meyer acquiesced. Evans resigned, but Meyer independently began to implement some of the changes. Taylor said of these changes that they were "in reality . . . just as near as they could get to our system."[17] Some of this work, including the use of detailed instruction cards, had to be jettisoned when workers considered it too authoritarian, but many elements remained. Among the new components of acceptable managerial power were the organization of work space and the greater managerial control over the production of work.

The Charlestown Navy Yard experienced similar resistance to Taylorite methods and also adapted. In 1912–1913, Assistant Secretary of the Navy Franklin Roosevelt investigated the utility of Taylor's system of management at the navy yard's hull division. Roosevelt, initially concerned that the system drove workers too hard, received a letter from a friend, Arthur Ballantine, and a visit from the chairman of the War Labor Policies Board, Felix Frankfurter, that convinced him to allow an unofficial study of Taylor's methods at the Charlestown Yard. Frankfurter barraged Roosevelt with statistics on the savings at the Watertown Arsenal that had resulted from the application of Taylor's methods.[18] The report sustained the efficiency of Taylor's methods. However, in 1915, before Roosevelt could act, Congress prohibited the introduction of time studies into naval installations.[19] Time study and bonus plans were the only elements of scientific management stopped by the legislation and, according to some sources, even they were not completely stopped.[20]

The Army appropriated Taylor's system more easily than did the Navy. Chief of Army Ordnance William Crozier, a sometimes overzealous supporter of Taylor, contacted Taylor in 1906 and reached an agreement with him in 1909.[21] Crozier, in distinction from his Naval colleagues, was given much greater autonomy. By 1911, the Watertown machine shop would become a model of Taylorian scientific efficiency.[22] In spite of a walkout strike against time studies and the Halsey premium (a system whereby the quickest time a job had been done was set as the standard and if workers completed the task in a shorter time they were paid an additional percentage), by 1913 it could be said of the arsenal that even the windows were washed scientifically.[23]

In March 1911, Major C.C. Williams was ordered to work with Carl Barth, one of Taylor's disciples, at Watertown Arsenal a few miles west of Boston. Williams, who later succeeded Crozier as chief of ordnance—a post he held from 1918 to 1930—became the chief ordnance officer to the American Expeditionary Force during World War I.[24] In June 1913, Taylorism was well enough in place at the Watertown arsenal so that it was self-sustaining, and there were no longer any outside consultants.[25] In distinction to the Mare Island facility, this system received a great deal of support from officers. Hugh Aitken explains their support as a function of their increased power and authority: "Most of the managing had actually been done by the master mechanic and the foremen. In part, the officers' firm belief in the efficiency of the new system may have been due to the fact that, under Taylorism, they felt that they, and not the workmen, were really managing the arsenal for the first time."[26]

Once again, many elements of scientific management were introduced, but only time studies provoked much resistance. When Dwight Merrick, a time study expert, began his study, which discriminated between waste effort and productive effort, a molder named Perkins used his pocket watch to time the complete job. The molders chaffed at the huge differences in times recorded by the two men and they challenged the work goal established by the faster time. Workers attempted to negotiate the differences in time with managers, a clear challenge to the supposed objectivity of time studies and scientifically set time standards. Everyone eventually agreed to compromise on the time standards.

But Merrick continued to conduct time studies even after compromise standards had been established. Workers were so protective of information that they resisted even when there were no immediate work consequences. One worker, a molder named Joseph Cooney, refused to continue at his work if Merrick continued to time him. He was dismissed and the rest of the line walked out with him, not against all elements of scientific management, but against the managers having free access to worker time information. This strike led to the eventual banning of time studies on government contract work, the same legislation that removed the issue from Roosevelt's desk. Most of the innovations Taylor and his disciples applied to Watertown Arsenal remained in place, however, particularly with the increased demand for production created by World War I.

Taylorite or similar methods of organization were felt throughout the military, not solely in ordnance production. In 1914, the Navy reported to the Senate, in an appeal for the passage of a bill for "Efficiency of Naval Militia" (H.R. 8667), that new organizations, military equipment, faster vessels, and professionalism demanded increased attention to the efficiency and funding of the naval militia.

The equipping of new organization, the new departure in the essential matter of target practice, the increased steaming by the Naval Militia vessels involve more expense. But these expenditures are so essentially in the line of increased professional efficiency that it is believed the results will justify the expense. It is estimated by the Navy Department that if this bill becomes a law the Organized Militia will rapidly grow to the strength of at least 10,000 efficient men capable of being on board ship in fighting trim on short notice. The benefit that would result, therefore, can scarcely be overestimated, in view of the fact that during the Spanish War it took six weeks to recruit 5,900 men in the regular naval service, a majority of whom were untrained, to a great extent, in naval warfare.[27]

Money was needed from government to ensure efficient conduct by naval militia. The widespread military adoption of new standards and plans for efficiency was justified on the basis of national need, strategic planning, American intellectual esteem, professionalism, and the importance of the government's recognition of new industrial standards.

In hearings conducted in 1916 to determine the value of Taylor's methods for the regulation of government work, Richard Feiss, a manufacturer of young men's clothing from Cleveland, Ohio, claimed that people working for the government actually worked for all Americans and should use, for their nation, the most efficient means possible. Taylor's methods, he claimed, applied to public as well as private shops.

They are working for me the same as my shop. We want the shops to be as efficient as possible. It is only the keynote to what we stand for in American life—better efficiency, better service to yourself and to your country and to your community at large. We want our Government workshops to represent them. We do not want them to condemn those means which make for efficiency and which stand alongside as an inspiration to the private worker.[28]

Feiss, in his defense of Taylor, demonstrated the power of a national identity to demand a new social order and the legitimation of a form of political authority. The impending conflagration of World War I buttressed demands for increased national efficiency, even at the cost of worker freedom. Henry Towne, of the Yale & Towne Manufacturing Company and a past president of the American Society of Mechanical Engineers, the society that published most of Taylor's written work, was authorized by the National Association of Manufacturers and by the Merchants Association of New York to appear before the House Committee on Labor. Towne was the creator of a method that closely resembled Taylor's system, a method that Taylor found very satisfactory except for its unscientific estimation of the highest production rates.[29] In his appearance before the committee, Towne predicted that increased efficiency was the guide through the world's impending military conflagration and, more significantly, a revolution of efficiency would follow the war.

Here we are to-day with most of the world in a whirlwind of a gigantic war, with uncertainty as to when we may be drawn into it, as we all hope may not be the case, but with the certainty that if we should be involved we will need every ounce of national efficiency of every kind, and that whatever may be the result of the war politically, there is going to be an economic revolution afterwards which will sweep the whole world in its influence and concerning which we do not yet know and can not yet foresee the effect upon this country, except to be very sure that anything we may do in the way of increased efficiency and preparedness is going to stand us in good stead, and probably will be needed badly. In the face of all these facts, to pass a law penalizing a system which overwhelmingly, as testified to, stands for efficiency, for economy, for better reward to labor, and higher production from labor and from machinery—in other words to not merely stop the wheels of progress but to set them spinning backward and say it is a crime—and we do not believe you will do it.[30]

Towne believed that new methods of management, like Taylor's, were the significant feature of the future; new forms of social control with more efficient wheels and cogs for the national machinery that must not be "set . . . spinning backward." From Towne's vantage point the future appeared to be one of nationalized bureaucratic rationality, one in which all of the wheels (big and little) spun toward a goal of national efficiency. Efficiency became the virtue of the future.

The supposed inefficiency of government work was often used to drive the adoption of more experimental methods, such as Taylorism. The increased efficiency achieved by the government, according to Evans, recommended the system to private industry. "The belief that all Government shops are inefficiently managed is very common among managers of commercial industrial establishments. . . . on the other hand it must be admitted that the Government has no monopoly of the inefficient establishments," he wrote in an article subtitled "The Government Has No Monopoly of Inefficient

Shops."³¹ Military shops illustrated methods that private employers could utilize to increase efficiency, and the recognition by the state of an intellectual system recommended it to other avenues of social life. Government shops also attempted to apply methods to make their employees as functional as private employees. "The officer in charge of a Government shop who wishes to manage it in the same manner as he would were he in commercial life, where the payment or non-payment of dividends would measure his success or failure as a manager, has some difficulties to overcome which he would not meet elsewhere."³² The significant problems to be overcome in government work included the increased difficulty in removing weak and inefficient employees and the difficulty in convincing managers that it was worth their time and trouble to apply new methods. Evans's reforms refined the relationship of government workers to government managers to more closely resemble that of private industry.

Testimony against the methods also suggested the symbolic importance of state recognition of the value of Taylorism. For example, the testimony of James O'Connoll, the president of the International Association of Machinists, feared the government imprimatur on Taylor-like methods.

It would give it the impetus of making it a practical proposition for every manufacturer of this country to say that the Government has given it its stamp of approval. The commission appointed by ex-President Roosevelt in connection with the miners—the chairman of this committee knows what impetus that gave toward that position or that decision of that committee. It was used immediately by the manufacturers all over this country because of the so-called open-shop theory expressed in that report, and they stated: "It is acquiesced in by the President of the United States and it is acquiesced in and given out by the commission appointed by him." And it became the watchword and byword of every hostile employer in this country.³³

Taylorism also became a watchword. The methods and powers associated with his name were widespread social phenomena that not only changed American work patterns, but made the notion of citizenship more assimilable with new forms of highly coercive power.

After demonstrating the possible value of Taylor's theories of scientific management to meet the increased demands for efficiency and increased toleration of centralization encouraged by World War I, management became a central aspect of the American military. The "science of personnel management and its widespread application to American industries," claimed William Leiserson in 1924, "have been due largely to the activities of war agencies established for the purpose."³⁴ "Though promulgated in the first decade of the twentieth century," affirms Joseph Dorfman concerning the methods of scientific management, "they were not generally adopted until World War I."³⁵ World War I began a process more fully extended in World War II. The American military of World War II was extensively organized according to Taylorist principles. There was much concern within the military over bureaucratic authority and organization. Taylorite methods helped answer some of the most salient questions facing the military as it entered World War II. How to ensure obedience? How to ensure that the production of needed goods got to the locations when they were needed? How to ensure identification with the goals and objectives of the war? Taylor's methods of organization and control were used extensively, if not explicitly, along the lines already sketched: increased authority of administrators, scientific studies, and consolidation of interests. The authority of administrators was vital to the Military's elaborate production and distribution needs.

As the government began to implement Taylor's theories in the postal service and in armament production, World War I drove ever more extensive adoption of systems of efficient management.[36] "The European war has developed into a high-powered advertisement for community organization," wrote Morris Cooke in 1917, "for the scientific in management and even for capacity in the individual. Notwithstanding much that might be cited to the contrary our great national desire is to be efficient in both government and industry."[37] Taylor believed that the application of his theories of management to the Army was one of the most promising of developments, a development encouraged by World War I.[38] Nelson claimed of Taylor's public utility that the "introduction of Taylorism at a private company had little impact outside the firm; the introduction of scientific management at a shipyard or arsenal often had wide-ranging external implications."[39]

If the Spanish-American War served as the catalyst for Taylor's studies, World War I cemented them into accepted order, and World War II further elaborated them into relations between citizens and institutions of state power. Wars encouraged the national designation of industrial labor. "Owing to the war emergency, public power became available to any private group or private individual who could attach a private strategy to the public cause," wrote Robert Cuff concerning World War I.[40] Wars extended the power of scientific management, and scientific management developed that power for the uses of the nation.

NOTES

1. Daniel Nelson, *Frederick W. Taylor and the Rise of Scientific Management* (Madison: University of Wisconsin Press, 1980), 154.

2. Guy Alchon, *The Invisible Hand of Planning: Capitalism, Social Science, and the State in the 1920s* (Princeton, N.J.: Princeton University Press, 1985), 17.

3. Charles Wrege and Ronald Greenwood, *Frederick W. Taylor: The Father of Scientific Management* (Homewood, Ill.: Business One Irwin, 1991), 94.

4. Frederick Winslow Taylor, *The Principles of Scientific Management*, in *Scientific Management* (New York: Frederick Taylor, 1911; reprint, New York: Harper & Row, 1947), 41–42.

5. Ibid., 46–47.

6. See Holden A. Evans, *One Man's Fight for a Better Navy* (New York: Dodd, Mead and Co., 1940), 182–83.

7. Holden A. Evans, *Cost Keeping and Scientific Management* (New York: McGraw-Hill Book Co., 1911), 10.

8. "The Taylor System in Government Shops: The Report of the House Committee to Investigate Various Systems of Shop Management Is in General Adverse," *The Iron Age* 89 (March 21, 1912): 746.

9. Holden A. Evans, "Reduction in Cost of Navy Yard Work," *American Machinist* 31 (June 30, 1910): 1201.

10. Ibid.

11. Ibid., 1202.

12. Holden A. Evans, "An Analysis of Machine-Shop Methods: The Government Has No Monopoly of Inefficient Shops," *American Machinist* 31 (1910): 569.

13. Nelson, *Frederick W. Taylor*, 158–59.

14. Ibid., 159.

15. Ibid.

16. Ibid., 160.

17. Ibid.

18. Franklin Roosevelt and Felix Frankfurter, *Roosevelt and Frankfurter: Their Correspondence*, annotated by Max Freedman (Boston: Atlantic Monthly Press, 1967), 11. After his meeting with Roosevelt, Frankfurter sent the following telegram to Ballantine: "HAD VERY SATISFACTORY TALK WITH ROOSEVELT. FEAR AS TO LOSS OF GOVERNMENT SERVICE OF MEN IN QUESTION ENTIRELY IDLE. DEPARTMENT ANXIOUS FOR EFFICIENCY AND ECONOMY, AS WELL AS PERMANENTLY SOUND LABOR CONDITIONS. OPPOSED TO TAYLOR SYSTEM AS SUCH, BUT EXPERIMENTING IN OTHER YARDS WITH VIEW TO ARRIVING AT OTHER ADEQUATE SYSTEM" (ibid., 11). While this telegram does express some hesitancy on Roosevelt's part to endorse Taylor's system, it also betrays support for elements of that system.

19. Kenneth S. Davis, *FDR: The Beckoning of Destiny, 1882–1928* (New York: G.P. Putnam's Sons, 1971), 316–18; Frank Freidel, *Franklin D. Roosevelt: The Apprenticeship* (Boston: Little, Brown, 1952), 196–201; Daniel R. Fusfeld, *The Economic Thought of Franklin D. Roosevelt and the Origins of the New Deal* (New York: Columbia University Press, 1956; reprint, New York: AMS Press, 1970), 67–69.

20. C. Bertrand Thompson reported in 1917 that the legislation proved ineffective, at least in the prohibition of bonus payments. "An error of the labor leaders in attaching this rider to the wrong bill, the payment of bonuses was continued." C. Bertrand Thompson, *The Theory and Practice of Scientific Management* (Boston: Houghton Mifflin, 1917), 93.

21. Hugh G.J. Aitken, *Scientific Management in Action: Taylorism at Watertown Arsenal, 1908–1915* (Princeton, N.J.: Princeton University Press, 1985), 61.

22. See *Reports of the Chief of Ordnance*, 1911, 1912, 1913, and 1914 (Washington, D.C.: Government Printing Office).

23. C.B. Wheeler, "Questionnaire—Scientific Management," National Archives, Record Group 156, Box 266, File 213, Schedule 1–3, Section 1, p. 11. Even though the Towne-Halsey Plan shared many elements with the Taylor plan, Taylor believed

his plan superior because of its ability to scientifically determine the proper time it takes to complete a task. The Towne-Halsey Plan, according to Taylor, encouraged workers to deceive managers concerning the amount of time it took to complete a task.

24. Aitken, *Scientific Management*, 63.
25. Ibid., 119.
26. Ibid., 120.
27. U.S. Congress, Senate, National Affairs Committee, *Efficiency of Naval Militia*, 63rd Cong., 2nd sess., January 22, 1914, Senate Report 167, 1:6552, p. 21.
28. U.S. Congress, House of Representatives, Richard Feiss testifying before the Committee on Labor, *Methods of Directing the Work of Government Employees*, A Bill to Regulate the Methods of Directing the Work of Government Employees, H.R. 8665, 64th Cong., 1st sess., *Congressional Record* (March 31, 1916), H-147-9, 133.
29. Taylor, *Shop Management*, 41. Taylor explained the difference in this way: "The essence of task management lies in the fact that the control of the speed problem rests entirely with the management; and, on the other hand, the true strength of the Towne-Halsey system rests upon the fact that under it the question of speed is settled entirely by the men without interference on the part of the management. Thus in both cases, though from diametrically opposite causes, there is undivided control, and this is the chief element needed for harmony." Ibid., 44–45.
30. U.S. Congress, House of Representatives, Henry Towne testifying before the Committee on Labor, *Methods of Directing the Work of Government Employees*, A Bill to Regulate the Methods of Directing the Work of Government Employees, H.R. 8665, 64th Cong., 1st sess., *Congressional Record* (March 31, 1916), H-147-9, 35.
31. Evans, "An Analysis," 568. Also see Evans, *Cost Keeping*, 170.
32. Evans, "An Analysis," 568.
33. U.S. Congress, House of Representatives, James O'Connoll testifying before the Committee on Labor, *Methods of Directing the Work of Government Employees*, A Bill to Regulate the Methods of Directing the Work of Government Employees, H.R. 8665, 64th Cong., 1st sess., *Congressional Record* (March 30, 1916), H-147-9, 36–37.
34. William M. Leiserson, *Adjusting Immigrant and Industry* (New York: Harper, 1924), 343.
35. Joseph Dorfman, *The Economic Mind in American Civilization*, Vol. 4 (New York: Viking Press, 1959), 60.
36. In 1916, the House of Representatives heard testimony concerning the use of speed tests among postal workers. "I will now cite a condition that prevails in the postal service that to my mind is without justification or excuse. I have presented to the committee copies of the department's speed standard, which in themselves are worthy of the serious thought and consideration of the members of the committee. The strain incident to keeping up with this so-called standard of efficiency is heartbreaking in the extreme, but the condition of the employees is aggravated by what is termed 'the secret tests.' Each carrier is subjected to this so-called speed test on one day of each month, the day and date being unknown to the carrier and the testing being secretly made. The purpose of these secret speed tests is to keep all the men working at top speed mentally and physically every minute each day, as the carriers do not know what day they are being tested. On the day a carrier is subjected to the test. I have been informed inspectors secretly count the pieces of mail of all classes that

the employee handles that day, before the carrier receives his mail for routing. Several weeks after these secret tests are made the employee receives a letter to the effect that he is 'not working up to a standard satisfactory to the office.' " So testified Edward Cantwell, Secretary National Association of Letter Carriers. U.S. Congress, House of Representatives, Edward Cantwell, Secretary, National Association of Letter Carriers, testifying before the Committee on Labor concerning the application of speed tests to postal employees, *Methods of Directing the Work of Government Employees*, A Bill to Regulate the Methods of Directing the Work of Government Employees, H.R. 8665, 64th Cong., 1st sess., *Congressional Record* (April 1, 1916), H-147-9, 249.

37. Morris Llewellyn Cooke, "Who Is Boss in Your Shop? Individual vs. Group Leadership, and Their Relation to Consent and the Ideals of Democracy," *Bulletin of the Taylor Society* 3, 4 (August 1917): 3.

38. Taylor to H.L. Gantt, January 3, 1907, Taylor Papers, File 120B, in Nelson, *Frederick W. Taylor*, 161.

39. Nelson, *Frederick W. Taylor*, 155.

40. Robert Cuff, "Business, the State, and World War I: The American Experience," in *War and Society in North America*, ed. J.L. Granatstein and R.D. Cuff (Toronto: Thomas Nelson and Sons, 1971), 6.

Chapter 3

"The Ultimate Strength of the Army": Managerial Bureaucracy in a Nation at War

> Looking for work in order to be paid: in civilized countries today almost all men are at one in doing that. For all of them work is a means and not an end in itself. Hence they are not very refined in their choice of work, if only it pays well.
> —Friedrich Nietzsche, *The Gay Science*, Book, 1, section 42

"The bureaucratization of organized warfare," Weber claimed, "may be carried through in the form of private capitalist enterprises, just like any other business."[1] This chapter examines the U.S. Army's utilization of managerial bureaucracies in World War II. Management and organization, perennial concerns of war, solidified under the nation-state to a new extent. Add to this the vast increase in the military as an institution of management, the new consolidation of authority in managers, and a consistent system of authority between the military and civilian production, and it can be said that the military of World War II was a far different institution than had ever before been fielded.[2] This chapter begins with an examination of several elements of the Army's extensive utilization of managerial bureaucracies. World War II presented the army with issues of production and distribution that had remarkable counterparts in industry—how to ensure that goods arrived on time and arrived where they were needed, that work was performed in the most efficient manner, that people worked together like a well-designed machine, and that people worked to achieve ends and goals "larger" than their own "interests." Next, this chapter examines the Army's basic structure and system of procurement. The system of procurement presented some of the trickiest points in the relationship between the military and private industrial discipline. Finally, this chapter examines the relationship between extensive systems of production and the intellectual understanding that invited citizens to imagine the nation as the meaning for much of their labor. As the nation made increased demands on civilian industrial production, the citizen's labor was more easily connected to national interests. A civilian's work increasingly belonged to the nation, which applied conceptions of an industrial division of labor to national citizenship. In this, way notions of industrial division of labor influenced pluralist notions of national citizenship—differences within the American national identity were increasingly conceived as differences necessary for national purpose.

SUPPORT

In December 1940, British Prime Minister Winston Churchill complained to his secretary of war that it took an additional 20,000 men to keep 15,000 soldiers in the field.[3] The surprising growth in the size of military bureaucracy greatly concerned many Americans as well. "The Army Ground Forces," the Army's final report bureaucratically confirmed, "repeatedly advised against further drain of manpower to noncombat functions and urged increases of allotment to combat forces. . . . Hopes of the War Department, in the months following 24 November 1942, to raise the proportion of combat units by reduction of overhead and service elements did not materialize."[4] The Weekly Bulletin from the Headquarters Army Ground Forces of November 1942 characteristically reminded staff of the importance of slimming support staff.

It has come to the attention of the War Department that the Army is too lavish with personnel for overhead functions and that tactical units expect too much of station complements. The result is that far too much personnel is assigned to overhead and there are continual demands for further increases. The ultimate strength of the Army is dependent upon the manpower available and every man devoted to overhead makes one less soldier available for the combat forces.[5]

By the end of 1942, the United States had an Army of 5 million people; of this number only 1,917,000 (38.3 percent) could be classified as ground troops.[6] Of the 16 million people who served in the U.S. military, 25 percent never left the United States, while less than 50 percent of those who did leave were ever in a battle zone.[7] The Army's own report of March 31, 1945 claimed that of 7,813,319 total persons, only 2,345,160 were in combat missions. Most of the remaining troops were in support or service positions, including combat support, combat service support, service support, training, and overhead.[8]

The massive amount of bureaucracy required to organize a twentieth-century military and to supply support and equipment to this highly mechanized force caused this significant lopsidedness.[9] Compared to World War I, America's forces in World War II were exceptionally top-heavy. The Army of 1945 was well over twice the size of the Army of 1918, the Army reported at the end of the war. "But," the report added, "the unit strength of combatant ground forces was not much greater than in 1918."[10] Even compared to the war still in common memory, the institutional bureaucracy had greatly expanded. The expansion increased the Army's reliance on new forms of bureaucratic authority, changed the work of the military, and foretold a change in American work more generally.

ORGANIZATION AND PROCUREMENT

On March 9, 1942, the Army was reorganized in what the Army's official history called "the most drastic and fundamental change which the War Department had experienced since the establishment of the General Staff by Elihu Root in 1903."[11] The Army Air Forces' desire for independence precipitated the reorganization, but the reorganization consolidated supply under General Somervell in the Army Service Forces (ASF).[12] Placing the different organizations under Somervell was an attempt to unite elements of procurement with supply. In addition, training functions of the four army commands created in 1932 were centralized in the Army Ground Forces. The preexisting structure of the Army had been formulated in 1918 by General John Pershing and remained basically unchanged until 1942. He adopted, partially from the French, a five-part division of functions to command his American Expeditionary Forces.[13] G-1 was in charge of personnel, G-2 controlled intelligence, G-3 carried out operations, G-4 ensured the availability of supplies, and G-5 carried out instruction and training. In 1921, the operations of the G-5 were divided between G-1 and G-2. This created, substantially, the structure of the Army going into World War II.

The military's most pressing problem of organization after World War I was the issue of procurement. Even after the National Defense Act of June 4, 1920, "no solution," was offered "to the basic issue of military versus civilian control of procurement."[14] When General Pershing became Chief of Staff on July 1, 1921, the issue continued. Pershing appointed a board of seven officers, led by Maj. Gen. James G. Harbord, to address the problem. The Harbord Board created a general staff system for the War Department. This organization system, for which Pershing was also responsible, "was the top management agency of the Military Establishment."[15] It overcame many earlier jurisdictional disputes. "Many different commands, supply bureaus, administrative bureaus, and other agencies might function as part of the War

Department, but all received top direction from the General Staff."[16] Pershing's reorganization clarified managerial authority, even though control of procurement, supply, and distribution continued to cause problems.

The appointment of Robert Patterson to the position of Under Secretary of War in charge of procurement and general economic mobilization contributed to the resolution of supply and distribution problems. Patterson hired a consulting firm to "scientifically" study the problem. The firm of Booz, Frey, Allen and Hamilton, having just completed a study of the Navy, examined the War Department's organization problems, particularly in the area of procurement and economic mobilization. At this time the Under Secretary's office controlled procurement and economic mobilization.[17] In the first year of Under Secretary Patterson's tenure, the personnel of this department multiplied fivefold.[18]

The Booz report recommended increased military authority for those involved in procurement, criticized the lack of scientific rigor in the statistical reporting methods of the division, and argued for an intensive strengthening of the department's administrative services, recommendations that could have come from the pen of Taylor.[19] The Booz report also suggested the clarification of the position of G-4, which at this time was in charge of procurement but could not issue orders for the production of goods, such orders being the purview of the Under Secretary of War. When Brig. Gen. Brehon B. Somervell became commander of G-4, he hired Goldthwaite Dorr to study the questions of supply organization. Dorr chaired an informal group that met to address these problems. "Its members worked individually on various assignments, and met in a 'hush-hush' atmosphere after regular working hours. The discussions were kept secret."[20] Eventually Dorr and the committee concluded that one individual should be in charge of the determination of requirements and the control of procurement.[21]

After much work and negotiation, on February 28, 1942, President Roosevelt ordered the completed plan to be put into effect, with General Somervell chosen to unite the functions of requirements and procurement. In March of that year, General Somervell began his responsibilities as commanding general of the Services of Supply, or, as it was more routinely called, the ASF.[22] With these changes, command in the Army became more centrally an element of organization and movement of goods and resources at maximum efficiency.[23]

The new setup of 9 March 1942 recognized an organizational need which had been evident in the top command of the Army, both overseas and in the United States, since World War I. This need was to handle all procurement and all supply operations as one integrated activity. No supply arm or service could do the job by itself. An army in combat had to have all its supplies, from weapons and ammunition to gasoline, food, and clothing, on a schedule which brought all of these items together in the right place at the right time. The ASF was the War Department's answer to this vital need in World War II.[24]

The ASF ensured for the War Department that all supplies arrived promptly where they were needed and when they were needed. This concern not only drove the creation of a more bureaucratic Army but made the military more like the rest of American industrial society.

Vast numbers of people in the military became managers. This shift in power to administrators consolidated decision making within bureaucracies. During World War II the War Department began an expansion that would eventually culminate in an organization of 2 million civilians, the largest of all agencies of the federal government and, fantastically, larger in size than the entire federal government at any previous period of time.[25]

The growth of administration as the majority occupation in virtually all fields, even war, with its consolidation of authority, exemplified the new conceptions of authority outlined by scientific management. The World War II American Army utilized many methods similar to those suggested by Taylor, including the introduction of Work Simplification Officers.

Work Simplification Officers applied the methods of Taylor to the work of the Army and brought about the attendant standardization of labor. "All our depots and warehouses are operating at top speed. We're operating on a bigger scale than anyone has every done before," sounded the narrator of *Attack on Hidden Waste*, an Army training film concerning work simplification, which touted the enormous benefits that the Army believed would result from closer attention to wasted movement and work. "I analyzed the job *scientifically*," the narrator explained. "Scientifically? How?" asked another voice. "Through Work Simplification. A planned program already in effect throughout all installations of the Army Service Forces." By studying the steps taken to complete a job and the movements associated with the work, the Work Simplification Officer sought ways for people to work more productively. This "technique" involved the filling out of "Gang Process Charts" by managers in order to learn how groups were working and then to devise better ways for them to work. "Gang Process Charts can be used to analyze almost any sort of a job: unloading a freight car, unloading a truck, loading a ship; work simplification can also be applied effectively to clerical jobs."[26]

"Process Charts" were filled out to improve the process individuals followed to complete jobs. Operations Studies were "the study of the work place of an individual with particular attention to elimination of waste movement." In a step-by-step manner, every movement by the worker was examined by the Work Simplification Officer to determine which were wasted, unbalanced, or inefficient. "Every movement is first carefully observed then written in sequence," explained the narrator of *Attack on Hidden Waste*. "In this case the work of each hand is studied and noted. By carefully analyzing the Before Study Operations Chart wasteful motions or idle intervals can be eliminated and a balance between the work done by each hand can be obtained. Such balance makes for easier and less tiring work for the operator."[27]

The Taylorite elimination of "wasted" effort removed much of the individual from the work. As Daniel Boorstin wrote, "To abolish the rule of thumb in factory work would excise a part of every worker's emotional investment and personal satisfaction. Could a worker now fail to feel that he was doing somebody else's job, or a job dictated by the machine? Rule of thumb was personal rule."[28] The application in business and the military of standard procedures reduced the experience of individualism in work.

Process Charts reordered the workplace. Military managers redesigned the workplace to maximize productive efficiency. Only the constant surveillance of motion, work, and organization would guarantee that America could meet the production challenge of World War II.

And what is your job? It's not just to operate on a bigger scale than ever before, not just to be content because you are doing a big job now, but to consider the problems of waste, to eliminate these problems, to keep everlastingly at the job of improving our supply system so that the goods may continue to reach the fighting front. By applying work simplification, by using its techniques on every phase of every job, big or little, the task can be done and your manpower headaches will be lessened. Not til *this is* done can you really feel proud, can you say, "we're doing all right."[29]

It was the job of workers to internalize the importance of streamlining and standardizing. Work simplification required workers to ask six basic questions: who, what, when, where, how, and why. The best answers to these questions supported the creation of standardized, administrative rules.

ADMINISTRATIVE RULES

The U.S. Army, its defenders claimed, was modern. Modernity in this instance referred to the Army's centralized creation of rules. "Army rules and order, while they are as dated as one would expect the regulations of a highly bureaucratic structure to be, nevertheless exert a modernizing influence on the Army. The social structure of the Army is gradually changing under the constant repetition of Army regulations."[30] This narrative of modernization relied on a faith in the eventual triumph of rational social organizations over medieval beliefs and irrational social hierarchies. There was widespread belief in the rationalizing nature of bureaucratic power, even in reports concerning the expanse of informal social organizations. "Although in theory a formal, rational, social organization governs every phase of the army life of enlisted men, in practice many army activities are controlled and carried on by informal social groups."[31] Compared to other militaries, the U.S. military was exceptionally "rational."

Rational administration was so highly mechanical, Martin Van Creveld noted, that "any- and every-thing was given a number. The official history is clogged with statistics, graphs, and tables; one of which, at any rate, is so complicated as to require ten pages of explanations."[32] The U.S. Army issued extensive regulations governing almost everything; its purpose, much like Taylor's, was to do everything the one best way. One observer reported:

In the technical units observed the minutiae of the daily job were prescribed in detailed technical orders, manuals, and directives, issued by higher headquarters and reaching the individual through the hierarchy of military authority. In some units these regulations ranged over such subjects as specifications for the size of the head of the arrow drawn on a map, hours of work, proper dress for work of various kinds, size of working shifts, nature of supervision, punctuation in work reports, courtesies to be shown to visiting officers, and standards of cleanliness.[33]

These next-to-godly orders concerning the devil of details attempted to fix the very best way of acting. Van Creveld concludes that "overall the U.S. Army's view of war was therefore considerably more managerial than the German one, putting far heavier emphasis on doctrine, planning, and control."[34] Planning every move in order to reduce wasted movement gave the military's administrators power over a range of actions that had been governed by the individual worker's discretion.

PROCUREMENT

Connections between the military and American society did not exist merely as common conceptions of managerial authority; they also existed as material connections between American industrial production and military organization. During World War II the American government's military exerted great control over industrial production. This control, generally centered in the administrative unit of the War Production Board (WPB), made the work of industry the work of a nation and involved two important aspects: (1) the state began to monitor and control business much more extensively and (2) the state's industrial organization began to affect the intellectual organization of the nation. This process of organization has often been called the organization of total war—in which every citizen became a soldier.[35] As the meaning of work aligned around the forces of nationalism, individual meanings for work were further driven underground.

It touched every aspect of the complex social and economic mechanism of the Nation. . . . In short, it involved a mass migration and a social and economic revolution of vast dimensions, much of it accomplished voluntarily under government direction, in order that our forces and those of our allies might have the superiority in weapons which is essential to victory in modern war.[36]

The U.S. government set up the WPB to monitor and control the relationship between business and the military—particularly the connections between industrial production and the military's needed equipment. "The normal functioning of the peacetime economy first had to be supplemented and ultimately had to be replaced by a system of centralized control."[37] "The national scheduling assignment might be described as the job of mobilizing the resources of the country by treating them as if they were the composite parts of a unified production complex."[38] Or, as the Army explained the challenges of organization in a companion volume: "the essence of economic mobilization for World War II was the development of a complex army of governmental agencies, activities, and controls for launching and managing the nation's war production program."[39] The WPB General Administrative Orders 2-23 and 2-33 (March 16, 1942 and April 22, 1942) allowed the military to place general preference, or P, orders with industry and organized the distribution of materials among manufacturers according to priority of production. During World War II, spending for defense consumed $304 billion of the $337 billion total spent by the U.S. government.[40] Control over this money was a significant source of power for the military.

As industrial production became closely tied to the military, there were disagreements over the control. "Since the American Revolution," Under Secretary Robert Patterson testified before Congress,

the Army and the Navy have been in charge of production of their weapons. The War Production Board is mobilizing the resources, facilities and materials (raw and semi-finished) necessary to such production and necessary also to civilian activities. It likewise allocates and controls the flow of materials so as to resolve conflicting demands of the Army, Navy, Maritime Commission, and other agencies and to adjust the program to available resources.[41]

The past demonstrated the need for military control of production and also provided examples of botched attempts at control. The entire nation began to function more as an industry—if goods backed up at one point, they were unavailable at another. The nation-state managed the movement of goods and money between different industries.

The creation of such a system addressed difficulties experienced during the previous world war, including the four-day closing in January 1918 of all factories east of the Mississippi by Harry Garfield in order to reduce pressure on distribution networks failing to keep up with industrial production. Former Harvard President Charles W. Eliot exclaimed concerning this failure, "The order itself inflicts a profound mortification on the American people, which, in my judgement, they will not forget for a long time. No one of the belligerent nations in Europe, except Russia, has been forced to admit such incompetence in public administration."[42] This embarrassing event encouraged the adoption of more rigorous methods of industrial regulation and planning.

Furthermore, in World War II there would be no silly regulations like that found in the National Defense Act of 1916, forbidding more than half of the officers of the General Staff from being located in Washington, D.C. at any one time.[43] "It is one of the inexplicable paradoxes of history," Britain's wartime prime minister, David Lloyd George, wrote after the war,

> That the greatest machine-producing nation on earth failed to turn out the mechanism of war after 18 months of sweating and toiling and hustling. . . . There were no braver or more fearless men in any Army, but the organization at home and behind the lines was not worthy of the reputation which American business men have deservedly won for smartness, promptitude and efficiency.[44]

The military believed, as did Taylor, that administrative control of knowledge and planning facilitated the mobilization of large-scale industrial production and offered a way to avoid such publicly embarrassing snafus. "THE ADMINISTRATIVE KEY to mass production is the painstaking planning, timing, and direction of the flow of materials and parts through the manufacturing process so that each item arrives at the final assembly line where and when it is needed." Mass production for the war machine conceived of the nation as an industry that needed organization and coordination in order to ensure that parts were distributed when and where needed. "Arrival ahead of time clutters up the production line or the factory with unnecessary materials. Arrival behind time interrupts the assembly operation and slows the production flow. This is the essence of the scheduling job in the individual plant expressed in its simplest terms." The need for this planning during a period of exceptionally high military demand placed planners in a position of authority over national industrial production. "In a larger sense, this is also the scheduling job in the national economy in time of war."[45] The nation at war was increasingly conceptualized as an industry.

In an effort to avoid a repeat of the embarrassing World War I performance, the United States began in the 1920s to plan for an M Day (Mobilization Day). The General Staff's plan for M Day required the extensive government takeover of industry according to the Industrial Mobilization Plan (IMP). The IMP proposed the creation of a highly centralized superagency to adequately plan organization of government agencies and to control the nation's industrial mobilization.[46] The IMP laid the groundwork for much of the control that actually occurred in World War II, particularly the methods of applying priority ratings to production. But one of the central elements, unified organizational control in the form of a highly centralized superagency that controlled economic mobilization, was rejected by President Roosevelt as imposing on his prerogatives to conduct war.[47]

Instead of approving this plan, the president reactivated the Advisory Commission to the Council of National Defense on May 29, 1940, which had technically remained after World War I.[48] As the management of the economy became more complex, the president created various offices and agencies to deal with more specific areas of concern, including the Office of Agricultural Defense Regulations, the Office of Price Administration and, most importantly, the Office of Production Management. Several additional boards and administrations were proposed and accepted until the eventual replacement of the entire system with the WPB, "which in many respects resembled the War Resource Administration proposed by the Industrial Mobilization Plan."[49] This reorganization on March 9, 1942 made Somervell responsible for both the Army's procurement and economic mobilization.[50] "The ASF organization brought together under one command all the scattered functions of the War Department concerned with services and materials."[51]

Scheduling and organization power also greatly influenced the authority imposed on civilian workers. Since military service reduced the domestic workforce, scheduling drove up the need for efficient production, both in the military and in domestic production, in order, to offset the loss in domestic workforce. After allowances for changes in price, according to the official War Department report, the annual gross national product of the United States increased by more than 50 percent between 1939 and 1944. One example of this increased production was Todd Shipyards. In 1941 Henry J. Kaiser, a former contractor and builder, greatly speeded up the production of ships at the Todd Shipyards. Before Kaiser applied methods of scientific management and production, the shipyards produced a merchant vessel in 300 days; by 1942 production time was reduced to 80 days, and by 1944 the shipyard produced a 10,000-ton Liberty ship in 17 days.[52]

Even in the short term, the domestic demand for production encouraged by the increase in military production affected the lives and expectations of workers. The military took roughly 10 million workers, creating a need for at least 7.5 million new workers—men and women not previously as directly involved in industrial production. These new workers produced with a high level of efficiency and represented, in part, the victory of less skilled and more easily replaceable labor. The average length of the work week for manufacturing concerns increased by 20 percent, from 37.7 hours to 45.2 hours. The average work week for construction workers increased from 32.4 to 39.5, while the work week for miners increased from 32.3 to 43.9 hours. As the Army's report concluded, "This mighty productive effort strained every industrial facility, the sources of all basic materials, and fabricated components, and the labor force available for employment. Under these extraordinarily demanding conditions the economic system was subject to stresses of the greatest severity. It became impossible to attain the desired volume and character of production under free market conditions."[53]

The great demand for productive forces encouraged the adoption of extensive state control of most major forms of production. Organization and coordination of production became a central concern for the nation-state and, significantly, introduced women into the workplace in greater numbers. Women went to work in administrative, bureaucratic, and industrial positions. This move gave women greater liberty to leave their homes but, perhaps, imprisoned them, like men, in systems of bureaucratic control. As unprecedented numbers of citizens went to work in hierarchical and bureaucratic systems, greater power was given to national-industrial systems of control and recognition.

Industrial discipline was further strengthened by the threat of military service.[54] Men in necessary industries received deferments; if these men failed to show up to work regularly, they could be reported to draft boards and given A-I status. These "work-or-fight" powers helped ensure obedience to industrial discipline.

In March 1943, the House Naval committee voted in favor of a bill, drafted by Texas Democrat Lyndon B. Johnson, to require employers holding war contracts or subcontracts to keep records of all unauthorized layoffs. The bill required employers to report the names of frequent absentees to their draft boards.[55] Johnson dramatized the need for legislative control over labor relations with the claim that absenteeism sank 42 Liberty ships in December alone, compared to the Nazis' 31.[56]

Regardless of congressional legislation, draft boards took their own actions. For example, the Reading Pennsylvania Draft Board No. 4 issued its own "work-or-fight" order. The notice informed local workers that the draft board would "reclassify for induction any war worker in Class 2-A, 2-B or 3-B whom it adjudges guilty of unnecessary absenteeism."[57] In that same month, the Labor-Management War Production Committee at the Monroe Calculating Machine Company's plant reported that its decision to report habitual absentees to draft boards for reclassification had reduced worker absenteeism by 30 percent.[58] There were other tactics that the Selective Service and War Manpower Commission utilized to ensure that workers understood they were involved in the war effort and were required to work. The War Manpower Commission's office in Philadelphia, for example, sent chronic absentees a letter: "Thank you very much for taking the day off. By so doing you help my cause in trying to beat a decadent democracy." The letter was signed, "Adolf Hitler." According to newspaper reports, the men returned to work and had not missed a single day.[59]

The threat of military service curtailed more than unofficial vacation days; they also proved useful to management as a way to discipline strikers. In Tuscaloosa, Alabama, Brig. Gen. Ben Smith, state director of Selective Service, ordered the local boards of Tuscaloosa to reclassify about 500 striking employees of the Central Foundry Company's plant at Holt, Alabama, as available for service. Gen. Smith wired Tuscaloosa Boards Nos. 1, 2, and 3 as follows: "Pursuant to classification circular No. 113, reclassification of registrants who are impeding the national defense program, you are directed to take the necessary action to immediately reclassify all registrants who are engaged in strike at Holt foundry and who have ceased to perform the job for which they were deferred. Give publicity to this telegram."[60]

The industrial power of the military over the national economy gave the military power over worker demands within that economy. Striking workers were faced with new threats, including the possible reassignment to the war. The use of the Selective Service as a strike-busting tool provoked angry response from labor. George Craig, CIO regional director for the Eastern Pennsylvania Region, wrote a letter in reaction to the June 9, 1941 order issued by Gen. Lewis Hershey, director of Selective Service, canceling draft deferments for striking workers:

A considerable number of cases have come to our attention in which the Local Draft Boards have re-classified strikers from deferment because of occupation to active service status. The effect of this classification is to make the Selective Service System a club over the heads of American workers, constantly threatening those in necessary occupations with induction into the Army if they dare exercise their rights to strike.[61]

One woman from Erie, Pennsylvania angrily wrote to Gen. Hershey, accusing him of undemocratic behavior.

On June 9th, by your order, the draft deferment of striking workmen was canceled. To my mind this order represents a clear violation of workers' rights, their legal rights to picket and strike. We are preparing to "defend" our democracy. Your order directly limits a democratic right of American workers. Shall we lose at home what we are preparing to defend by arms here or abroad?[62]

Most of the arguments in protest of this order compared it to supposed Nazi attempts at forced labor and noted the irony that the fight for democracy required the sacrifice of democracy. Members of the Draft Welfare Committee of one CIO affiliate wrote to Roosevelt in protest of the measure, which they felt was an undemocratic attempt to control labor.

We strongly oppose such an order and feel that you are sanctioning an undemocratic procedure. This order is definitely a strike breaking, union busting weapon. To attempt to regiment workers, to stop their fight for better conditions, for a higher standard of living and all that we call the American way of living is a *disgrace* to the traditions for which our forefathers fought![63]

American labor resented the utilization of draft law to subvert strikes, but Congress was encouraged by such efforts to further reign in labor. By May 1943, the Senate approved the Connally bill, which empowered the president to take over striking plants. In June, the House approved even more extensive powers. The president vetoed the final Smith-Connally bill, but Congress swiftly overturned his veto, giving the president the power to take over striking plants important to the war effort and making it a crime to encourage strikes in those plants. Because Roosevelt needed to maintain political ties to labor, the act was not as crippling to unions as it originally appeared to both critics and supporters.[64]

Workers were elements in the national machinery that needed to function in the interest of the nation and the war, a fact ten strikers at the American Chain and Cable Company discovered when the Selective Service Board removed their draft deferments in order to force a conclusion to the strike.[65] Government control of production was only one example of the connections between industrial production and the war, which, in effect, turned all citizens, at least conceptually, into soldiers.

The Army training film *Enough and On Time* taught a lesson to the entire range of support crew, from industrial worker to front line distributor, concerning the importance of goods arriving on schedule where they belonged. This new organization of the Army symbolized the closer ties between industrial war production and men on the front lines, blurring, as did the growth of miliary bureaucracy, the understanding of war as something that only occurs where men fight. This film traced the cause of some absent fuses, which resulted in deaths. Beginning with the people responsible for the manufacture of these fuses, the investigator found that some civilian workers in an ordnance plant were responsible for the missing fuses because of absent-minded handling of crates. "General," the lead investigator began, "I'm looking for some murderers." As the film concludes, pictures of the men responsible are overlaid with the scenes of men dying, clearly connecting industrial labor to warfare.[66]

Total war, then, is a great equalizer. It levels class distinctions. By subjugating both armed and unarmed members of the community to the danger of violent death, modern war creates a community of equals. Heroism under these conditions is no longer a military virtue only. The heroes of this war are not the unknown soldiers but the unknown common men and women, whether or not they wear uniforms.[67]

Regardless of dress appearance, the intellectual style of the nation mirrored the industrial division of labor.

Every national was conceived of as a soldier. This "total war" contributed to the nationalization of identification and the bureaucratization of authority. One particularly telling example was the poster produced by the Works Progress Administration that paired a riveter and a machine gunner. "Give 'Em Both Barrels," the poster advised. Industrial workers were equated with soldiers. Another poster exhorted, "You are a production Soldier: America's first line of defense."[68] Jobs of industrial production were done, it was hoped, in the name of the nation. The nation became a source of legitimacy for those jobs as the nation worked to make sure that production was carried out in its name. All had their national jobs to perform; everyone became a worker for the nation. Total war, in this way, contributed to the understanding of citizens as parts of a national machine. In much the same way as all workers contributed to a corporation, all citizens had their different role to play in the nation.

This centralization around the nation-state was not without its divisions. Local communities and states, for example, still exerted authority. In the case of the Selective Service System, this division worked to amplify the power of the nation-state. States or local communities were not powers exerted against the national power, but identities and powers that worked with the nation-state, powers that were essentially harnessed to the national chariot. This utilization of differences became a central element in the consolidation of national power. World War II occurred in an era in which differences would be organized not as alternative and possibly competitive centers of interest and community, but as bureaucratic differences that required order. Differences became elements that could be put to different uses and had different elements valuable to the nation-state.

NOTES

1. Max Weber, *Economy and Society*, Vol. II (Berkeley: University of California Press, 1978), 981.

2. "Only since the peace of Tilsit [in 1807,]" Weber claimed, "has the concentration of the means of warfare in the hands of the state definitely come about" (*Economy and Society*, Vol. II, 982). Even during the American Civil War, officers were elected by the men who served under but were not necessarily appointed by presidential authority; these men typically were called together by a prominent local individual. "In practice, the election of officers was of a *pro forma* ratification of the role that a prominent planter, lawyer, or other individual had taken in recruiting a company or a regiment. Sometimes a wealthy man also paid for the uniforms and equipment of a unit he had recruited." James M. McPherson, *Battle Cry of Freedom* (New York: Oxford University Press, 1988), 318. Samuel Huntington claims that, "if it were necessary to give a precise date to the origin of the military profession, August 6, 1808 would have to be chosen." Huntington, *The Soldier and the State* (New York: Vintage Books, 1964), 30. This was the date on which the Prussian government issued a pronouncement of the qualification of officers that most recognizably conforms to modern notions of official duty.

3. Winston Churchill, *The Second World War*, Vol. 2 (Boston: Houghton Mifflin, 1985), 619–21.

4. Kent Roberts Greenfield, Robert R. Palmer, and Bell I. Wiley, "Ground Forces in the Army: A Statistical Study," in *The Organization of Ground Combat Troops* (Washington, D.C.: Historical Division Department of the Army, 1947), 175.

5. Weekly Bulletin, Headquarters Army Ground Forces, D.C. Number 3, 24 November 1942, Quotation from War Department letter AG 320.2 (11-4-42) OB-I-A, 9 November 1942, National Archives, Record Group 337, AGF 341, Box 586, Binder 5.

6. John Ellis, *The Sharp End: The Fighting Man in World War II* (New York: Charles Scribner's Sons, 1980), 157.

7. Michael C.C. Adams, *The Best War Ever: America and World War II* (Baltimore, Md.: Johns Hopkins University Press, 1994), 70.

8. Greenfield et al., *The Organization of Ground Combat Troops*, 170.

9. The Taylor system was remarkable in its production of "non-producers" and tended to raise the ratio of overhead costs to labor costs. Carl Barth attempted to make this clear during the Watertown Arsenals adoption of Taylor's methods. "Under a Taylor System of Management the ratio between indirect and direct labor ... will be absolutely incomparable with this ratio under the kind of management and the system of cost accounting now in operation at the Watertown Arsenal," he wrote in his initial report to Crozier. Barth to Crozier, April 17, 1909, ODR, Watertown Arsenal Document File, Box 1052, File 10206–10222, in Hugh G.J. Aitken, *Scientific Management in Action: Taylorism at Watertown Arsenal, 1908-1915* (Princeton, N.J.: Princeton University Press, 1985), 88. Or as Taylor wrote in *Shop Management*: "The belief is almost universal among manufacturers that for economy the number of brain workers, or non-producers, as they are called, should be as small as possible in proportion to the number of producers, *i.e.*, those who actually work with their hands. An examination of the most successful establishments will, however, show that the reverse is true." Taylor, *Shop Management*, in *Scientific Management* (New York: Frederick Taylor, 1911; reprint, New York: Harper & Row, 1947), 121.

10. Robert R. Palmer, "Mobilization of the Ground Army," in Greenfield et al., *The Organization of Ground Combat Troops*, 190.

11. O.L. Nelson, *National Security and the General Staff*, p. 335, quoted in John D. Millett, *The Organization and Role of the Army Service Forces* (Washington, D.C.: Office of the Chief of Military History Department of the Army, 1954), 36.

12. "The new setup of 9 March 1942 recognized an organizational need which had been evident in the top command of the Army, both overseas and in the United States, since World War I. This need was to handle all procurement and all supply operations as one integrated activity." Millett, *Organization and Role*, 38.

13. Some elements of the French military had been substantially remodified along Taylor's principles. Government-operated arsenals adopted Taylor's methods, and Taylor had been personally involved in changes at Michelin. Furthermore, Renault, the company that had supplied most of the American tanks in World War I, and Panhard also adopted Taylor's methods. In 1913, Renault workers struck against scientific management because, according to Taylor, Renault had attempted to proceed too rapidly. Nelson, *National Security*, 179; Lyndall F. Urwick, ed., *The Golden Book of Management: A Historical Record of the Life and Work of Seventy Pioneers* (London: N. Neame, 1956), 56. See also Aimee Moutet, "Les origines du systeme de Taylor en France: Le point de vue patronal (1907-1914)," *Le Mouvement Social* 93 (October–December 1975): 15-49; Paul Devinat, *Scientific Management in Europe* (Geneva: International Labour Office, 1927), 23; and Charles S. Maier, "Between Taylorism and Technocracy: European Ideologies and the Vision of Industrial Productivity in the 1920s," *Journal of Contemporary History* 5 (1970): 27-61. Walter Millis discusses America's reliance on France for tanks in *Arms and Men* (New York: Putnam Books, 1956), 261–62. For an excellent study of the political struggles in France and Germany between Taylorians and Fatigue, or Science of

Work, studies, see Anson Rabinbach, *The Human Motor: Energy, Fatigue, and the Origins of Modernity* (Berkeley: University of California Press, 1992).

14. Millett, *Organization and Role*, 15.
15. Ibid., 18.
16. Ibid.
17. Ibid., 26.
18. Ibid., 27.
19. Booz, Frey, Allen, and Hamilton, "Surveys of the Office of the Under Secretary of War," 20 December 1941, Under Secretary's Office, referenced in ibid., 27.
20. Millett, *Organization and Role*, 30.
21. Ibid., 31.
22. Ibid., 36.
23. The lack of coordination between tactical command and supply command was one of the issues that the reorganization attempted to resolve. Ibid., 24.
24. "The Reorganization of the War Department," in ibid., 38.
25. R. Eberton Smith, *The Army and Economic Mobilization* (Washington, D.C.: Office of the Chief of Military History, 1959), 105.
26. All quotations in this paragraph are from *Attack on Hidden Waste*, Army Pictorial Service, National Archives, Record Group 111, Series M/1073.
27. *Attack on Hidden Waste*.
28. Daniel Boorstin, *The Americans: The Democratic Experience* (New York: Random House, 1973), 369.
29. *Attack on Hidden Waste*.
30. Arnold Rose, "The Social Structure of the Army," *The American Journal of Sociology* 51, 5 (March 1946): 364.
31. Anonymous, "Informal Social Organization in the Army," *The American Journal of Sociology* 51, 5 (March 1946): 365.
32. Martin Van Creveld, *Fighting Power: German and U.S. Army Performance, 1939–1945* (Westport, Conn.: Greenwood Press, 1982), 63–64.
33. Anonymous, "Informal Social Organization," 365.
34. Van Creveld, *Fighting Power*, 33.
35. "Total war is not altogether a moral phenomenon, a result of wickedness," wrote Hans Speier, a professor of sociology in the Gradate Faculty of Political and Social Science, New School for Social Research, New York City. "It is the war of the machine age, with its applied science, widespread literacy, and the worship of efficient organization." Total war, he suggested, owed much to scientific management. Hans Speier, "The Effect of War on the Social Order," *The Annals of the American Academy of Political and Social Science* 218 (November 1941): 89. It is worth remembering Hannah Arendt's comments on the re-creation of total war. "There is *first* the fact that the seeds of total war developed as early as the First World War, when the distinction between soldiers and civilians was no longer respected because it was inconsistent with the new weapons then used. To be sure, this distinction itself had been a relatively modern achievement, and its practical abolition meant no more than the reversion of warfare to the day when the Romans wiped Carthage off the face of the earth. Under modern circumstances, however, this appearance or reappearance of total war has a very important political significance insofar as it contradicts the basic assumptions upon which the relationship between the military and the civilian branches of government rests: it is the function of the army to protect and to defend

the civilian population . . . until today the strategy of deterrence has openly changed the role of the military from that of a protector into that of a belated and essentially futile avenger." Hannah Arendt, *On Revolution* (New York: Viking Compass, 1965), 5.

36. Troyer S. Anderson, "Munitions for the Army—A Five Year Report on the Procurement of Munitions by the War Department Under the Direction of the Under Secretary of War (9 April 1946)," U.S. Army, Office of the Chief of Military History, 2–3, in Smith, *The Army and Economic Mobilization*, 30–31.

37. David Novick, Melvin Anshen, and W.C. Truppner, *Wartime Production Controls* (New York: Columbia University Press, 1949), 15.

38. Ibid., 268.

39. Smith, *The Army and Economic Mobilization*, 8.

40. Ibid., 4.

41. Robert P. Patterson, "Responsibility for Military Procurement Before the Senate Special Committee Investigating the National Defense Program," 77th Congress, 2nd Session, 16 December 1942, in Millett, *Organization and Role*, Appendix H, 458.

42. David Kennedy, *Over Here: The First World War and American Society* (New York: Oxford University Press, 1980), 124.

43. Smith, *The Army and Economic Mobilization*, 36.

44. David Lloyd George, *War Memoirs of David Lloyd George*, Vol. 2 (London: Odhams Press, 1942), 1831, 1833.

45. Novick et al., *Wartime Production Controls*, 268.

46. Smith, *The Army and Economic Mobilization*, 86.

47. Ibid., 89, 98–99.

48. Ibid., 103.

49. Ibid., 105.

50. Ibid., 112.

51. Ibid., 115.

52. Gerald D. Nash, *The Great Depression and World War II: Organizing America, 1933–1945* (New York: St. Martin's Press, 1979), 137.

53. Novick et al., *Wartime Production Controls*, 15.

54. And strengthened by the taint of disservice. Reportedly, "a machine company in Connecticut announced it will award each week a plaque, inscribed with a swastika, to the department or section having the highest percentage of absentees." George Stimpson, "Some Absenteeism Cures Hold Harsh Note," Cedar Rapids, Iowa *Gazette*, March 14, 1943.

55. " 'Work or Fight' Bill May Be Approved by Committee Today," Washington, D.C. *Star*, March 12, 1943.

56. "Victims of Absenteeism," Macon, Ga. *Telegraph*, March 2, 1943.

57. "Absenteeism to Bring Draft Reclassification," Washington, D.C. *Star*, March 9, 1943.

58. "Draft Threat Reduces Absenteeism in Plant," Washington, D.C. *Star*, March 7, 1943.

59. "Acting On 'Work or Fight' Order," Allentown, Pa. *Morning Call*, March 4, 1943.

60. "Alabama Draft Chief Orders 500 Strikers Reclassified," Washington, D.C. *Star*, March 20, 1943.

61. George Craig, letter to Lewis Hershey, August 26, 1941, National Archives, Record Group 147, Stack Area 17W4, Row 11, Compartment 02, Entry 2, Records of the Selective Service System, Box 33.

62. Katherine Bogart Ross, letter to Gen. Lewis Hershey, October 14, 1941, Erie, Pennsylvania, National Archives, Record Group 147, Stack Area 17W4, Row 11, Compartment 02, Entry 2, Records of the Selective Service System, Box 33.

63. Draft Welfare Committee, United Office and Professional Workers of America, New York, letter to President F.D.Roosevelt, June 9, 1941, National Archives, Record Group 147, Stack Area 17W4, Row 11, Compartment 02, Entry 2, Records of the Selective Service System, Box 33.

64. Richard Polenberg, *War and Society: The United States, 1941–1945* (New York: J.B. Lippincott, 1972), 167–69.

65. War Department Memo, "Strike at American Chain and Cable Company, Nonessen, Pennsylvania," September 10, 1941, National Archives, Record Group 147, Stack Area 17W4, Row 11, Compartment 02, Entry 2, Records of the Selective Service System, Box 33.

66. *Enough and on Time*, War Department, Signal Corps, National Archives, Record Group 111, Series TF/2094.

67. Speier, "The Effect of War," 90–91.

68. Adams, *The Best War Ever*, 74.

Chapter 4

Tests and Nuts: Testing and the Organization of Citizens

> A "scientific" interpretation of the world, as you understand it, might therefore still be one of the *most stupid* of all possible interpretations of the world, meaning that it would be one of the poorest in meaning. This thought is intended for the ears and consciences of our mechanists who nowadays like to pass as philosophers and insist that mechanics is the doctrine of the first and last laws on which all existence must be based as on a ground floor. But an essentially mechanical world would be an essentially *meaningless* world.
> —Friedrich Nietzsche, *The Gay Science*, Book 5, section 373

This chapter explores the military's collection of information about recruits. During World War II the military utilized physical and mental examinations and tests much more thoroughly than ever before, including tests given by psychiatrists. "And another mistake we could have made and didn't," reported Brigadier General Hugh Johnson, concerning World War I induction,

all the psychiatrists, all the nuts of various kinds . . . they came in with fancy, patent medicine schemes, and one of them was that we should sit there and have the draft boards pass on the qualifications of the soldiers before they were drafted and taken to the camps, to determine whether they ought to be brigadier generals or privates in the rear rank.[1]

World War II made the mistake—tests and nuts proliferated as the military scrutinized recruits, compiled extensive studies, and sought to place inductees in their proper organizational position with the proper attitude.

One of the most significant characteristics of the U.S. Army, like American society more generally, was the collection and organization of information. In this, both participated in the social trend exemplified by Taylorite scientific management. Taylor emphasized the importance of the careful, "scientific" collection, organization, and utilization of performance information. "What the writer wishes particularly to emphasize," wrote Taylor, "is that this whole system rests upon an accurate and scientific study of unit times, which is by far the most important element in scientific management."[2] The cultural trends exemplified by Taylor demanded the investigation of "facts," and increasingly the facts were social. The authors of *Wartime Production Controls* claimed accumulation of social information was crucial to the military's success in the war.

> It is only through the intelligent use and interpretation of such information that the nation's resources can be allocated so as to maximize the effective contribution of both the military and civilian sectors of the war economy. This fundamental responsibility for the collection, tabulation, and interpretation of statistical information was central to the successful execution of the entire war program.[3]

Beginning with an examination of the Army's system of induction, this chapter examines the Army's collection of information about recruits and soldiers. The military conducted detailed studies of the physical capacities and dimensions of the physical bodies of recruits which contributed to the military's ability to place these recruits in the jobs for which they were physically suited. This process also increased the physical standardization enacted by the military on the physical body and, much more significantly than ever before, to study the mental state of the recruit in an effort to place the recruits in the proper intellectual order.

Studies of recruits began on October 16, 1940, the day all men in the United States had to register for military service. The overwhelming acceptance by the public of this registration revealed the power of the nation-state and the legitimacy of exceptional powers of coercion. National power, particularly the intellectual power involved in imagining yourself as part of the nation, during World War II deviated from national power during World War I in its acceptance of racial, religious, and ethnic diversity. World War I produced a large demand for homogeneity, as many people believed that particulars of some identities threatened national unity and should be suppressed or destroyed. Gen. Leonard Wood was only one proponent of using World War I as a way to Americanize racial and ethnic differences so that everyone would "speak American and think American."[4] During World War

II, on the other hand, the nation did not demand homogeneity so much as diversity united for a common national purpose. Personal and group traits were legitimated by their utility in a national division of labor. The social understanding that affirmed difference within a workplace began to function within the nation. In fact, compared to World War I, there was relatively little demand for citizens to lose ethnic, religious, or racial traits that might distinguish them from their fellow citizens. Therefore, instead of appearing as challenges to a national identity, as during World War I, these traits appeared as elements of a national identity, with each part serving a different function. This pluralism corresponded to the valuation of an industrial division of labor like that associated with Taylorism. Industrial society was increasingly explained as an association of diversity necessary for the correct functioning of a corporation, even as the nation was increasingly explained in a similar way. Differences were necessary because workers/citizens had different functions to perform for the social body.

INDUCTION

On October 16, 1940, between 16 million and 17 million men registered with Selective Service in accordance with the Selective Training and Service Act of 1940. There were isolated resistances to draft registration. "Of course not all were eager. Some were unwilling. Some even stayed away entirely, but the latter were obviously a tiny, fragmentary minority."[5] Free citizens and non-citizens accepted reluctantly and enthusiastically the demand by the state that they offer personal information to the state in preparation for war. Positive accounts of draft registration highlighted the ability of the state to call upon a wide variety of ethnicities, races, and classes to respond to its needs, revealing a pluralism reliant on the maintenance of differences.

After suggesting that emotionalism was at a much lower ebb than twenty-three years earlier, when men registered for World War I, newspapers praised the professional way that citizens registered. "Registration for the draft yesterday went on in an orderly, business like, matter-of-fact manner. The men went to the designated places, and the work was carried through in routine fashion."[6] The acceptance was very businesslike, especially in its reliance on a conception of the value of differences that work together. Many different ethnicities, races, religions, and cultures became elements in the American nation—a pluralism that allowed for many differences, as long as those differences worked for the good of the nation.

"Sixteen million strong and more—sons of the poor and wealthy," newspaper reports rejoiced, "truck drivers, Hollywood glamour boys, big league ball players, shifty-eyed waterfront drifters, college students, aliens devoid of English—they streamed in and out of the registration places throughout a day unparalleled in American history." The rich and the poor, the famous and the unknown, all united under the flag of the nation. Not only were classes united but races came together, not in a boiling cauldron, but into a relationship that relied on differences.

Henry Ford II, grandson of the automobile manufacturer, stood side by side with a Filipino domestic at a municipal building in suburban Detroit awaiting his turn to sign up.... Four Chinese boys were first in line at Philadelphia headquarters. They signed their names in Chinese characters.... A Shreveport Negro presented himself, carrying a suit case packed, saying he was ready to go to war.

All of these different races, ethnicities, classes, and religious groups came together for the benefit of the nation. "And so it went," repeated the Associated Press in newspapers across the nation. "In the aggregate they formed a motley but mighty army from which picked men will be drawn to swell the nation's armed forces."[7]

This draft, like its predecessor in 1917, demonstrated all over again that the United States is a polyglot nation, home of every racial strain on earth. And representatives of every race went freely to their appointed places and supplied the information that, in these times of emergency, may one day put them not only in uniform but also behind guns whose targets are not paper. The descendants of the Mayflower families, the sons of Germans, Irish, English, Chinese, Japanese, Hungarian, Italian, Rumanian, Turkish parents stood in line awaiting their turns. They answered eleven identical questions, they received identical cards that they must carry with them always. And the spirit they displayed was a calm, cooperative spirit. There was horseplay in some registration lines, typical soldierly grumbling about delay in others, but no instances of violence.[8]

Cooperation and efficiency were the watchwords for the stories of diversity united to register for the draft. Registration and classification of those millions was one of the central and most widely shared experiences of World War II for males and was conducted with incredible efficiency. Hugh Johnson, one of the two people most responsible for the operation of the draft in World War I, made early pleas on the basis of efficiency to pass the Burke-Wadsworth bill, which authorized the registration. "While the kind of organization we set up in 1917 can begin to select men in a few weeks, it can't get into its full scientific and equitable efficiency in less than four months—not until registration and classification of millions are complete."[9]

Central to efficient registration was the acquisition of information to influence the classification of soldiers. A soldier's military life began with a ritual emblematic of military life, and the late twentieth century more generally—filling out forms. Men reported their names and addresses to the government and filled out a seven-page questionnaire. For many recruits, reporting to the nation-state was a novel experience (in 1940 only three out of a hundred citizens had ever filled out federal income tax forms).[10] The completion of this form and questionnaire symbolized their entrance into the military's world of social studies. "Everybody, by this time, is accustomed to filling out endless questionnaires," a newspaper remarked. "Nobody seemed to think it was anything out of the ordinary," the report stated, suggesting with the back of the hand that it was unusual.[11] The sorts of disciplines needed for people to reveal personal information had become, by 1940, relatively commonplace in terms of employment but somewhat new when dealing with the nation-state.

The form that men completed on October 16, 1940 contained only eleven questions: name, address, age, telephone number, place of birth, citizenship, name of person who would always know their address, relationship of that person, address of that person, employer's name, and place of employment. This, however, was only the beginning. After completing the form, the registrant filled out a registration card—a white, 2.5" × 3.5" card that registrants carried at all times as proof of enlistment.[12]

The cards, it turned out, were useful for policing drinking ages and keeping youngsters out of juke joints as well as putting men in the military.[13] The cards became highly demanded black market items for draft dodgers, workers, and underage drinkers.[14] The FBI even made headlines in San Francisco in June 1943 for "smashing" a "high school draft card ring."[15]

The short, eleven-question form recruits filled out was sent to a location central to many draft boards, most often an armory. There, workers grouped cards by draft board area, usually an area of about 30,000 persons. By the very next day, October 17, 1940, local draft boards shuffled their cards and affixed serial numbers to them. In Washington, D.C., numbers from one to the highest in any single state were placed in the same big fishbowl used for the World War I draft. President Franklin Roosevelt used the same ladle and blindfold that Woodrow Wilson used in that draft to select the initial draft numbers.[16]

After all of these numbers were drawn, the order of induction was generally known. Draft boards then sent out much more comprehensive questionnaires to registrants at a rate of thirty to fifty per day according to lottery number. Within five days, recruits were to return these questionnaires to their draft boards. This form was a seven-page, highly detailed study of "all facts about himself that have bearing on whether he should be called to serve."[17] After completing this form, recruits were called to their local draft board, which was composed of three men appointed by the president at the recommendation of the governor. There they submitted to a number of tests and inquisitions.

World War II presented an opportunity for the extension of the power of social scientific knowledge. The military, in association with academic social scientists, began an encyclopedic compilation of information about recruits.[18] Michael Adams has referred to this as one of the problems of military induction. "The root problem here lay in a reliance on behavioral science techniques that were pioneered in America but that were at a relatively early and crude stage of development. . . . This was one of the worst aspects of the growth of the organization society, with its insistence on machine like regularity."[19]

Like scientific managers, social scientists learned that there was power in the control and professionalization of knowledge. "Behavioral scientists suggested that you could quickly and easily deal with large masses of humanity through the application of standardized test questions. . . . Social scientists tried to apply industrial, production line, quality control techniques to people," Michael Adams concluded.[20] The application of quality control by the military began one of the largest social science projects ever attempted. Power in an administrative state relied on accurate understanding and organization of its "human resources."

It quickly became apparent to people involved in these examinations that the information could be used for more than simply the military induction process. In Patterson, New Jersey, health officer Dr. Frederick P. Lee, "realizing that physical examinations of draftees opened a new field for case finding," requested that the Board of Health station a nurse at the Newark induction station. The nurse's job was to collect the names and addresses of all men rejected for health reasons. The local draft board then ordered rejected draftees to report to the local clinic for examination. This order by the draft board received an almost 100 percent response through the use of "the Selective Service system as a case-finding medium."[21] But these studies did more that simply aid in policing or control.

Medical and social science professions used elements of Taylor's organization of production to meet the mass demands of the military. The military demanded, for the purposes of standardization, that rules be established over almost all vagaries concerning the best ways to do almost anything. The rule making even applied to the professionals that served the Army. For example, the Army's dental staff circulated a letter detailing their refusal to set a specific number of teeth necessary to chew Army rations in order to set clear standards for denture distribution.[22] In this case, the military's demand for standardized rules clashed with the dentists' understanding of the many different ways of chewing. There were too many variables in chewing to standardize it for optimal efficiency, the dentists claimed.

It is impractical and militarily and professionally inexpedient to declare that a given minimum number of natural teeth are necessary to masticate the Army ration. The size, shape, condition, and position of the dental arches, as well as the teeth, are all determining factors in a diagnosis and decision. When comparing individuals, even though each has the same number of natural teeth, there is a vast difference in occlusal patterns and chewing efficiency.[23]

Recruits underwent a battery of physical tests to ensure that they could efficiently perform many tasks essential to their military service, including mastication. Beginning with the urine test, typically given in a large room with rows of containers that had "to be done like this so as not to take a month to get a bunch through the routine," the Army quickly marched recruits through their physicals, but the examinations typically took most of a day. Everything was checked, including, eyes, ears, and teeth.[24] The Selective Service examiners received clear instructions on the grading of recruits according to their physical abilities. In spite of the complaints of dentists, the Selective Service regulations set out rules governing the classification of recruits according to the number and positions of their teeth. "A minimum of 3 serviceable natural masticating teeth above and 3 below opposing and 3 serviceable natural incisors above and 3 below opposing. (Therefore, the minimum requirements consist of a total of 6 masticating teeth and of 6 incisor teeth.) All of these teeth must be so opposed as to serve the purpose of incision and mastication."[25]

The military's standardization of the body was an element in the Cheshire process, in which the individual's body disappeared except for its parts, which were ordered according to their efficient functioning. In conjunction with the training that the recruits underwent, standardization of the function of body parts revised the understanding of the individual and the body; as the body became more standardized, less individual, and functioned more as a machine, conceptions of individualism had to lurk in what was common as well as what was unknowable.

Changes in the understanding of the self and the body ran into a problem during induction—a problem related to sexuality. Since the birth of the "homosexual" at the dawn of the twentieth century, sexuality was read as the truth of the self displayed through physical action. Sex was not something people occasionally did, but became an action that betrayed the true self.

By World War II, however, desire, in this case sexual, became something that lurked, regardless of action. Psychiatrists were put in charge of analyzing communication for any trace of disorderly sexual desire. Confession betrayed desires. In an inverse relation to the way the "homosexual" first appeared in American political discourse, that is, instead of action betraying the truth of the self, communication could betray truths that existed regardless of action.

The Army film *Introduction to the Army* attempted to prepare recruits for mental and physical examination. "Somewhere along the line you're going to lose your clothes for the rest of the trip. This is where you better check any bashfulness you may still have, cause here's where all privacy ends. Did you ever have one of those dreams about being out someplace and suddenly realizing you didn't have any pants on? Well, this is it."[26]

Bashfulness would not remove recruits from the demand to reveal their physical body, their personal attitudes, and their dreams. The mental examinations conducted on the recruits focused on their sexuality. *Introduction to the Army*, which virtually all new inductees watched, portrayed the psychological interview given to high school graduates.[27] "Since you are a high school graduate you won't have to take the psychological test they give to nongrads. But you will be interviewed by psychiatrists along with all the rest. They've got to know how you will adjust yourself to the Army. If you've got what it takes to make a soldier."

Apparently, what it took to be a soldier was an affection for girls. The film cut to the interview between Johnny and the psychiatrist, who asked Johnny: "Are you married, Jones?"

"No sir," Johnny replied.

"Do you like, aah, going around with girls?"

"Well, I didn't before kindergarten, but after that I was crazy about them," responded Johnny.

As Johnny left the interview room the camera recorded his conversation with himself: "Do I like girls!?"

Johnny's scripted answer betrayed a crucial slip: he was asked if he liked to "go around with girls," an action of physical accompaniment, yet his answer conveyed a mental state of being "crazy" about them. This move from action as the revelation of the self to unseen desires as the "truth" of the self was an important occurrence of the early twentieth century, an occurrence hastened by the work that scientific methods of management in business and the military did to erode the body (and action) as the truth of the individual.

The military's scrutiny of sexual desire also reified the position of women as objects of male desire, which was a significant component in the all-male environment of the military. Army films consistently made women objects of desire, a project that utilized this historical social order to solidify the increased power of the nation.

Sexual identities aided in the defense of troubled gender boundaries created by the eventual mass movement of women into industrial and bureaucratic positions, as well as the homosocial society of military life. Furthermore, democracy had taken on feminine meanings in the face of the fascist obsession with masculine metaphors. Defenders of the masculinity of America were determined to demonstrate that America was masculine and hard, not soft and feminine. Clarence A. Dykstra declared in his first public statements as Selective Service director that "those who had thought we were soft and supine and, as a democracy, could not move with effectiveness, may be disappointed."[28] Response to the call for registration gave the executive officer of Selective Service, Lieutenant Colonel Lewis B. Hershey, a feeling of pride in American manhood. "Anyone who watched these Americans at the places of registration must have sensed a great surging pride, for America's manhood was parading through those places of registration today, America's youth upon whom the nation depends for preservation."[29] Conceptions of masculinity, like many truths dependent on the body, were called into question by changes in work. The homosocial world of the military also created tensions concerning sexual identity, which were manifested during the induction process through close scrutiny of homosexual interest.

The tests and nuts that Hugh Johnson feared brought a new elaboration of scientific studies to the recruit. For the first time, a large percentage of Americans submitted to psychological testing. In World War I the military conducted fairly extensive tests of the physical properties of the recruits, and attempted to standardize them by work performance. In World War II the program was directed to the mental properties of the recruits. By directing such studies to the attitudes, values, and opinions of recruits, these very personal attributes increasingly appeared less personal and more standardized.

If the inductee had failed to graduate from high school and failed the Mental Qualification Test, he was given two more tests. The Block Counting Test DST-10 was administered first, since it was perceived to be the easiest. This was followed with the Concrete Directions Test. "No man will be recommended for induction on the basis of individual tests unless he has passed *both* the Block Counting Test and The Concrete Directions Test." Of course, failing all of these tests did not ensure an inductee of freedom. After failing these tests they were then interviewed, "to detect malingering and check for inconsistencies. Such interviews will be individual, and will be conducted by specially trained personnel. When practicable, the interview may be combined with the individual tests referred to in paragraph 4d." If a soldier was thus rejected, his form 221 was marked "disqualified for military service by reason of failure to meet minimum intelligence standards." For soldiers who passed, a Report of Mental Status was forwarded to their reception centers.[30] Soldiers rejected by psychological personnel could be granted 4-F status for "any serious mental or neurological disorder," including:

a. Insanity, b. Epilepsy, . . . Post-encephalitic syndrome, Imbecility, Drug Addiction, Chronic alcoholism, Severe stammering, Psychoneuroses and constitutional psychopathic states, Chronic essential chorea, Syphilis of central nervous system, Post-traumatic cerebral syndrome, Multiple sclerosis, Paraplegia or hemiplegia, Syringomyelia, Muscular atrophies and dystrophies, Hysterical paralysis, Neuritis or neuralgia, Brain tumors, Cerebral arteriosclerosis . . . t. Sexual perversion.[31]

Sexual perversion, the final category of rejection, was listed as a serious mental disorder that psychological personnel were directed to search out, but symptoms of sexual perversion were never explained. Several types of insanity were explained including:

Dementia praecox.—Look for indifference, apathy, withdrawal from environment, ideas of reference and persecution, feelings of the mind being tampered with, or thought being controlled by hypnotic, spiritualistic, or other mysterious agencies, hallucinations of hearing, bodily hallucinations, frequently of electrical or sexual character, meaningless smiles, in general, inappropriate emotional reactions and lack of connectedness in conversation. There may be sudden emotional or motor outbursts. The history of family life and of school, vocational, or personal career will usually show erratic and more or less irrational conduct.[32]

This manual of rules governing the Selective Service listed physical signs of attitudes, teaching examiners to read the physical body for signs of mental health, feelings, and thoughts. The mental and physical state of malingering was also on the list of signs to note. "Persons of intelligence and education have more difficulty in deceiving, as they are bound to express themselves freely. If they are reticent in these matters they arouse suspicion by their reticence. Those who talk freely may be counted on to say things at variance with the existence of the disease of which they complain."[33] The higher the level of education, the greater the difficulty in deception through speech, since the educated were prone to speak freely. The determination to read speech for clues that could give away the hidden desires and attitudes was an element of power at this time.

Everyone was expected to speak freely, or at least answer written questions freely. The Army's film *Classification of Enlisted Men, Personnel Placement in the Army* conveniently explained the Army's procedure for creating a mental characterization for recruits. The film began with an account of the different backgrounds of four men—their different skills, hobbies, and occupations. "Men from every walk of life. A mass that must be sorted and selected."[34] The men in the film began their military careers with a test. This test, the Army General Classification Test (AGCT), produced a number that would attach to the recruit for the duration of their Army careers. "Not an IQ test," the narrator assured the recruits, "but rather a comparative rating test."

"Now begins your mental calisthenics," the narrator of the basic training film *Introduction to the Army* informed the viewer and his newly inducted next-door neighbor.

First you'll take the Army General Classification Test. Take a tip from me and do your best on this test, and all the others you take at the reception center. The scores you make will have a lot to do with deciding what kind of an Army job you'll get. If you get stuck on one question skip it and go to the next one. Those forty minutes will be up before you know it.[35]

The recruit's performance during these forty minutes placed them in one of five categories. As the neighbor correctly explained, a recruit's score affected the sorts of jobs he could be assigned to, including such routine jobs as driving. "It does not appear to be practical or economical, considering the projected employment and urgent need of subject units," an Army memorandum of September 1943, claimed, "to attempt to produce 'safe and skillful' drivers from personnel having low AGCT scores." This memorandum further directed attention to the Training Manual: "Test of intelligence.—Persons very low in intelligence are unlikely to respond successfully to emergencies on the road. It would be wise to exclude from driver training anyone who has received the grade V (or a score of 60 or less) on the Army General Classification Test. This information may be available in company records."[36]

The AGCT test relied on answers to questions to determine individual characteristics of recruits. Answers supplied knowledge of the truth of the recruits; not answers to what they could do or what skills they possessed, but answers concerning whether recruits would ever be able to perform hypothetical tasks. The idea that people could make themselves into many different selves through different actions met the conception of the self as destined for machinelike utility within its one best location, thereby taking much of the individualism out of most jobs.[37]

After the recruits completed the AGCT test, they were interviewed in order to determine the recruits' knowledge and skills in different areas of employment. "Every reception center has specially trained interviewers, many of them selectees themselves. They are sympathetic, yet each one is an expert in drawing out all of the information necessary for this primary classification," the narrator informed the viewer. The interviewers used two books, the *Dictionary of Occupational Titles* and the *Oral Trade Test Manual*, to determine exactly what jobs the recruits had performed in civilian life and to judge their knowledge of those jobs.[38]

After this interview the inductee went to the classifier, who studied the facts collected by the interviewer and the score on the AGCT. The classifier assigned the recruit a serial number that designated the inductee's most suitable jobs. Office workers punched this number as slots into the recruit's information card. By cutting slots in the cards, office workers could isolate recruits with the necessary job number by placing the cards on a wire rack. The rack had wires specially gauged for different occupations; a card that designated the chosen occupation would have slots instead of holes and would fall off, thus isolating soldiers suited to particular jobs. These men were distributed to the locations and occupations where they were most needed by the core placement center.

This institutional account of the citizen was also based on a faith that the world could be properly ordered—that for every person there was a proper place, a belief that contributed to the growing relativism fostered by the military. At least in some ways it was important for people to be different. This relativism was caged by its required capacity to support the state, so that differences were valuable if they supported the state and the war effort. But even with this cage of recognition, the military was contributing to a growing relativism concerning physical capacity and ability, a contribution that was also made to the mental ability and capacity of recruits.

The institutional labor that the military performed contributed to the notion of the citizen or subject as a plurality. As recruits were expected to have some task that they could perform as well as anyone else, their subjectivity was attached to that task, but this did not mean that the citizen did not have elements of the skills or drives necessary to perform others. The citizen was increasingly understood to be constructed from a plurality of elements, some of which could specially contribute to the power of the nation, but all were aspects of the citizen.

The psychiatric profession immediately benefitted from the Army's growing information machinery of induction. Two psychiatrists, Harry Stack Sullivan and Winfred Overholser, realized that the mass military inductions supplied a perfect avenue for the application of psychiatric principles to an extremely large, if incredibly male portion of American society. These two psychiatrists, in conjunction with Harry A. Steckel, chairman of the American Psychiatric Association's Military Mobilization Committee, developed the military's psychiatric screening program.[39]

The psychiatrists sold the military on this program with the promise of reducing the after-war psychiatric expenses.[40] They argued that the psychiatric causalities of World War I had cost the government $1 billion, and those patients occupied more than half of the beds in all Veterans Administration hospitals.[41] The psychiatrists promised that their expertise would reduce these figures in the next war.[42] They also asserted that their skills could quickly and cheaply return soldiers to the front lines.[43] Finally, they demonstrated the value of "Mental Hygiene" to deal quickly and efficiently with psychosomatic complaints. "Through a reduction in psychosomatic complaints, 122 to 531 man-hours of training time have been saved during the basic training period of a single company; and in a total of 5 companies tested, 996 man-hours were saved during the basic training period of a single company," wrote Robert Cohen.[44] Efficiency was, of course, one of the major selling points: "The intelligent handling of psychiatric problems in the Navy during the last war was effective in improving the general efficiency of the personnel of the fleet."[45]

Psychiatry played a quite different role in the military of World War I. In World War I the attention of most of the psychiatrists involved in military work was directed to understanding the ways that the brain made sense of stimuli to help commanders focus their minds much more efficiently. As Hugo Munsterberg claimed:

It is a psychotechnical science which cannot acknowledge barriers where the human mind is working in the interplay of social energies. Commanding a ship or fulfilling the orders of the commander, shaping the plans of a battle or pointing the gun, directing a submarine or aiming a torpedo, sending the wireless message or even feeding the engines in the hold of the ship while the cannons are thundering, is an activity of the mind, and it is not only the right, but the duty, of the psychologist to consider conscientiously whether his science may not be applied in this realm of human efficiency too.[46]

Munsterberg developed "a careful psychological study . . . devoted to the mental conditions of the localization of sound."[47] He also developed a test that supposedly isolated individuals most reliable to make quick, yet sane judgements. What little attention these studies paid to sailors or soldiers was typically directed to studies of crowd psychology. "One psychological fact ought to stand in the foreground and ought never to be forgotten," wrote Munsterberg in 1913. "The many are not simply a large number of single minds; they are not only many, but they are at the same time one. They are held together—more, they are forged together into one compact mental mass in which no single mind which entered has remained unchanged in its structure or in its energies."[48] The work of psychiatrists in World War I was directed to understanding how many became one, while World War II hunted for traces of non-useful individualism in every person. No attention is given in Munsterberg's account to the necessity of producing desire in the soldiers in order to get them to perform or obey—the predominant theme of World War II psychiatry. Obedience is produced from social cohesion and mimesis. "I say the spirit of obedience is in itself fostered by the increased suggestibility with its imitativeness. To be obedient is the common function of all the men. They feel themselves as parts of that one unified organic fighting-machine which can fulfil its purpose only if strict discipline controls it, and the willingness to submit therefore becomes infectious."[49] What little psychiatric studies utilized in World War I focused on forging the many into one. In World War II the state became far more interested in ordering the thoughts and feelings of citizens. No longer content with the extensive power of a Hobbesian state, this state became socially managed—it undertook massive efforts to scrutinize and adjust the thoughts and desires of citizens. "Just as World War I gave new impetus to the study of human *aptitudes*," Stouffer claimed in the Army's final report on psychological testing, "so World War II has given new impetus to the study of *attitudes*."[50]

In November 1940, the Selective Service issued the first directive arising from the plans of Sullivan and Overholser. Medical Circular No. 1 was issued to more than 30,000 volunteer physicians at local draft boards. This circular provided the simplest explanation possible of the five categories of handicap, later expanded to eight, that might reveal a recruit's potential psychiatric weaknesses. Additionally, in May 1941, the Army Surgeon General's Office issued its own circular, and in January the Navy issued a directive. On the first day of June 1943, the standards governing "the mental screening and classification of Selective Service registrants" were revised. These revisions applied to all branches of the armed forces.[51] The new procedure was "designed to qualify for induction into the armed forces, those men possessing mental capacity above the lower three-fifths of Grade V as measured by the Army General Classification Test."

The recruit's initial interaction with the military began with the military's compilation of personal information. The military, like Taylor's managers and in a fashion that exemplified the future of the American state, produced extensive bureaucracies for the accumulation of social information. These studies shared with Taylor's industrial studies a desire to correctly order the world, placing everything and everyone in their proper position—a desire extended, if not brought on, by the dislocation of the national-capital system. The studies were extensively conducted by the Research Branch of the Information and Education Division of the United States Army. "Never before," the introductory paragraph to the final report claimed, "had modern methods of social science been employed on so large a scale, by such competent technicians."[52]

The work of compiling and organizing statistics on the attitudes, as well as aptitudes, of recruits was viewed by the questioners as work that could produce a more transparent society.[53] It promised the dissolution of animosities and conflicts that disrupted social order. Social science and scientific management promised to order human relationships correctly.

> They were bound together by a common ideal to present conclusions arising out of ascertained factual material. They were loyal, patriotic, and moved by the hope that their specialized efforts might make some contribution to winning the war. But there was also in them a deeper motivation. They believed that in this major application of the scientific approach to human problems might be found keys to the improvement of human relationships.[54]

The keys to this kingdom of social order required the unlocking of secret and hidden dimensions and attitudes of recruits. By revealing the nooks and crannies of the citizen, science could address the problems of human interaction. One possible solution offered by social science was the identification of citizens with the demand for social truth. The desire for factual social knowledge was a demand with which all could identify and take to be necessary for humanity.

> The search for factual knowledge provides a common meeting ground for all creeds and races. Such a meeting ground exists already in the physical sciences which, at least in the Western democracies, know no national boundaries. Perhaps this new approach could be extended to those human and emotional problems towards whose solution so little progress has been made during thousands of years of intuitive and hortatory approach. This may not have been the major motivation of the Research Staff. But the thought was in their minds. It lent a sort of consecration to their efforts to protect the integrity of their work.[55]

The Taylorite demand for accurate information could not only produce useful factual information concerning human behavior, but did itself rely on a demand for "truth" that could modify human behavior. This consecrated desire lent itself to an attempt to control human behavior. Human behavior, it was understood, could be modified and controlled through good administration. Management based on accurate knowledge could, it was believed, correctly organize social relations.

A major purpose of the Research Staff was to provide a base of factual knowledge which would help the Director of the Army Information and Education Division in his administrative and policy decisions. This purpose was abundantly fulfilled. . . . For the first time on such a scale, the attempt to direct human behavior was, in part at least, based on scientific evidence. If this method could be developed and more widely used, it might provide further impetus for a great advance in the social relations of man. To that hope these volumes are dedicated.[56]

World War II presented one of the most significant moments in the study of social management. Management at this time required the scientific determination of attitudes and opinions. It was expressed in the image of an orderly pluralism in which social differences were valuable if they worked for the promotion of the nation. This orderly pluralism, a conception of order related to the order of industrial division of labor, was further consolidated by management elements common to the industrial workplace—particularly the managed control of details of action and the creation of an identity of interests.

The study of attitudes was made feasible by the increased professionalism of psychiatry and the advent of opinion poll methods. George Gallup, for example, began his national studies in October 1935.[57] The attempt to learn of the "inner" thoughts and beliefs of the subject distinguished this new approach from earlier types of social management.

Studies of attitudes betrayed a greater attention to the belief in the consistent subject, the attributes of which were attainable through the proper questions. The answers to these questions revealed, it was believed, the strengths and weaknesses of the subject. These questions revealed "what the soldier thinks," not simply what the soldier could do.[58] And this information, it was believed, would contribute to better soldiers and a better society. K.M. Bowman defended the military's use of psychiatry in the pages of *The American Mercury*:

There was a great deal of criticism of the Navy in that it was felt that the screening done at the induction centers was all that was necessary, but we have found that by our double method, we have saved thousands of men from complete psychiatric breakdowns, and as the wisdom of our policy is becoming more apparent, and as the war goes on, the benefits we earn by returning men to civil life where they will be useful citizens will justify the additional time spent in observation at our training stations. . . . The ill winds of war have blown some good in that they have given physicians an opportunity to estimate more closely the role of the intangible—the psychological factors in our daily lives.[59]

During World War II the military utilized physical and mental examinations and tests much more thoroughly than ever before, including tests given by psychiatrists.

NOTES

1. Brig. Gen. Hugh Johnson, Notes of Lecture Delivered at the Army War College, Washington, D.C., October 20, 1939, National Archives, Record Group 147, Stack Area 17W4, Row 11, Compartment 02, Entry 2, Records of the Selective Service System, Box 33.
2. Frederick Winslow Taylor, *Shop Management*, in *Scientific Management* (New York: Frederick Taylor, 1911; reprint, New York: Harper & Row, 1947), 58.
3. David Novick, Melvin Anshen, and W.C. Truppner, *Wartime Production Controls* (New York: Columbia University Press, 1949), 360.
4. Leonard Wood, "Heat Up the Melting Pot," Philadelphia, Pa. *Independent*, July 3, 1916, 15.
5. Associated Press, "16,000,000 in Nation Sign Up for Duty in Draft Army," Buffalo, N.Y. *Courier-Express*, October 17, 1940, also in Schenectady, N.Y. *Gazette*, October 17, 1940, and Troy, N.Y. *Record*, October 17, 1940.
6. "The Selective Draft Now and in 1917," Schenectady, N.Y. *Union-Star*, October 17, 1940.
7. Associated Press, "16,000,000 in Nation Sign Up for Duty in Draft Army."
8. "Procedure Smooth," *New York Times*, October 17, 1940.
9. "Selective Service—Now," Radio Address of Gen. Hugh S. Johnson over Station WJSV, Columbia Broadcasting Service, Washington, D.C., August 23, 1940, National Archives, Record Group 147, Stack Area 17W4, Row 11, Compartment 02, Entry 2, Records of the Selective Service System, Box 33.
10. Lee B. Kennett, *G. I.: The American Soldier in World War II* (Norman: University of Oklahoma Press, 1997), 7.
11. "The Selective Draft Now and in 1917."
12. "Process of Draft Is Given in Detail," *New York Times*, October 13, 1940.
13. "Chief of Police Jess Filby has instructed police to ask to see the draft registration cards of youthful-appearing beer drinkers. If they can't show the card they won't be permitted to remain and the operator will be notified to exclude them in the future under penalty of an ordinance which forbids juveniles in a beer parlor." "Absence of Draft Cards Bars Boys from Joints," Topeka, Kans. *Capital*, February 20, 1943.
14. "Boards Expose Racket in Sale of Draft Cards," Philadelphia, Pa. *Inquirer*, June 10, 1943.
15. "S.F. Draft Card Ring: School Boys Held," San Francisco *News*, June 19, 1943; and "High School Draft Card Ring Smashed by G-Men," Oakland, Calif. *Post Enquirer*, June 19, 1943.
16. "The ladle, hewn from an oak beam of Independence Hall, Philadelphia, and the blindfold, made from a cover on a chair in Independence Hall used by delegates signing the Declaration of Independence, have been in Col. Morris's possession since he blindfolded President Wilson twenty-two years ago and handed him the ladle to stir draft numbers inclosed in capsules," reported the New York *Herald Tribune*.

"Blind and Ladle of 1918 Sought for Draft Draw," New York *Herald Tribune*, October 18, 1940.

17. "Process of Draft Is Given in Detail." For an actual copy of the questionnaire, see "The Questionnaire Which Selective Service Registrants Will Fill Out After Oct. 16," Buffalo, N.Y. *Evening News*, October 12, 1940.

18. The German Army, on the other hand, explicitly forbade Taylor-style induction testing. "The organization of examinations," Van Creveld explains, "on a conveyor belt principle, with a separate physical examining each organ, was explicitly forbidden. The number each physician could see each day was limited to 80." See Generalstab, ed., Heeres Dienstvorschrift 81/15, *Wehrmachtersatzbestimmungen bei besonderen Einsatz* (Berlin, 1942), pp. 34–36, and Generalstab, ed., Heeres Dienstvorschrift 252/1, *Vorschrift uber militarartzliche Untersuchungen der Wehrmacht*, part I (Berlin, 1937), p. 6, in Martin Van Creveld, *Fighting Power: German and U.S. Army Performance, 1939–1945* (Westport, Conn.: Greenwood Press, 1982), 66.

19. Michael C.C. Adams, *The Best War Ever: America and World War II* (Baltimore, Md.: Johns Hopkins University Press, 1994), 79.

20. Ibid.

21. "Paterson Shows Way to Get Health Records of Rejected Men," Patterson, N.J. *Call*, March 3, 1943.

22. Dental problems were the largest causes of rejections. Mental and nervous problems were fifth, just before defective lungs. "Army Accepts Diseased Men," San Francisco *News*, April 21, 1943.

23. Office of the Surgeon General, Memo of (3 Oct. 1943) GNGAP-I, 3d Ind., Headquarters Army Ground Forces, Army War College, Washington, D.C., to: Commanding General, XIII Corps, Fort DuPont, Delaware; National Archives, Record Group 337, Box 584, AGF 341 (c), Binder no. 4; quotation from paragraph 2, Circular Letter No. 114, 22 June 1943.

24. Introduction to the Army, War Department, Army Signal Corps, National Archives, Record Group 111, Series TF/2067.

25. *Selective Service Regulations, First Edition*, September 23, 1940 to February 1, 1942 (Washington, D.C.: Government Printing Office, 1944), National Archives, MR 1-9, Section VII, 31, Record Group 147, Stack Area 17W4, Row 12, Compartment 12, Entry 37, Records of the Selective Service System, Box 1.

26. Introduction to the Army.

27. After June 1, 1943, Selective Service registrants, if high school graduates, could skip mental tests in favor of oral interviews if they brought with them a transcript of scholastic credits, high school diploma or additional education summary card. "Bellaire Draft Officials Receive New Regulation," Wheeling, W.Va. *Intelligencer*, May 28, 1943; "Draftees Asked to Bring Evidence of Graduation," Charleston, W.Va. *Gazette*, May 27, 1943.

28. "Army Call Shows Democracy Isn't Soft, Dykstra Asserts," Buffalo, N.Y. *News*, October 17, 1940.

29. Associated Press, "16,000,000 in Nation Sign Up for Duty in Draft Army."

30. George Evans, by Command of Lt. Gen. Brehon B. Somervell, "Mental Induction Standards and Procedures," 11 May 1943, National Archives, Record Group 337, AGF 353, Entry 55, Box 677.

31. *Selective Service Regulations, First Edition*.

32. Ibid.
33. Ibid.
34. *Classification of Enlisted Men, Personnel Placement in the Army*, Office of War Information, Bureau of Motion Pictures, 1942, National Archives, Record Group 111, Series TF/.0578, 1942.
35. *Introduction to the Army*.
36. Headquarters Third Army, Fort Sam Houston, Texas, "Enlisted Personnel for Quartermaster Troop Transport Companies," to: Commanding General, Army Ground Forces, Army War College, Washington, D.C., 13 September 1943, National Archives, Record Group 337, AGF 353, Entry 55, Box 665.
37. The categories of this test also applied racist social understandings with the force of science. The Army's tests created tension in the placement of "colored" soldiers within colored units and the equal distribution of soldiers who scored in the fourth and fifth classes. "Reference is made to Paragraph 5 of basic communication. In this connection, a check of the AGCT groups of white battalions shows that all of the white battalions have less than 45 per cent Grades 4 and 5. A check of the colored battalions indicates that 84 per cent of the men are either Grades 4 or 5." Headquarters, IRTC, Fort McClellan, Alabama, to: Commanding General, Replacement and School Command, Birmingham, Alabama, 21 September 1943, National Archives, Record Group 337, AGF 353.01, Entry 55, Box 715. As one anonymous enlistee explained concerning racist treatment in the military: "I had envisioned the Army as being a vast military machine, working with utmost precision. Instead I found it to be, for the Negro, a place impregnated with suppression and racial prejudice." The military's machine, which partially mixed up ethnic and racial identities of recruits, also solidified and consolidated some of these identities. "This is the age of science," this enlistee continued, "of steel—of speed and modernization." He had entered the military with the expectation that the machine's demand for efficiency and interchangability would increase equality. After all, "it is no time to let petty indifferences stand in the way of a nation in great need of defense, on the brink of great crisis!" Anonymous, "Jim Crow in the Army Camps," *The Crisis* 47, 12 (December 1940), in Herbert Aptheker, ed., *A Documentary History of the Negro People in the United States, Vol. 4: 1933–1945* (New York: Citadel Press, 1992), 397.
38. *Classification of Enlisted Men, Personnel Placement in the Army*.
39. Allan Berube, *Coming Out Under Fire: The History of Gay Men and Women in World War Two* (New York: The Free Press, 1990), 9.
40. "The number of doughboys who broke under that strain was so large that in the summer of 1918 General John J. Pershing cabled the War Department from France, urging that future draftees be screened to winnow out those who would be most susceptible to 'shell shock.' Nearly a hundred thousand such cases entered Army hospitals through 1919, and in caring for them after the war the Veterans Administration spent close to a billion dollars." Kennett, *G. I.*, 28.
41. Berube, *Coming Out Under Fire*, 10. See also Harry Stack Sullivan, "Psychiatry and the National Defense," *Psychiatry* 4 (May 1941): 202.
42. There was some interest in the immediately useful aspects of psychiatry in World War I, but on a much smaller scale than World War II would allow. For the official account of Army psychiatry see Pearce Bailey, Frankwood Williams, and Paul Komora, *The Medical Department of the United States Army in the World War, Vol. X: Neuropsychiatry* (Washington, D.C.: Government Printing Office, 1929).

43. *Field Psychiatry for the General Medical Officer*, PMF 5011, adapted from a British Training Film by the Army Pictorial Services Signal Corps, National Archives, Record Group 111, Series M/1167.

44. Robert Cohen, "Mental Hygiene for the Trainee: A Method for Fortifying the Army's Manpower," *The American Journal of Psychiatry* 100, 1 (July 1943): 71.

45. Forrest Harrison, "Psychiatry in the Navy," *War Medicine* 3, 2 (February 1943): 114.

46. Hugo Munsterberg, "Psychology and the Navy," *The North American Review* 197 (February 1913): 160.

47. Ibid., 161.

48. Ibid., 165.

49. Ibid., 170.

50. Samuel Stouffer, Edward Suchman, Leland DeVinney, Shirley Star, and Robin Williams, Jr., *The American Soldier, Vol. 1: Adjustment During Army Life* (Princeton, N.J.: Princeton University Press, 1949), 5.

51. Evans, "Mental Induction Standards and Procedures."

52. Frederick Osborn, "Foreword," to Samuel Stouffer, Edward Suchman, Leland DeVinney, Shirley Star, and Robin Williams, Jr., *The American Soldier, Vol. 1: Adjustment During Army Life* (Princeton, N.J.: Princeton University Press, 1949), vii.

53. See Bailey, Williams, and Komora, *The Medical Department of the United States Army in the World War, Vol. X: Neuropsychiatry*. This account deals in depth with the roles of the National Committee for Mental Hygiene (NCMH) in promoting psychiatry within the military. When the organization of neuropsychiatric units were recommended by the Surgeon General for military training units in World War I the NCMH did the actual organizing.

54. Osborn, "Foreword," viii.

55. Ibid.

56. Ibid., ix.

57. George Gallup, *The Gallup Poll, Public Opinion 1935–1971* (New York: Random House, 1972), v.

58. In December 1942, the Research Branch published a compendium of graphically represented research with the title *What the Soldier Thinks*. After this publication the Chief of Staff eventually ordered that *What the Soldier Thinks* be prepared monthly as a periodical for distribution to officers throughout the Army. The publication, first appearing in December 1943, was to be distributed to officers in staff and command positions down to the regimental level. Stouffer et al., *The American Soldier, Vol. 1*, 10.

59. K.M. Bowman, "Psychiatry at War," *The American Mercury* 59, 249 (September 1944): 340.

Chapter 5

A "Different Breed of Cat": Military Intelligence and Intellect Militant

> A society in which corruption spreads is accused of exhaustion; and it is obvious that the esteem for war and the pleasure in war diminish, while the comforts of life are now desired just as ardently as warlike and athletic honors were formerly. But what is generally overlooked is that the ancient national energy and national passion that became gloriously visible in war and warlike games have now been transmuted into countless private passions and have merely become less visible.
> —Friedrich Nietzsche, *The Gay Science*, Book 1, section 23

After registration, induction, examination, and classification, soldiers met Army discipline. Military discipline contributed to the creation of what one commentator for the *New York Times* called a "different breed of cat.... questioning everything from God Almighty to themselves."[1] The military experience contributed to a growing alienation from social order. Physical discipline and mental testing removed notions of individualism from a wide range of the recruit's actions. These twin moves changed the meaning of individualism: on the one hand people relied less on meaning and recognition by others, while on the other hand their own actions became much more highly influenced by others. Individualism became hidden and meaning became mysterious. "Deep beneath the surface of men's consciousness lie attitudes and impulses that may be altered," wrote Gordon Wright, "often in incalculable ways, by the strain of protracted war. Thus the Second World War seems to have initiated or reinforced trends toward a mood of lawlessness, toward a confusion and corruption of values, toward a decline in man's belief in a rational universe."[2] In the twilight of the rational universe, people caught glimpses of a new individualism produced through discipline.

Reception centers were the first stop for the newly inducted soldiers. "Brother, this is where your Army discipline begins," claimed the training film *Introduction to the Army*, concerning the soldiers' arrival at the reception center.[3] They usually stayed from four to seven days. Immediately organized into rosters and supplied roster numbers, they were then tested and studied in greater detail. Physical examinations constructed the recruits' "physical profile—which simply means what kind of military service you are physically fit to handle," as "Johnny" explained to his next door neighbor in the film. Draftees were also fingerprinted and given G.I. clothes. "Here's where you shed your civvies and draw your G.I. clothes, from skin out."

Drawing the G.I. from the skin began with training and drills aimed at the body of the recruit. At the reception centers, soldiers began to learn particulars of Army discipline: always step out with the left foot first and wear your hat two fingers above the left eye. During basic training these standards of order became highly regimented. The Army's steps toward physical discipline ordered, placed, and paced the physical bodies of draftees.

DISCIPLINE

In the reception centers draftees were taught to stand, move, and drill "like a soldier." This discipline taught soldiers the myriad rules governing the positioning of the body and its parts, so that the "mind and body work together" in a harmony of elements. Military drill taught the recruits obedience, first and foremost. "Habits of precision and response to a leader's order and the spirit of cohesion developed by executing drill in unison with others." Obedience was also an important strategy of order that came to bear fruits of control for the Army because of its ability to particularize body parts and body movements. Basically, military training turned the bodies of recruits into well-ordered machines, reducing the individualism found in movement and performance and standardizing the individual's body.[4]

For example, new soldiers learned the position of attention. "Heels are on the same line, or as near each other as the conformation of the man permits. The feet are turned out equally forming an angle of forty-five degrees." Even the angle of the soldier's feet was not too insignificant a detail for the attention of the instructor. "The weight of the body is resting squarely on the heels and balls of both feet. . . . the knees are straight without stiffness," while "the hips are drawn back slightly and level." The soldier's chest was expected to be "lifted and arched. Shoulders are square and falling equally." From these double right angles hung arms "straight down without stiffness." Hands did not escape scrutiny and control. "The thumbs are along the seams of the trousers. The back of the hands are out and the fingers held naturally." Meanwhile, at the top of the order, "the head is held erect and squarely to the front with the chin drawn in so that the axis of the head and neck are vertical." The windows of the soul were "straight to the front."[5]

Even commands concerning rest had specific meanings and heavily prescribed movements. At "Command Rest" soldiers could move one foot and the rest of the body, but the other foot had to remain in the position of attention. Typically, at "Command Rest" soldiers talked. The "At Ease" command required soldiers to keep quiet. Their foot movements were more specifically ordered. Soldiers could move their left foot but not the right foot, which remained at attention. The "Parade Rest" command instructed soldiers to move the left foot twelve inches away from the right foot. Legs were kept straight, equal weight was kept on both legs, and the thumb and fingers of the right hand grasped the left thumb. When the call to "Fall In" was given, soldiers formed ranks and spaced themselves from each other by the length of their left arm. "Close Interval" called for them to put left hand on hip and position themselves so that their left elbow just touched their neighbor.

In the spirit of Taylor, the Army's instructional film observed that "all movements may be divided into numbered motions," and these numbered motions were called out for the soldiers to perform. "When each man functions properly as an individual his entire outfit operates at greatest efficiency." Teaching soldiers control over even the smallest of details, taught them the selflessness of physical details, even as it taught them obedience and community. "Careful study and constant practice of these positions and facings is essential for the mastery of drill and intelligent execution of orders constitute vital links in the evolution of a well-trained soldier." Being a well-trained soldier kept the individual alive but destroyed the conception of individualism displayed in movement and behavior.[6]

The military further disciplined the body through time regimentation. Basic training disciplined the recruit with schedules and clocks. They were taught to obey the instructions of managers in small particular decisions, leaving the more general decisions for those in authority. Every action finds its proper place and time, as determined by the military. Every job is to be completed as others commanded.

In December 1944, the basic training schedule at Infantry Replacement Training Center in Camp Fannin, Texas placed the beginning of the day at 5:55 A.M., with reveille and roll call at 6:05 A.M. The soldiers were to wash, dress, and fall in by 6:20 A.M., from which they marched to the mess hall. They were allowed twenty minutes for breakfast, from which they returned to their barracks, policed the area, prepared their equipment, and made the forty-minute march to the training site. Activities at the training site were scheduled from 8:00 A.M. until 5:30 P.M. After supper at 7:00 P.M., the men marched back to their bunks where, after various housekeeping choirs, they were given thirty minutes to prepare for bed. Lights went out at 9:45 P.M. The recruit's day was a highly scheduled lesson in obedience to time organization.[7] Discipline reduced the expression of individualism in work and action; the recruit became a body.

The use of his time is scheduled for him by the staff of the induction center. The first thing that he must learn is that there is a time for everything. When this time is, and how much is allowed, is determined by the institution and not by the recruit. The second thing he must learn is that how this is to be used is defined by the institution, except the rare "free time." Third, the institution defines how the task allotted to a given time is to be accomplished. Fourth, the recruit learns that he does everything in formation, that is, with his group. In short, the recruit is no longer an individual, with the right of personal choices, alternatives and decisions. Instead, he is, in informal army usage, "a body." This "body" must be trained to act without question or hesitation to institutional stimuli. The loss of choice and initiative develops in him a sense of dependency on the institution for decisions.[8]

The body became dependent on national institutions for direction. In this way the military nationalized many folk patterns of behavior. To nationalize subjects by replacing past communities and social patterns with national connections, the military sent recruits to camps and forts scattered across the United States. Training camps disciplined the recruits' bodies and reordered their minds—cutting connections to earlier social groupings and identities, establishing new ways to interact with groups and new relationships to identities, and contributing to an individualism free from religious, ethnic, and social restraints. The military fostered individualism by separating its recruits from communities of value and meaning (religion, class, and family in particular). Military discipline constructed powerful forms of obedience but also begot new forms of independence.

REMOVING PAST COMMUNITIES

"The essential fact," Brotz and Wilson reported, "about induction, reception-center, and basic training experience is the knifing-off of past experience. Nothing in one's past seems relevant unless, possibly, a capacity for adaptation and the ability to assume a new role."[9] Military training cut the recruits off from their past and forced them to adapt to a new world with new rules. "Those who are unable to do so fall readily into the psychoneurotic category and may get medical discharges. . . . The sense of being thrust into a completely alien role and some feeling of personal degradation is common to a large number of recruits."[10] This ability to "assume a new role" in a new order of things became one of the defining characteristics of the modern consciousness nationally expounded by the state.[11]

The adaptable actor created here received dialogue and stage direction from others. Basic training undercut the authority that had previously constituted the recruits' subjectivity in such a way as to give them the basis for making important decisions. For example, the state had to undermine the trustworthiness of social and religious prohibitions against killing other human beings. In so doing, the military substituted its own authority for that of the groups and institutions from which the soldier had previously drawn moral guidance. Of course, some resisted, but not many and not very effectively. Edward Graf, who was inducted in spite of his request for conscientious objector status, refused to obey orders and refused to take the army's money. He was court-martialed and convicted.[12]

This deconstruction of personality worked not only upon enlisted men. Officer training, according to a member of the Research Board who successfully completed that training, went through a substantially similar process.

The practices start with the assumption that self-selection has been effective to the extent that candidates are highly motivated to become officers. The hopeful candidate is now subjected to a nearly catastrophic experience, which breaks down to a large extent his previous personality organization. His previous valuations fail him and in order to find a basis for self-respect, he must adopt new standards or escape from the field. . . . At the same time new, appropriate attitudes are built up and established. The catastrophic experience provides a kind of purgatory, a definite demarcation from the candidate's enlisted incarnation that puts a barrier between the new officer and his enlisted memories. It has some of the characteristics of a conversion experience, or the ordeal of the medieval knight.[13]

This infernal machine destroyed the earlier connections that had supplied the subjects with social connections and moral guidelines, but also reoriented the soldier in new directions.

The effect of this ordeal on the officer candidate is not only to attack his previous personality, but to exert a positive influence in the desired direction. The extremely rigorous training and the tremendous pressure resulting from the number that are failed mainly served to induce the critical situation. The constant threat of "washing out" of OCS increased subjective pressure and provided a most effective punishment for stamping incorrect behavior.[14]

This stamping was carried out, according to the Research Report, through a significant interest in "chicken," that is, obsessive attention to detail.

Other features of the ordeal are an extremely "GI" atmosphere, gigging, hazing, "bracing," and a general apotheosis of "chicken" (that is, petty detail). Aside from constituting a frontal attack on any civilian residue in the candidate's personality, these practices also involve the learning of new habits and values. Become oneself "GI," identifying with rather than resisting "chicken" values, is an adjustive response.[15]

This focus upon petty "chicken" issues organized attention to the importance of little details. According to the Research Branch's final report, the most common complaint enlisted men lodged against officers was that there was "Too much 'chicken' to put up with."[16]

"The soldier, so recently a civilian," wrote an Army psychiatrist, "is called upon to make difficult adjustments at a most unusual tempo and in an atmosphere of authority and discipline which are foreign to everyday life. The loss of individuality, the change in the most detailed habits of life and the hovering imminence of death bring about inevitable problems."[17] Changes in the small habits of life compounded the relativism created by the military through bodily control. Foods, hygiene habits, and recreation all presented the soldier with changeable facts of life. The replacement of social orders (in this case local mores) demonstrated the authoritarianism in any social order, even those they called home, including language. In World War II some draft boards communicated in non-English languages, including, in the case of one Chicago draft board, Chinese. Initially the Selective Service rejected draftees for not speaking or reading English, but the local boards eventually convinced the Selective Service to change this policy. The change required that the military teach recruits English. Eight hundred thousand inductees eventually circulated through Special Training Units, where they learned to read English using *Meet Private Pete* and *Private Pete Eats His Dinner*.[18] The Private Pete series was supplemented with the filmstrip, *The Story of Private Pete*, which attempted to teach a vocabulary of forty-six words.[19] The 65th Infantry Puerto Rican Regiment was an all-Spanish-speaking unit.[20] The replacement center, however, refused to consider placement within that regiment as an option for non–Puerto Rican Spanish speakers who had exceptional difficulty learning English in the Special Training Units.[21] Soldiers were to learn English. The military, in this way, promoted a more nationalized culture.

Compared to the Army of World War I, the Army of World War II was far more homogenous in terms of language and was more successful in removing recruits from ethnic and local communities. For example, in World War I at Camp Gordon, Georgia, Italians and Slavs made up two separate companies, and the officers in charge were fluent in the respective languages (and cuisines). Even in the midst of World War I the military was considered an important element in Americanization, which provoked some complaints from officers. "It may rightly be claimed that such segregation of races into regiments, etc., does not make American citizens, and possibly this is true, but we are not in this war to make more American citizens, we are in to win the war," argued one World War I staff report.[22]

Even though racial segregation still existed in the military during World War II, there was a push by the military to reduce racism and to disperse ethnicities. *Introduction to the Army*, the War Department training film shown to recruits at their induction, teased and admonished the recruit who packed for his stay at the reception center. "Just bring a toothbrush," the narrator intoned, "and sense of humor."[23] The narrator was less congenial concerning the baggage that should be forgotten at home.

> But what you mustn't bring is a load of stupid prejudices. If you've got any leave them at home. It's no use saying that lots of us don't have them, that it won't take a lot of time for the world to get rid of them. But as I say, don't bring them into the Army. Take people as they come. In the Army it's the kind of soldier a man makes, that counts.[24]

From the very first step of selection the military began to destabilize some prejudices and community identification, whether racial, ethnic, regional, or religious. Of course, some of the group identifications remained and were of use to the military.

God and Country, a training film from 1942, starred Ronald Reagan as a Catholic chaplain. He played the Catholic in a story of three chaplains: Catholic, Protestant, and Jewish. These three roommates begin chaplain training together, where they became close friends. The film proceeds through several moments of switching. In one hospital scene the Protestant has to step in for the Catholic. In a similar, if more humorous, scene, the Jewish chaplain informs the Catholic chaplain that he has found him an Irish tenor for his transport show. "What's his name?" the priest asked. "Saul Rosenfield," is the humorous, if predictable reply. The film concluded, after the touching death of Ronald Reagan's character, with the flags of Christianity, Judaism, and the United States appearing in the sky, illuminated by a heavenly light. This narrative homogenized two major forms of monotheism in favor of possibly the twentieth century's most powerful form of connection and purpose, the nation-state. In a similar vein, the military tried to dissolve the salience of connections, like varieties of monotheism, in favor of the nation-state; after all, these training exercises asserted, we are all Americans.

The American Army, like the industrial organizations within American society, opted for the power to organize and administer, and soldiers were taught to obey this form of authority. The military was in the war to win it, but nationalizing the recruits did not hamper the winning.

In spite of highly differentiated jobs, the Army decided to train recruits according to a standard program, even though World War II was being fought in many different theaters under many different conditions. The training occurred in three stages: First, the most basic training attempted to change the recruit from a citizen into a soldier. This training, which the Army often referred to as "branch immaterial training," physically conditioned the recruits to be soldiers, teaching them how to conduct themselves in their new social surroundings. The second phase developed the soldiers' specialties. Army Ground Forces had a third level of training with their weapons. The third level for Army Service Forces taught soldiers their non-combat specialties. Specialties were very narrowly defined: "The Army trained both cooks and bakers at Fort Sheridan, Wyoming, but it did not teach them each other's specialty. Mechanics were trained to work on diesel or gasoline engines, but not on both."[25]

THE INDIVIDUAL

"It is of the utmost importance," Taylor claimed in *Shop Management*, "in starting to make a change that the energies of the management should be centered upon one single workman, and that no further attempt at improvement should be made until entire success has been secured in this case."[26] Methods applied by Taylor and by the military separated workers from sources of power, like class, ethnicity, neighborhood, work group, and work gang. This loss of power reduced the workers' ability to "soldier" or "goldbrick"— to perform less work than they really could. Reducing the assimilative, mimetic, or authoritative power of local groups disentangled the subject from a set of social authorities and created new elements of control or, perhaps more accurately, the production of individualism produced new elements of control.

The removal of soldiers from their earlier connections can also be seen in the Army training film *Fighting Men: Baptism of Fire*.[27] Like the baptisms of old, this marked a separation of a new life from an old one. The fire referenced in the title was both the battle with the enemy and the battle with the self in order to enter combat. This battle with the self, the film asserted, was the most difficult fight and could only be won by forgetting home, family, and other social ties, mothers and girlfriends in particular. "You've gotta forget your civilian life," the central character's best buddy informs him.

"It's a past we can't get back to . . . not for a long time maybe. Now here's the way it works, you're going into battle, right away you start thinking about home, then you start thinking about all the things that can keep you from getting back there again. The result: you're too scared to start thinking about your job, and if you want to come back this is one job you've gotta think about."
"Yeah, I get it."

As the troop transport drove into the night, our hero, "Jim," thought of home, his parents and "his girl." "I've got to forget them. I've got to forget them," he repeated to himself. Soldiers who failed to forget past communities risked "cryptic nostalgia."[28]

He can be described as a person who has not as yet severed his ties with home and is completely immersed in thoughts of family and friends. . . . This continual preoccupation with thoughts of home and friends causes an air of abstraction. . . . It is a home fixation rather than a home sickness. A recruit simply is unable to get his mind off home, and the continues to live in the old environment rather than actively merging himself with the new one. . . . When present during the training period it interferes with efficient performance and may lead to disciplinary difficulties."[29]

A good interview with a psychiatrist was usually all it took to "return a recruit to efficiency," psychiatrists claimed.[30] Nostalgia was a significant block to morale. "A most important factor in attaining morale among fighting men," wrote David Flicker and Paul Weiss, "is the preventing or overcoming of nostalgia."[31] Flicker and Weiss, of the Station Hospital in Camp Blanding, Florida, cited Friedrich Engels approvingly in their account of the necessity of dissolving family ties if other identities are to form. The defeat of nostalgia required the severing of ties to communities of alternative understanding in favor of the "herd," to use Engels' word for the nation.[32]

Basic training also involved the instruction of the soldiers in the myriad of rules that existed in Army life. "Few social institutions, unless it would be monastic organizations, have such an elaborate body of formal rules and regulations to anticipate all the minutiae of life as does an army, with punishment specified for infraction."[33] The most important work of these codes of infraction and the enforcement of punishment for infraction was the internalization of the rules. "Yet these codified rules and regulations backed by authoritarian power and enforced in extreme cases by formal court-martial proceedings can be ineffective as devices for social control unless those who enforce them are indoctrinated in their enforcement and those who obey them are indoctrinated in obedience."[34] This process taught soldiers to identify with a social position from which the rules appeared legitimate. Soldiers internalized the legitimacy of a new set of rights and wrongs and a new set of authorities.

By indoctrination of enforcement and obedience is meant not merely knowledge of the official penalties for infraction, but rather willing acceptance of the necessities of enforcement and obedience. It meant the development of a social climate in which one's *fellows* as well as one's *superiors* serve as checks on a tendency to infraction and, ultimately, the internalization of the controls such that an individual's "conscience" inhibits infraction even when there is no likelihood of detection by either superiors or fellows.[35]

These new authorities were generally established as bureaucracies and as bureaucratic authority.

Nationalism benefitted from the erosions of earlier connections. As local groups became less powerful sources of identity, the nation-state became a more powerful source of identity. Additionally, social obedience was secured through a consciousness of a national division of labor. The social consciousness Taylor strove so hard to produce assured workers not only that their interests were the same as the managers and owners, but that the world was so well ordered that there was a place for everyone in a scientifically managed world within a system of connections between business and government. Professional and managerial authority in both business and government received the strongest validation.

Combat, with its destruction of life, also presented important intellectual challenges. The instantaneous dissolution of life corroded notions of rationality and meaning in the universe, highlighting the fact that people disappear without a trace. In an interview with one veteran, Fred Nauheim (5th US Armored Division) recorded the following account of death:

[T]hey got an empty ... [rations] box from us. What they found of [the captain] went off in that. Must have caught an 88 ... but good. Just think of that. A guy grows up, maybe makes something of himself, probably got a helluva good education, nice home, wife and kids back home thinking about him, waiting for him, and just because he was in the wrong place at the right time yesterday, all that's left can rattle around in a frigging cardboard box. Jesus Christ, that's something isn't it?[36]

In combat, soldiers came face to face with the end of their time. Such an abrupt transformation from living, breathing being to the contents of a ration box taught lessons of the pointlessness of existence: life can disappear almost without a trace.

In 1941, in response to an article in *Life* magazine critical of morale in the military, the *New York Times* began to explore the attitudes of soldiers. The War Department gave Hilton H. Railey, the *Times* correspondent, complete access to military training facilities. After talking to over a thousand men, he dispatched a 200-page report to Washington. In fulfillment of a pledge to the War Department, the document was not published, since it described remarkably disorganized and unsupportive troops. Railey found the soldier to be a virtual Deleuzian war machine—a group of men in a state of constant flux, making war against state forms of organization and control. "Command," Railey wrote, "vintage of 1917 (pretty general), appears naively and disconcertingly unaware that its men, vintage of 1940, are *a different breed of cat*.... The Present breed (mark well) is questioning everything from God Almighty to themselves."[37] The breakdown of identity connections created individuals substantially removed from common, historic means of social control. This adjustment was explored by the Army through studies of the intellectual transformations of soldiers and the intellectual motivations for fighting.

Beginning on December 8, 1941, the day after Pearl Harbor, until the end of the war, the Research Branch interviewed more than a half million soldiers and administered over 200 different questionnaires, many of which contained more than 100 separate questions.[38] The studies revealed that many soldiers had little interest in reasons or willingness to express reasons for fighting. They fought because they had to. The military responded to these dismal studies with a greater encouragement to soldiers to identify with the aims of the war. Yet, remarkably, many soldiers were willing participants in the war, even though they were unable to give an account of the connection between the war's purposes and their own interests. "It may be said that except for a very limited number of men, *little feeling of personal commitment to the war emerged.* The war was accepted passively as a national necessity, but this acceptance was not internalized as a sense of personal responsibility."[39]

The general picture in this volume of men preoccupied with minimizing their discomforts, acquiring higher rank or pay, securing safe jobs which would offer training useful in civilian life, displaying aggressions against the Army in many different ways, and in getting out of the Army as fast as possible does not suggest a particularly inspired work performance in the American Army.[40]

While in the Army the men resisted many elements of military authority, including the lack of explanation of orders and the lack of independent thought. As one interviewee reported:

If each man along the line got all the information and passed it on, the privates would know what to do and how to do it, but as things are now, many absurdities, much delay, many mistakes and, not the least important, much lack of interest, result from the fact that the man who has to do something doesn't know enough of the why and wherefore. And this is encouraged rather than discouraged by the Army.[41]

Soldiers also rebelled against the Army's hierarchical arrangement. "The Army is the biggest breaker of morale," reported one recruit. "The Army idea of class distinction between officers and men is all wrong. The Army does not take advantage of its man resources. Men do not like to be treated as if they were just toys and dogs for someone to play with."[42] Soldiers also learned to hate the methods of discipline for their standardization. "I think," reported a soldier, "we should do away with the close-order drill which only makes you respond to orders without thinking. In the wars of today I should think the soldier would have to think and use his judgement rather than do just what is shouted at him like a reflex action."[43] Service in the military strongly increased criticism of the military. The Army's final report stated that "at later stages of the war, men tended to have less favorable attitudes toward officers than did men in the same rank and longevity groups in earlier surveys."[44]

Military psychiatrists worried that this lack of personal identification with the war would increase the war's psychological costs. "It is possible that the minimal character of ideological motivation increased the psychological cost of the war. Army psychiatrists thought so and the Surgeon General's Office cooperated energetically with the Information and Education Division in seeking to help men merge personal desires with the issues of war." This attempt to merge desires applied Taylor's strategies of scientific management to soldiers. Taylor attempted to synthesize the interests of the workers and the interests of management. The military scrutinized the attitudes and opinions of soldiers in an attempt to justify the organization of interests so that their interests were the interests of the nation.

To this end, the Army worked to change the interests of soldiers. "The pervasiveness of the attitudes we have been describing was the subject of enough official concern to the Army to call forth efforts to indoctrinate the men explicitly, with the purpose of strengthening their convictions and promoting a stronger sense of personal commitment."[45] "If, it was reasoned, attitudes toward the war could be improved, then personal commitment would be heightened. Some of the reservations which made the men's commitment a limited one might be removed."[46] Through indoctrination the military attempted to overcome the elements in the soldier's subjectivity and social networks that might limit the power of the state as the center of validation and recognition. "The study of the tremendously important factor of morale in warfare must be undertaken in times of peace and preparation, so that its accepted principles many be firmly and scientifically applied when the enemy strikes. Morale can be created, planned and deliberately engineered, even though knowledge of its psychology is meager."[47] The military tried to consolidate positive morale in the soldiers by a variety of means but, as a soldier in the Persian Gulf Command pointed out, "the distinction made between officers and men is so great that it spoils any attempt to raise our morale by movies and footballs. All we ask is to be treated like Americans once again."[48] "It is said," reported another soldier in the same command, that "the American soldier is fighting for freedom and justice and equality. Somehow the army ways represent the very things we are fighting against."[49] Even as the military increased its attempts to adjust the attitudes of soldiers through movies and sports, the disciplines of the military and the shock of war undercut these attempts. The Army's final report concerning the use of films for motivation concluded, "the films had no effects on items prepared for the purpose of measuring effects on the men's motivations to serve as soldiers, which was considered the ultimate objective of the orientation program."[50] In this report they further admitted that movies could not significantly offset the effects of Army life. "But the longer the individual is in the Army, the more his morale may be adversely affected through disillusionment about Army life. Hence in the correlation of increments a real causal relationship between indoctrination and 'morale' may be obscured by a third factor."[51] Against the more extensive adjustments enacted by military service and discipline, movies had little chance of resisting social alienation.

CONCLUSION

The chapters in Part II have explored the American military's contributions to discipline in World War II. This elaboration of Weber's claim that discipline begins in the Army has explored three possible meanings to that claim. The first is the discipline of the bureaucratic authority. Second, the military disciplined the body of recruits into time schedules and national authority. Finally, the military worked to construct American citizens as collections of quantifiable characteristics.

The military contributed to constructions of citizenship in three ways. First, through the maintenance of national authority, which extended elements of bureaucratic authority and elaborated on significant connections between industry and military. Second, the military broke up the significant social relationships that had organized the subject's world. This breakup denaturalized the subject's relationship to groups and to concerns that those groups had informed, such as identity, social value, and rules of obedience. Third, the military contributed to the organization of authority around bureaucratic institutions that separated significant questions from individuals.

This chapter has, through the institutions of the military, explored connections between disciplines of surveillance, schedules, bureaucratic authority, and the powers of the national-capital system, revealing that powerful conceptions of legitimate authority served to unite the behaviors induced and maintained by the American nation-state and the system of managerial capitalism.

NOTES

1. Hilton H. Railey, "Morale in the U.S. Army: An Appreciation," written for the *New York Times*, September 29, 1941, quoted in Lee B. Kennett, *G. I.: The American Soldier in World War II* (Norman: University of Oklahoma Press, 1997), 70.

2. Gordon Wright, *The Ordeal of Total War: 1939–1945* (New York: Harper & Row, 1968), 236.

3. *Introduction to the Army*, War Department, Army Signal Corps, National Archives, Records Group 111, Series TF/2067, 1941.

4. All quotations in this paragraph are from *Instruction of the Soldier, Dismounted, Without Arms, Positions and Facings*, War Department, Army Signal Corps, National Archives, Records Group 111, Series TF/0248, 1941.

5. All quotations in this paragraph are from *Instruction of the Soldier*.

6. Ibid.

7. Kennett, *G. I.*, 53.

8. A.B. Hollingshead, "Adjustment to Military Life," *American Journal of Sociology* 51 (1946): 441.

9. H. Brotz and E. Wilson, "Characteristics of Military Society," *American Journal of Sociology* 51 (1946): 374.

10. Ibid.

11. This is intended to suggest Nietzsche's discussion of Americans in *The Gay Science*, Book 5, section 356. "The individual becomes convinced that he can do just about everything and *can manage almost any role,* and everybody experiments with himself, improvises, makes new experiments, enjoys his experiments; and all nature ceases and becomes art.... To say it briefly (for a long time people will still keep silent about it): What will not be built any more henceforth, and *cannot* be built any more, is—a society in the old sense of that word; to build that, everything is lacking, above

all the material. *All of us are no longer material for a society*; this is a truth for which the time has come."

12. "Judge Denies Soldier's Plea as Objector," Little Rock, *Arkansas Democrat*, March 4, 1943; "Soldier to Seek Release from Army," Little Rock, Ark. *Gazette*, March 4, 1943.

13. Samuel Stouffer, Edward Suchman, Leland DeVinney, Shirley Star, and Robin Williams, Jr., *The American Soldier, Vol. 1: Adjustment During Army Life* (Princeton, N.J.: Princeton University Press, 1949), 389.

14. Ibid., 390.

15. Ibid.

16. Ibid., 396.

17. Harry Freedman, "The Services of the Military Mental Hygiene Unit," *American Journal of Psychiatry* 100, 1 (July 1943): 34.

18. Kennett, G. I., 18.

19. Alonzo G. Grace, *Educational Lessons from Wartime Training* (Washington, D.C.: American Council on Education, 1948), 52.

20. Capt. B.G. Nix, A.G.D. Assistant Adjutant, Headquarters, Tank Destroyer Replacement Training Center, North Camp Hood, Texas, 10 November 1943. Subject: Request for Reassignment of Non-English Enlisted Men. To: Commanding General, Replacement and School Command, AGF, Birmingham 3, Alabama. National Archives, Record Group 337, AGF 341, Entry 55, Box 587, Binder 7.

21. "The transfers of Privates Enreque Arroyo, 32862825, and Rafael H. Chavez, 39133494, are not favorable considered. It is desired that these enlisted men be reported to this headquarters on regular availability report upon completion of basic training." Headquarters Army Ground Forces, Army War College, 24 November 1943, to: Commanding General, Tank Destroyer Replacement Training Center, North Camp Hood, Texas, by Command of Lt. Gen. Lesley J. McNair, National Archives, Record Group 337, AGF 341, Entry 55, Box 587, Binder 7.

22. David Kennedy, *Over Here: The First World War and American Society* (New York: Oxford University Press, 1980), 158.

23. *Introduction to the Army*.

24. Ibid.

25. Kennett, G. I., 47.

26. Frederick Winslow Taylor, *Shop Management*, in *Scientific Management* (New York: Frederick Taylor, 1911; reprint, New York: Harper & Row, 1947), 192.

27. *Fighting Men, Baptism of Fire*, War Department, Army Signal Corps, National Archives, Records Group 111, Series TF/2014, 1943.

28. C.L. Wittson, H.I. Harris, and W.A. Hunt, "Detection of the Neuropsychiatrically Unfit," *U.S. Naval Military Bulletin* 40 (April 1942): 340–46.

29. C.L. Wittson, H.I. Harris, and W.A. Hunt, "Cryptic Nostalgia," *War Medicine* 3, 1 (January 1943): 58–59.

30. Ibid., 59.

31. David Flicker and Paul Weiss, "Nostalgia and Its Military Implications," *War Medicine* 4, 4 (October 1943): 380.

32. Ibid., 381.

33. Stouffer et al., *The American Soldier, Vol. 1*, 410.

34. Ibid.

35. Ibid.

36. F. Nauheim, *Behold the Upright* (New York: Apollo Books, 1970), 39, in John Ellis, *The Sharp End: The Fighting Man in World War II* (New York: Charles Scribner's Sons, 1980), 114.

37. Kennett, *G. I.*, 70; Railey, "Morale in the U.S. Army."

38. Stouffer et al., *The American Soldier, Vol. 1*, 12. See the appendix to volume II of the study for a list of the principle studies.

39. Stouffer et al., *The American Soldier, Vol. 1*, 449.

40. Ibid., 485.

41. Ibid., 70.

42. Ibid., 74.

43. Ibid., 78.

44. Ibid., 364.

45. Ibid., 458–59.

46. Ibid., 459.

47. Forrest Harrison, "Psychiatry in the Navy," *War Medicine* 3, 2 (February 1943): 135.

48. Stouffer et al., *The American Soldier, Vol. 1*, 371.

49. Ibid., 372.

50. Carl I. Hovland, Arthur Lumsdaine, and Fred Sheffield, *The American Soldier, Vol. 3: Experiments on Mass Communication* (Princeton, N.J.: Princeton University Press, 1949), 64–65.

51. Ibid., 78.

Part III

Harmonious Curriculums: Education and the Nation-State

Chapter 6

Industrial Subjects: Education and Efficiency

> That is how education always proceeds: one tries to condition an individual by various attractions and advantages to adopt a way of thinking and behaving that, once it has become a habit, instinct, and passion, will dominate him *to his own ultimate disadvantage* but "for the general good."
>
> —Friedrich Nietzsche, *The Gay Science*, Book 1, section 21

The twilight of the nineteenth century witnessed the creation of new systems of education. By the 1930s and 1940s, many early reforms, including increased administrative power, education surveys, and extensive testing, were commonplace. Early applications of scientific management to education dealt with education systems as if they were businesses. Education, it was widely concluded, needed to produce its product more efficiently. Consolidation of administrative authority, testing, and the more efficient organization of the school building, the student's day, and the student's studies promised to make education as efficient as iron production. This chapter introduces education's attempts in the early part of the twentieth century to accommodate itself to the increased social demand for measurable efficiency—a demand asserted with increased gusto during World War II. "The impact of war upon institutions of higher education is direct and disconcerting," wrote editors of *The*

Annals of American Academy of Political and Social Science. Furthermore, this direct and disconcerting impact should be studied:

> There is always a danger that in focusing attention on disturbing influences of the moment one will overlook the fact that in spite of all the losses which accompany disruption there are potential gains that spring from the possibility of introducing changes. The effect of the war on higher education has been adverse, no doubt of that; but at the same time, the war has made it necessary to break with traditional modes of thought and action.[1]

In many ways, however, the war reinforced contemporary modes of thought and action, particularly the twentieth-century interest in attuning education to the demands of industrial efficiency and national recognition power at (perhaps) a disadvantage for the individual, if maybe for the individual's *ultimate* advantage.

EFFICIENCY

Most of the criticism of education in the early twentieth century was directed at its lack of efficiency and its need for scientific management. For example, an Iowa school superintendent in 1911 wrote in the *American School Board Journal* that "what we need is more efficient management of the old system instead of something new."[2] However, efficient management, on the model of Taylor's scientific management, was quite new. Simon Patten wrote for the *Educational Review* that schools should, like businesses, be made to demonstrate their success rates. Why should New York, Patten asked, "support inefficient school teachers instead of efficient milk inspectors? Must definite reforms with measurable results give way that an antiquated school system may grind out its useless product?"[3] It was widely believed among educators that they were being "compelled to face a powerful adverse public criticism—a criticism not of the existence or public support of the schools but rather of their efficiency."[4] Application might have begun slowly but, it was believed, educators would quickly implement the new standards of efficiency. "Where one school superintendent, principal or trustee now talks of applying business tests to school management, there are one hundred who have not yet seen how much better the efficiency test is than the hit-or-miss goodness test of the present day."[5] James Phinney Munroe, president of the National Society for the Promotion of Industrial Education, chairman of the Massachusetts Commission for the Blind, chairman of the Committee on Education of the Boston Chamber of Commerce, and secretary of the Corporation, Massachusetts Institute of Technology, began his 1912 book *New Demands in Education* with a statement of the value of efficiency: "The fundamental demand in education, as in everything else is for efficiency—physical efficiency, mental efficiency, moral efficiency."[6]

In February 1911, J. George Becht, principal of the State Normal School in Claxton, Pennsylvania, addressed the meeting of the Department of the Superintendence of the National Education Association on ways to increase scholastic efficiency. The solution, Becht proffered, was Frederick W. Taylor. Becht praised the efforts of Taylor, offered examples of the methods of scientific management, and proclaimed Taylorism the key to eliminating inefficiency in education.[7] Later that year, the High School Teacher's Association of New York City committed three years to "Efficiency in the High Schools through the Application of the Principles of Scientific Management," as the resulting bulletins were titled.[8] The annual meeting of the National Education Association in 1912 contained a wide assortment of presentations incorporating methods of increased efficiency for education. C.A. Fullerton presented a paper entitled "The Principles of Scientific Management Applied to Teaching Music in the Public Schools." "As sure as daylight follows the dawn," he concluded, "this higher standard of efficiency will be applied to all phases of education, including religious education, and the sooner the better."[9] The application of scientific management to religious education and music presented challenges, but challenges that would eventually be met.

One reason why better progress has been made in reducing the technique of the factory to a scientific basis than in the technique of public school music is that success in the technique of the factory is measured by dollars and cents and the results are not questioned. It is not so easy to measure success in the development of an art—and the appreciation of beauty. Technical skill in the factory means the ability to turn out so many articles per day. Technical skill in music means the ability to perform music, but its value depends on the power to interpret music in an artistic manner and also on the taste used in selecting music that is worth performing.[10]

Education, especially in areas like religion and music, offered new challenges to the application of efficiency, but there was a widespread demand that education meet these challenges. Lively attacks on inefficient education came from many directions, including popular magazines such as the *Saturday Evening Post* and *Ladies' Home Journal*.[11] In November 1912, *Ladies' Home Journal* collected and published accounts by important educators concerning the ills of American education. James E. Russell, dean of Teacher's College, claimed that "our educational system is wasteful and inefficient." H. Martyn Hart, dean of St. Johns Cathedral in Denver, made an almost identical claim and argued that this inefficiency led to a variety of social ills. "The crime which stalks almost unblushingly through the land; the want of responsibility which defames our social honor; the appalling frequency of divorce; the utter lack of self-control; the abundant use of illicit means to gain political positions; are all traceable to its one great and crying defect—inefficiency."[12]

Giving education a better, more efficient organization and plan would aid in the fight against crime, corruption, and divorce and make students more efficient workers. The fight for our social honor waged by the schools would be aided, many reformers believed, by increasing the power and control of administrators and managers.

The application of scientific management methods meant several things: (1) more efficient administration, (2) more efficient educational methods, (3) more standardized studies of schools, and (4) more standardized testing of students. Administrators approached their fields of opportunity with assurances of increased efficiency.

ADMINISTRATION

"Modern demands," the Commissioner of Education for Massachusetts, David Snedden, carefully explained, "assume that public school administration is a complex affair; that from many fields of science, applications of modern methods should be made, and that a premium should be put upon the development of professional experts, opening for them deserved fields of opportunity."[13] David Tyack and Elisabeth Hansot wrote of this period: "The twentieth-century managers sought to 'take schools out of politics' and to shift decision making upward and inward in hierarchical systems of management."[14]

Two administrators in particular, Frank Spaulding and John Franklin Bobbitt, conducted extensive tests and studies promoting the applicability of scientific management to education. Spaulding, superintendent of schools at Newton, Massachusetts, was a leader in the movement to apply the methods of business to the work of education. As "the cost issue grew more intense," he wrote of his first tenure as superintendent, "the subject of education in relation to cost became the dominant theme of my annual reports."[15] The application of business methods to education directed Spaulding's reports to a greater concern for facts that could be quantifiably tallied, like costs. Spaulding used the cost accounting methods that he associated with Taylor to determine the value of different classes. Studies of needs and production, he believed, would determine the value of various types of instruction. For example, cost efficiency studies could determine the value of education courses, like Greek.

Thus confronted, do we feel like denying the equivalency of these values—we cannot deny our responsibility for fixing them as they are? This is a wholesome feeling, if it leads to a wiser assignment of values in future. Greater wisdom in these assignments will come, not by reference to any supposedly fixed and inherent values in these subjects themselves, but from a study of local conditions and needs. I know nothing about the absolute value of a recitation in Greek as compared with a recitation in French or in English. I am convinced, however, by very concrete and quite local considerations, that when the obligations of the present year expire, we ought to purchase no more Greek instruction at the rate of 5.9 pupil-recitations for a dollar. The price must go down, or we shall invest in something else.[16]

Greek, proven inefficient, should be replaced with a more efficient language or purchased at a much lower cost. Spaulding's cost accounting methods of administration scarcely proved anything about Greek unknown to generations of schoolchildren, but they did demonstrate the sorts of decisions increasingly controlled by administrators.

Bobbitt, who received his Ph.D. under the direction of G. Stanley Hall at Clark University, proposed the introduction of Taylor's methods as a way to increase efficiency through the increase in administrative power. Efficiency depended, Bobbitt believed, on "centralization of authority and definite direction by the supervisors of all processes performed."[17]

Teachers cannot be permitted to follow caprice in method. When a method which is clearly superior to all other methods has been discovered, it alone can be employed. To neglect this function and to excuse one's negligence by proclaiming the value of the freedom of the teacher was perhaps justifiable under our earlier empiricism, when the superiors were merely promoted teachers and on the scientific side at least knew little more about standards and methods than the rank and file.[18]

The increasingly professional administrative staff should set up new methods and standards, professionalism obtained through universities and actualized through studies, and tests. No longer should teachers practice rule-of-thumb methods; administrators, paid to study problems like the most effective means of testing, would scientifically study and compare different methods and would standardize such methods after the very best way had been determined.

TESTING AND SOCIAL SCIENCE

The shift in authority from teachers to professionally trained administrators strengthened the authority of statistical studies. Schools incorporated Taylorite methods by conducting and submitting to a variety of tests.[19] Several tests were developed in order to apply scientific measurement to student performance. S.A. Courtis developed an arithmetic test, Thorndike and Ayres developed a handwriting scale, and Thorndike and Hillegas developed a scale for measuring English competency. Callahan has concluded that "educators from all over the country engaged in this activity by developing rating sheets or offering suggestions to the profession on ways and means of increasing efficiency."[20] For example, in 1937, Cecil B. Read wrote a short monograph, principally for teachers, comparing the time of students using three different methods of solving algebraic problems. He attempted to discover the most efficient means of solving algebraic equations. (Isaac Newton's method came out ahead.)[21]

The testing of teachers further aided in the growth of administrative power, an important element in the adaptation of Taylor's methods to education.

For example, Joseph Taylor, district superintendent of schools in New York City, created charts that rated teachers according to many different details of teaching, including the evaluation of the time it took them to pass out and collect papers.[22] Administrators in virtually all large cities, reported the *American School Board Journal*, undertook "elaborate plans for rating the work of instructors."[23]

In addition to his cost-cutting methods, Spaulding created a system of measurement by which to judge textbooks. In much the same manner in which Taylor standardized the tools for industrial work, Spaulding attempted to standardize the tools of educators. "Textbooks are tools. To be serviceable, they must be adapted, like other tools, to three considerations: the end to be accomplished by their use, the material in connection with which they are to be used, and the needs of the user."[24]

School administrators tracked student performances, as well as teacher performances, through a consolidation of information and methods such as the now ubiquitous report card. "Several groups of New York Principals have recently formulated a card report record," wrote William Allen in 1907, "calling for facts that some day every school will be expected to answer, as to the child's pedagogical and physical progress during school life."[25] The report card would contain and report the measured results of student actions at various demarcated grades of study.

Schools increasingly tested students concerning their skills in various avenues of instruction, aptitudes, and personalities in order to determine the most efficient methods of education. For example, in May 1915, *The American School Board Journal* printed a student efficiency test, which included such questions as, "Do you sleep with at least one window open?" and "Have you a bank account?"[26] These questions informed educators of the habits of the best students.

Testing also involved the supposed testing of intelligence. Alfred Binet developed the first important intelligence test in France in 1905. Lewis Terman at Stanford, Robert Yerkes at Harvard, and Henry Goddard at the Vineland Training School in New Jersey imported and promoted intelligence testing in the United States. They claimed these tests exposed innate intelligence. Terman published his Americanized "Stanford-Binet" test in 1916. He believed that the test could determine productive and efficient citizens. For those who did not meet his standards he recommended sterilization. "In the near future intelligence tests will bring tens of thousands of these high-grade defectives under the surveillance and protection of society. This will ultimately result in curtailing the reproduction of feeble-mindedness and in the elimination of an enormous amount of crime, pauperism, and industrial inefficiency."[27]

Intellectual testing of students coupled with sterilization encouraged, according to Terman, industrial efficiency. When Terman got down to racist brass tacks, he wrote of "Spanish-Indian and Mexican families of the South-west and also among negroes," that children of these groups "cannot master abstractions, but they can often be made efficient workers."[28] Social scientific testing helped determine who belonged in what relationship to the means of production and the means of reproduction. In the seventeen-year period after 1905, eighteen states passed bills that allowed the sterilization of natural criminals and the feeble-minded. These bills became laws in fifteen states.[29] By 1941, 38,087 people had been sterilized in the United States.[30] Testing greatly contributed to the desire to see the world as naturally ordered according to a plan whereby the rich, powerful, and managerial were justly in their positions, as were the poor, ignorant, and managed. This understanding required that the world, individuals, movements and fields of study be broken-up into organizable parts. Furthermore, as this example makes clear, these differences were internalized to the physical, genetic make-up of the subject.

The social understanding of a division of labor made it possible to imagine a society in which different people performed very different tasks. The attempt to find in skin color and action internal meanings was a significant aspect of early-twentieth-century social order. This conception changed during the century, as the truth of the individual moved from action and visible manifestation to the invisible and hidden.

INFORMATION CONSOLIDATION

Like so many aspects of social life in the early twentieth century, education came under thrall of statistical studies. Social science explored more and more areas of life to determine their precise contents and meanings. In 1933, Henry Suzzalo, president of the Carnegie Foundation for the Advancement of Teaching, arranged for Walter Crosby Eells of Stanford to conduct a survey of educational surveys. This study of the influence of social science on the study of education suggested the value of statistics and America's extensive faith in them.

On the whole, it would seem that the surveyors of our higher education have not been by any means exempt from the passion for statistics that has come to possess the American mind. The industrious collection of facts alone does not constitute science or the scientific method; interpretations, with understanding and intelligence, must follow, by whatever method good judgment indicates. Here as elsewhere statistics are no adequate substitute for common sense.[31]

Howard Savage's foreword to this study exclaimed, "even a cursory examination of the pages that follow reveals that the survey as defined by Professor Eells has played a not inconspicuous part in the development of higher education from 1908, the year of the inception of the Oberlin study, until the present day."[32] Scientific surveys, this study claimed, distinguished education in the twentieth century. Eells further claimed that one of the notable motivations for these studies was the interest in efficiency and coordination established by Frederick W. Taylor.

The underlying forces which brought educational surveys into existence resembled the economic, social and scientific forces which brought the efficiency expert into business and industry. The early years of the twentieth century were characterized by the consolidation of great business and industrial enterprises and a resultant emphasis upon efficiency and economy. They were marked by the development of the Taylor movement for efficiency engineering. Intensive scientific studies of industrial processes were made by Dr. Frederick Winslow Taylor and his associates; extensive examinations or surveys were made of the organization and products of great industrial combinations. The reorganization of large-scale American industry was based upon studies which in reality were often industrial surveys, although not always called by that name. Since many of the men who were industrial and commercial leaders were also members of the boards of trustees of leading state and private institutions of higher learning, it was natural that the methods of efficiency in business which they were finding so effective should be suggested as well to the colleges and universities.[33]

The fact that the men positioned in the boards of most major universities also conducted most of the national industrial production disclosed candidly the influence of business methods, such as Taylorism, on the business of universities. The forces that brought the efficiency expert to business also created education surveys.

STRUCTURE: DIVISION AND ORGANIZATION

In 1912, Theodore Mitchell gave a presidential address to the Schoolmasters Association of New York and Vicinity. In this address, Mitchell challenged the educators to work harder to promote efficiency. The studies and tests led to more efficient control of education, its standardization, and its reorganization in the most efficient manner possible.

It must give way to an ideal of timesaving through preparation for dealing expeditiously and variously with a variety of needs, to the end that maximum results may be attained under pressure of time and with economy of material. By better use of ground space, by better setting of machinery, by better placing of raw material, by the cutting down of labor motions, by producing harder and more lasting cutting tools—by these and other means the factories have increased their output, have lowered the cost of production, have met the demands of their very existence. In a word they have learned to "speed up," not only without placing fresh labor burdens on the workman but on the contrary, with beneficial results in the matter of energy expended and wages earned. And we teachers ought to do the same. We should be compelled to, were we, like members of other professions, as often under watchful, critical adult eyes—were our mistakes to carry as quickly as do theirs, the penalty of almost immediate retribution. We are curiously protected in inefficiency."[34]

Experiments needed to be conducted to determine the correct times for the production of goods and for particular movements. In his earliest account of scientific management, Taylor asserted "that this whole system rests upon an accurate and scientific study of unit times, which is by far the most important element in scientific management."[35] The scientific determination of unit times divided work into its simplest and most easily measurable parts, then proceeded to pare these parts down to the quickest possible accomplishment time. Once the quickest time for steps had been determined, managers could figure out proper completion times for entire jobs. Managers who made workers produce at this rate had standards which they could claim as neutral. Worker resentment could be mollified by appeal to these seemingly neutral standards. In this way, work could be speeded up without the managers appearing overly disciplinary. It was not their fault, it was the standards.

Education did a great deal of paring and organizing of elements of life. One of Franklin Bobbitt's contributions to education's adoption of Taylorism was his division of studies into "ten areas that make up the layman's daily living."[36] Once life had been divided into its elements, these parts could be more efficiently managed. In 1945, in a critique of the Harvard faculties 1945 report *General Education in a Free Society*, Bobbitt, sounding very much like Taylor, suggested that "the ten areas of living that he had identified ought to be scientifically investigated in order to determine their precise components and what was necessary in order to perform them efficiently."[37] In 1941, Bobbitt published his account of the curriculum of the "newer" education, and claimed that "eighteen areas of human living, however, appear to cover it with at least reasonable completeness."[38] Bobbitt argued that education for citizenship was "one of the most necessary of educational responsibilities." Education should "bring the population to a clear and well-matured understanding of the coordinate status of all of the legitimate agencies of the Great Cooperative Enterprise, and of the need for so managing the social order that all are brought to operate harmoniously and efficiently."[39]

An additional program, commonly called the Platoon Plan or Gary Plan, developed to make better use of space and tools, made it cost effective for schools to build specialized facilities. It was, according to Roscoe Case, "a movement for the break-up" of fixed types of schools.[40] This plan was based, according to Ellwood Cubberley, "on sound thinking as to the new educational needs arising from the profound industrial and social change taking place in American life and the American home."[41] The Gary Plan, begun by William A. Wirt, superintendent of schools in Gary, Indiana, attempted to apply industrial methods to schools. A student of John Dewey's at the University of Chicago, Wirt developed a system whereby educational pursuits that needed special equipment or space (i.e., physical education or chemistry) would be built into the school buildings. When changing topics of instruction, students would change the room in which they were instructed. In this manner, groups of students could use highly specialized facilities for short periods of time and then move to a different room, leaving the first room to be occupied by a new group of students. By 1925, this plan was in place in 632 schools in 126 cities, and by 1929, similar plans were in use in 1,068 schools in 202 cities for 730,000 students.[42] Their attempt to deal with the rapidly growing industrial area of Gary created, John Franklin Bobbitt claimed "a thoroughly modern school plant, equipped with every modern necessity; then to operate it according to recently developed principles of scientific management, so as to get a maximum of service from a school plant and teaching staff of minimum size."[43]

The Gary Plan emphasized four elements: (1) the efficient use of space, (2) child growth and child nature, (3) training in citizenship, and (4) the spirit of progress. All four elements contributed to the changes taking place in American society. The efficient utilization of school space was part of the long trend, epitomized by Taylor, to order space in the most efficient manner possible. The standardized approach to child growth was fostered by the increased standardization of all aspects of life. Training in citizenship promoted a social understanding in which children learned the importance of different parts working together for the whole.

The necessity for a division of labor in the various projects which must be worked out in school life is conducive to early growth of the democratic spirit; and the assumption of one's share of responsibility, not only to one's group but in terms of the best interests of the entire school world, contributes generously to character building. Since purposeful activity is in keeping with the nature of the child, interest results to a degree beyond the expectations of the most enthusiastic exponents of the platoon plan.[44]

Progress was the wheel that connected the desires of students to the education system. Thus, because the world was improving, they believed that they were ensured a good place in the social order of the future. This system relied on a division of projects into various stages so that students learned the importance of difference to the completion of the whole. Students also learned to think of their interests as the same as those of the "entire school world." This system of education supplied the child with purposeful activity—that is, activity with a social goal.

Early-twentieth-century applications of Taylorite theories to education mostly regeared the physical world of education. Administrative authority was enhanced through testing of teachers and students. Studies of school programs were nationalized in an effort to standardize procedure. Like the rational reorganization of the workplace in factories, the physical plant of school buildings was reorganized. By World War II, the mental landscape became the location of rational ordering, and methods of industrial order were applied to the desires and drives of the citizen.

WORLD WAR II: PRODUCTION PLAN

"During World War II educators witnessed the successful prosecution of the greatest emergency training program in all history," Alonzo Grace concluded concerning the wartime education effort. "More than ten million men and women," he elaborated, "were taught to perform expertly the vast range of duties necessary to the effective conduct of modern technological warfare." Participants in this vast educational program worked together through difference for the advance of the national industrial machinery. "The students in this program came from every section of American life. The things they were taught were of almost incredible variety. Every available means of instruction was brought to bear. No expense was spared in getting the desired results. It was an educational undertaking of tremendous scope and magnitude."[45]

Social efficiency, Herbert Kliebard reported, returned to the forefront of American education reform during World War II: "it was once more social efficiency that moved to center stage."[46] "In this day," Frank Schultz, dean of the Division of General Science, South Dakota State College of Agriculture and Mechanic Arts, wrote in 1944, "when the 'scientific' approach to the solution of educational problems is quite generally accepted, it is axiomatic that planning of any sort should be based upon a sound analysis of facts and hypotheses."[47] A study by the Stanford University School of Education faculty concerning America's education needs during wartime looked at the efficiency possible through reorganization via Taylor's methods:

There are fairly good grounds for believing that a reorganization of school hours and terms would facilitate physical efficiency. The new plan would provide rest alternating with activity; food and diversion through the day; a quarter system, with a week of vacation between the quarters; and with a month of vacation once a year. Where workers are on a long-term job, a half day off in the mid-week and another full day and a half of rest and diversion weekly are an aid to health.[48]

The Stanford faculty explicitly relied on notions of assembly-line work in this understanding of pacing and organization. "On the assembly line, in column, or at tasks in the school, persons of like speed should be put together."[49] World War II consolidated efficiency as the goal of education. "Our schools are a part of, not apart from, our government and our many social, economic, and intellectual enterprises."[50] As a part of the means of governance, the schools attempted to speed up their production of workers and recruits, as well as perform a range of social functions in the interest of the nation.

NOTES

1. T.R. McConnell and Malcolm M. Willey, eds., Foreword to the issue on "Higher Education and the War," *The Annals of The American Academy of Political and Social Science* 231 (January 1944): vii.
2. E.T. Armstrong, "Is Our Present High School System Inefficient?" *American School Board Journal* 42, 4.
3. Simon Patten, "An Economic Measure of School Efficiency," *Educational Review* 41 (May 1911): 467–69.
4. National Education Administration (N.E.A.), *Proceedings* (1911), 519, in Raymond Callahan, *Education and the Cult of Efficiency* (Chicago: University of Chicago Press, 1962), 49.
5. William Allen, *Efficient Democracy* (New York: Dodd, Mead and Co., 1902), 111.
6. James Phinney Munroe, *New Demands in Education* (Garden City, N.Y.: Doubleday, Page & Co., 1912), v.
7. N.E.A., *Proceedings* (1911), 221.
8. *Efficiency in High Schools: Studies, 1911–14, in the Application of the Principles of Scientific Management to High School Problems* (a collection of bulletins of the High School Teachers Association of New York City), vii.
9. Callahan, *Education and the Cult of Efficiency*, 60.
10. N.E.A., *Proceedings* (1912), 1017–20, in Callahan, *Education and the Cult of Efficiency*, 61.
11. See William Hughes Mearns, "Our Medieval High Schools—Shall We Educate Children for the Twelfth or the Twentieth Century?" *Saturday Evening Post* 184 (March 2, 1912), 18–19; Maude Radford Warren, "Medieval Methods for Modern Children," *Saturday Evening Post* 182 (March 12, 1912); Maude Radford Warren, "The Case of Seventeen Million Children—Is Our Public-School System Proving an Utter Failure?" *Ladies' Home Journal* 29 (August 1912); William McAndrew, "The Danger of Running a Fool Factory," *Ladies' Home Journal* 29 (September 1912).
12. H. Martyn Hart, *Ladies' Home Journal* 29 (November 1912): 9.
13. David Snedden, "Combining Efficiency and Democracy in Educational Administration," *The American School Board Journal* 42, 1 (January 1911): 3.
14. David Tyack and Elisabeth Hansot, *Managers of Virtue: Public School Leadership in America, 1820–1980* (New York: Basic Books, 1982), 107.
15. Frank E. Spaulding, *School Superintendent in Action in Five Cities* (Rindge, N.H.: R.R. Smith, 1955), 393.
16. Callahan, *Education and the Cult of Efficiency*, 73.
17. John Franklin Bobbitt, *The Curriculum of Modern Education* (New York: McGraw-Hill Book Co., 1941), 89.
18. Ibid., 95.
19. Giles M. Ruch and George D. Stoddard, *Tests and Measurements in High School Instruction* (Yonkers, N.Y. and Chicago: World Book Co., 1927); William Anderson McCall, *How to Measure in Education* (New York: Macmillan, 1922); Norman Fenton and Dean A. Worcester, *An Introduction to Educational Measurements* (New York: Ginn & Co., 1928).
20. Callahan, *Education and the Cult of Efficiency*, 101.
21. Cecil B. Read, "Efficiency of Methods in Solving Algebraic Equations,"

Bulletin, Municipal University of Wichita (University Studies Bulletin No. 3, Wichita, Kans.) 12, 1 (1937): 29.
22. Callahan, *Education and the Cult of Efficiency*, 104.
23. Ibid.
24. Frank E. Spaulding, *Measuring Textbooks* (New York: Newson and Co., 1922), 3.
25. Allen, *Efficient Democracy*, 136.
26. *American School Board Journal* 50 (May 1915): 50.
27. L.M. Terman, *The Measurement of Intelligence* (Boston: Houghton Mifflin, 1916), 6–7.
28. Ibid., 91–92.
29. Philip R. Reilly, *The Surgical Solution: A History of Involuntary Sterilization in the United States* (Baltimore, Md.: Johns Hopkins University Press, 1991), 45.
30. Ibid., 97.
31. Howard J. Savage, Foreword to Walter Crosby Eells, *Surveys of American Higher Education* (New York: The Carnegie Foundation for the Advancement of Teaching, 1937), iv–v.
32. Ibid., iii.
33. Eells, *Surveys of American Higher Education*, 56–57.
34. Theodore C. Mitchell, "Loss of Efficiency in the Recitation," *Educational Review* 45 (January 1913): 27–28.
35. Frederick Winslow Taylor, *Shop Management*, in *Scientific Management* (New York: Frederick Taylor, 1911; reprint, New York: Harper & Row, 1947), 58.
36. John Franklin Bobbitt, "Harvard Reaffirms the Academic Tradition," *The School Review* 54 (1946): 327.
37. Herbert M. Kliebard, *The Struggle for the American Curriculum* (New York: Routledge, 1995), 211–12.
38. Bobbitt, *The Curriculum of Modern Education*, 6.
39. Ibid., 347.
40. Roscoe David Case, *The Platoon School in America* (Stanford, Calif.: Stanford University Press, 1931), vii.
41. Ellwood P. Cubberley, "Foreword," to Case, *The Platoon School in America*, viii.
42. Case, *The Platoon School in America*, 30.
43. John Franklin Bobbitt, "The Elimination of Waste in Education," *The Elementary School Teacher* 12, 6 (February 1912): 260.
44. Case, *The Platoon School in America*, 12.
45. Alonzo G. Grace, *Educational Lessons from Wartime Training* (Washington, D.C.: American Council on Education, 1948), v.
46. Kliebard, *The Struggle for the American Curriculum*, 206.
47. Frank Schultz, "Basic Research Needed for Postwar Educational Planning," *The American School Board Journal* 108, 6 (June 1944): 30.
48. Stanford University School of Education Faculty, *Education in Wartime and After* (New York: D. Appleton-Century Co., 1943), 83.
49. Ibid.
50. Jesse Sears, *Public School Administration* (New York: The Ronald Press, 1947), iv.

Chapter 7

Expansive Perceptions: Pluralism and American Education

> Our pleasure in ourselves tries to maintain itself by again and again changing something new *into ourselves*; that is what possession means.
> —Friedrich Nietzsche, *The Gay Science*, Book 1, section 14

The organization of parts to benefit the whole, a model borrowed from an industrial division of labor, organized the sense of American society fostered by wartime schools. Curriculum changes during the war demonstrated the roles that different identities played in the drama of America. What was called "intercultural education" conceived of national unity as a collection of recognized differences—changing something new into ourselves—and became important in many different disciplines. Educational methods of the war period relied on the power to recognize difference and put differences to the service of the nation in a manner exploited in military registration and in businesslike division of labor.

The education faculty at Stanford reminded teachers that, especially during wartime, one of the most important areas for curricular development was the education for racial tolerance. "More difficult is the teaching of respect for differences in ideas and beliefs."[1] This teaching of respect for differences was one of the most significant wartime elaborations of state power. Differences—racial, ethnic, economic, or religious—became valuable because they were seen as having contributed to the greatness of American society.

The American Council on Education issued a statement in June 1940 entitled "Education and the National Defense," which attempted to persuade readers to avoid the Americanization programs of World War I. "The language or literature of no country should be eliminated from the curriculum; so-called 'hundred per cent' campaigns should be kept out of the classroom; personal or social discrimination because of racial or national origins should not be tolerated."[2] These attempts to avoid racial discrimination were direct responses to the attempts at "Americanization" during World War I.[3]

Unity, obviously, was of great concern during World War II. There were many possible alternatives to American unity: sexual, racial, ethnic, religious, and class differences all presented possible alternatives and challenges to feelings of belonging to a national identity. Education and schooling promised a powerful and permanent way to achieve national unity. "Of all our institutions, the schools have the greatest obligation and responsibility for developing in these young people a love for democracy," explained the faculty of Stanford University's school of education, "which will give the nation the oneness of feeling and purpose necessary for winning the war."[4] This demand for unity was immediately explained as requiring a faith in democracy and increased tolerance for racial diversity, not to be confused with a unity of cultural homogeneity.

To develop this unity of purpose and action, the schools' task is twofold: first, to help youth develop a deep and abiding loyalty to American democracy, and second, to help unify the various racial and national strands among the American people without destroying their cultural diversity. If they can accomplish this twofold task, the schools will have made not only a great contribution to the war effort, but to the preservation of American life.[5]

The war required unity, but America also required diversity. Schools were to bring Americans together without destroying America's cultural heterogeneity. (And here the possessive is most appropriate.) "To them [schools] have been entrusted the children from all economic levels, from every walk of life, from all the racial and national groups which together make up the American people."[6] To protect this trust, the schools should protect and not destroy the cultural diversity of American society.

These various groups were valued because of their contributions to America. As suggested by the University of Chicago Educational Monograph article on wartime readings for the middle grades: "We need units of work about the various nationality and racial groups that make up America. An understanding of people may be gained by studying the contribution that representatives of different groups have made to our heritage and to life today."[7]

Instead of requiring that all Americans become similar in cultural traits, what was increasingly required was an understanding of the different ways that different cultures contributed to the greatness of America—with every part performing a different function.

One odd example of this unity was the harmonic scale. George Kingsley Zipf discovered that if the cities of the United States are arranged in size they formed the harmonic mathematical series, $1, 1/2, 1/3, 1/4 \ldots 1/n$. Zipf's study made the American nation-state the order in which all the tonal differences of American geography were brought together. This "first-class contribution to social science" was not true for the individual states. This harmonic series demonstrated, the author claimed, American national integration, since harmony required different notes to come together in a larger pattern.[8] More circumspect scholars suggested that differences would not disappear as a result of Americanization but would remain as valuable elements of America. Horace Kallen's "ethnic federation" theory and Kimball Young's "sociological" theory both suggested that America would benefit from the differences of immigrants.[9] In March 1942, Harold Hoskins suggested that the melting pot should be thrown aside in favor of orchestral harmony. "Our American ideal should be expressed not in terms of a 'melting pot' with its somewhat mournful implication of uniformity," he claimed, "but rather in terms of an orchestra, in which each racial group, like an orchestral choir, contributes its special, different tone to the rich ensemble of the whole."[10] Kallen borrowed this language to suggest that "Majorities are orchestrations of the different; minorities are dissociations of the different."[11]

"Our problem," *The American School Board Journal* explained in an article subtitled "For a Better America We Must Harmonize," was "to discover materials and to adopt methods which will develop in our children a strong loyalty to America, without destroying their individual ethnic loyalties, and without losing important, inherent values in their individual group cultures."[12] Ethnic differences would be kept alive to aid in the recognition that citizens would feel in the nation-state. "This writer has found in his own experience that nothing engenders in a pupil more pride in America than to discover that his own people have played a part in making America, and that his own native culture has contributed to the beauty and strength of America."[13] "A by-product of this emphasis on the fact that the United States is a country of many stocks and cultural backgrounds has been a renewed interest on the part of all groups in their particular backgrounds," concluded Marian Schibsby, associate director of the Common Council for American Unity in New York City. Colleges played an important role in constructing American national history as the history of various groups contributing to the nation of the United States. "Colleges and schools are encouraging their students to seek out the roots of their heritage and to trace the history in this country of the group from which they stem."[14]

The foreword to *The Annals of the American Academy of Political and Social Science* of September 1942, an issue that explored "Minority Peoples in a Nation at War," counseled that minorities should understand their interests to be synchronized with those of the United States. "To the extent that these minorities remain unconvinced—because of their divergent traditions, ways of life, and the discrimination suffered at the hands of the old-American white majority—that their interests are identified with those of the Nation as a whole, to that extent the Nation will fall short of achieving its maximum effectiveness in the war."[15] But this consolidation of interest, the editors assured the readers, should be by the means of "positive measure rather than by the regressive devices likely to be engendered by war spirit."[16] The ability to turn differences into positives instead of negatives was one of the significant shifts in social organization and social power in the World War II period and became one of the central tasks of education.

INTERCULTURAL EDUCATION

By World War II, "intercultural education" became popular among educators. This movement was critical of the enforced nationalism common during World War I, and of such ideas as Israel Zangwell's famous melting pot.[17] The yearbook for the National Council for the Social Studies criticized the idea of the melting pot as "an unwholesome standardization" which took away from "the continuation of the foreign heritage."[18]

> The intense wave of nationalism which followed the last war culminated in our Americanization programs, the Ku Klux Klan outrages, the quota laws, and the reversal of our policy of an open door for all who wished to come. The loyalty and patriotism which our naturalized citizens had exhibited during the war were forgotten in the economic difficulties of the post-war period. . . . Strong-armed Americanization programs which "forced the alien to accept American customs and ideals, and implied that what immigrants brought with them and contributed to the common life was of little value," were put into effect.[19]

Reed Ueda has written that "World War II was a turning point in official attitudes toward ethnic and racial barriers."[20] This shift, particularly revealing when compared to World War I, moved from cultural homogeneity to cultural pluralism—but this was a pluralism harnessed to the service of the nation.

Ruth Benedict, writing in the *Annals* in 1941, looked to education to solve America's race problem. "Our great public educational system offers incomparable opportunity for improvement of cultural relations in America," she began, "and it is no small matter that the methods used should be well chosen." These programs promoted cultural diversity in the interest of the nation.

At present the philosophy of such programs is based on perpetuation of cultural diversity. Such diversity is extolled as a national asset, and the programs center around having different groups dramatize their customs in assembly programs, around sponsoring get-togethers where one group is singled out as guests to be received by the community, and around teaching in special "tolerance" sessions the cultural achievements of immigrants in their own country and the individual achievements of immigrants in America.

These programs "are carried out in the name of giving minorities a more secure place in America and of integrating our population,"[21] Franklin Roosevelt said to the National Association for the Advancement of Colored People, on June 25, 1938; "for it is evident that no democracy can long survive which does not accept as fundamental to its very existence the recognition of the rights of its minorities."[22] Stanford Education faculty understood this organization of racial and ethnic difference in the service of the nation as the trigger of national power:

Appreciating the cultural heritage and the contributions to American life made by the various cultural groups in American life. The keystone of our national strength is that we are not one race, one religion, or one culture but rather that we are one hundred and thirty million people with a rich heritage of many different customs, traditions, cultural and social backgrounds, each of which has contributed something of value to American life.[23]

This national pluralism relied on the overlapping conceptions of social power and goals between the nation-state and industry. That is, the differences required by industry were perceived to be comparable to the differences needed by the nation-state. These differences would have to be properly organized if the United States was to win the war. As Grayson Kefauver, Dean of the Stanford School of Education, wrote in the preface to the school's book *Education in Wartime and After*: "Total war demands the mobilization of the total resources of the country. Just as business cannot continue as usual, education cannot continue as usual."[24]

It is true, of course, that it takes many kinds of people to win a war and to make a world. Everyone brings to the effort a unique contribution of aptitude, talent, and experience. This war will be won by the concerted action of such unique personalities, each one giving the utmost in terms of what he has to offer.[25]

Our differences were not liabilities that should be modified but valuable possibilities when recognized by the nation or utilized by industry. Industrial division of labor became the model of social unity, even as schools and industry joined together in the promotion of American nationalism.

"As the war effort got under way," wrote Walter Magill, in an address before the Pennsylvania County Superintendents' Association at the University of Pennsylvania in 1944, "the schools and industry became closely integrated, and as this developed the efficiency of the instruction increased proportionately."²⁶

The December 1941 report of the Planning Commission of the National Council of Teachers of English, "The Role of the Teacher of English in Wartime," established some objectives for teachers of English during the war. One of their guidelines suggested the importance of intercultural recognition and valuation as a means of winning the war.

> c) In the development of democratic unity we aim to recognize the rights and contributions of minorities in this country as well as those of majorities, especially of the Negro, the Semitic peoples, and those loyal aliens who may be under suspicion at the moment because of descent from enemy nations.
>
> d) At the same time, we seek to promote through the study of literature a sense of unity among the various sections of our country and among the various social and economic groups represented in our national life.²⁷

Language education also demonstrated a change in attitude to national, racial, ethnic, and social differences. Instead of the repudiation of non-English languages, as in World War I, there was a push to promote language acquisition.

> The practice prevalent in America during World War I was to frown upon the language and culture of the enemy and to repudiate anything that pertained to him. In World War II we, as a nation, adopted a totally different point of view. Instead of denouncing German, Italian, or Japanese, the languages of the enemy, the various branches of the services put forth every effort to have their personnel learn them. And, what is more important, to learn them so well in some instances as to be able to converse effectively with natives! How this point of view, this right-about-face attitude, toward the languages of the enemy nations came about is a phenomenon which we are not to explain here.²⁸

There were, however, considerable rifts in this national order. Racism still proved a powerful force in American political culture, especially as directed against "blacks": "The fact that America denies tolerance, freedom, and equality of opportunity to large numbers of American citizens in our minority groups has, of course, made us vulnerable to charges from our enemies that we do not practice the democratic ideal which we preach."²⁹

This new organization of difference under the recognition power of the nation-state also displayed a significantly distinct understanding of race and a new word, "racism." This new meaning for the idea of race included several seemingly discordant elements. Race was increasingly understood to have no biological basis. Yet, perhaps not surprisingly, as race was increasingly understood to be mutable, it was concurrently deemed to be culturally significant for the nation and its retention was encouraged. The elements retained were to be those beneficial to the nation-state.

RACISM

The period from the turn of the twentieth century to World War I had witnessed the development of a new organization and meaning for racism. Race, increasingly associated with a distinction between black and white (with white being the assimilation of various European groups under a new title), allowed for the quick adoption of recent European immigrants into an racially coded nation.[30] This process was exceptionally detrimental for those coded black, since to be white was to a significant degree to be American. This exclusion of blacks from the American identity was most notably diagnosed by W.E.B. Du Bois in *The Souls of Black Folk* and his wish "to make it possible for a man to be both a Negro and an American."[31]

This turn-of-the-century racial organization brought with it powerful demands for cultural assimilation into a supposed American identity. By the late 1930s this organization shifted. Instead of being threats to the nation, cultural, racial, and ethnic differences were valuable aspects of America. Increasingly, people looked for "themselves" in the nation—that is, they listened to and told stories of the contributions made by people who shared some of their own characteristics. Differences became valuable as they found their proper position and role in American life. This shift greatly expanded the behaviors, beliefs, and actions to which the nation-state laid claim.

Racial, religious, and cultural differences ordered the unstable American social organization. Tremors of relativity were postponed through assurances that identities were admired by others, an assurance that could come from the nation-state or from others. An important aspect of the remaining distinction between black and white was that the proper positions for blacks within this scene were in positions of servitude and in positions of approval. The representations of blacks in positions of servitude came from an old American tradition of representation, but the question of approval, while not new, reveals an increasing relativism in which positions of some security were achieved through the realization that others want your position. That is, whites aware of their own insecurity and lack look to others for recognition and for models of self-sufficiency, and look to blacks for assurances that they are models of self-sufficiency for others.

For example, the June 10, 1939 *New Yorker* revealed the roles of blacks in the construction and maintenance of a white middle class. These examples are somewhat removed from education but clearly demonstrate the role of a racial division in maintaining assurance. In several advertisements blacks played prominent roles as approving and affirming onlookers, demonstrating the value of the actions and products presented in the advertisements. One advertisement, for Mount Vernon Whiskey, successfully organized connections between the onlooking black server, the national founding fathers, and the consumption of consumer goods. The advertisement praised the 150-year-old hospitality of Mount Vernon rye with a drawing of four bewigged founding fathers luxuriantly sipping "a glass of hospitality" as the black server glances at the reader of the advertisement, assuring them of the truth of the picture and the value of a life of leisure.[32]

The advertisement for Sanka Coffee that also appeared in the June 10, 1939 *New Yorker* is perhaps one of the best examples of the intersections between race and class. The advertisement, as most material in the *New Yorker*, was geared to approving the values and ways of life of the middle and upper classes in the United States. The plot of the Sanka advertisement involved the attempt of a white upper-middle-class woman to win the affections of her husband's rich aunt, "Jim's Aunt Daisy . . . the wealthy old thundercloud." She gained these affections by teaching the aunt the rewards of Sanka Coffee—she could have her after-dinner coffee treat and sleep soundly at night. Three of the six sketches that conveyed the narrative contained the presence of the black maid. In her first scene the maid looked on as Aunt Daisy bellowed her refusal of after-dinner coffee. The maid's face, especially her wide eyes, displayed the fear of the diners. In her final scene the maid smiled approvingly as "the old girl drank two cups!"[33]

In the same issue of the *New Yorker*, Christian Peper Tobacco Co. featured an approving black man in their advertisement for London Dock Tobacco. The advertisement featured an approving array of onlookers as an upper-class man smoked his pipe, checked his train schedule, and waited at the train station to depart on his honeymoon. The two most prominent onlookers were his recent bride and the railway porter. The caption appears to be spoken by both of these onlookers: "Ah! He Smokes That Aromatic London Dock Tobacco!"[34] The onlookers assured the participants of the value of their actions. The advertisements created an imagined identification with the whites but additionally created a symbolic identification with the blacks. That is, the advertisements appealed to a desire to be seen as the object of accomplishment and completeness that the desire itself revealed to be lacking. The imagined identification betrayed the way people wished others would perceive them; the symbolic identification revealed the way we see our selves, as unstable and uncertain.[35]

Race became "retainable" at the point that it became "discardable." This mutability revealed a further contingency—a radical lack of stability in our belief in what we should be and what we should do. An instability that for the moment promoted the interests of the nation and worked as an element in national power. In World War II this power required the recognition of contributions by various differences to the achievements of the nation and required that citizens expect to see themselves reflected in the nation.

In June 1940, Congress passed the Alien Registration Act, which required that the alien population of the United States register with the Justice Department. "Therefore, for the first time in the history of our Nation," concluded Donald Perry, "a complete inventory was to be made of noncitizens."[36]

The state required increased knowledge concerning possible alternative identities—that is, greater knowledge of elements of personal identity. The Works Progress Administration, the Justice Department, and the United States Office of Education sponsored the National Citizenship Education Program to nationalize and assimilate aliens into American society.

One of the most striking failures of cultural pluralism to protect a minority as long as they functioned in the interest of the nation was the decision by the Western Defense Command to evacuate and imprison in concentration camps Japanese Americans. Lieutenant General J.L. DeWitt, commanding officer of the Western Defense Command, issued orders on March 24, 1942 that affected virtually all Japanese in the states of Oregon, California, Washington, and Arizona.[37] All of 112,000 citizens and aliens of Japanese decent were removed from military areas and placed in concentration camps under the supervision of the Army. "The inability of many Americans, official and unofficial, to understand the 'oriental mind' came out strongly in the testimony."[38] Many authors attempted to cast the concentration of Japanese as an attempt by the government to protect them. "A better case can be made" for internment, "however, for the need to protect the Japanese from mob violence due to the hysteria and resentment caused by the war situation."[39] Certainly a self-serving interpretation, but also telling of the need for this action to be interpreted in terms of national recognition and protection of difference. Shotaro Frank Miyamoto suggested that even "some Japanese have accepted the evacuation as a protective measure against majority group hostility."[40]

The application of Executive Order 9102, which created the War Relocation Authority (WRA) and the exclusion of Japanese Americans from the western United States, uniquely configured issues of citizenship, work, and management. Of central concern to the WRA was the contribution that the internees could make to the national war economy. It was in this vein that the camps functioned as training grounds for bureaucratic work. Furthermore, the internment of citizens in racial concentration camps contributed to the general trend consolidating citizenship as a juridic relationship to the state—that is, citizenship question would after this time become highly associated with issues of equal treatment by the state as guaranteed in the Fourteenth Amendment. Additionally, the camps functioned as a laboratory for many of the political trends already discussed—the increased attention on the part of the state to the facts of life of citizens, particularly facts that were perceived as possibly conducive to changing attitudes and beliefs.

At a meeting held on April 7 in Salt Lake City to discuss the relocation camps, Milton S. Eisenhower, director of the program, focused attention on the need to make sure that the labor of the internees was not wasted. "Admitting candidly at the start that the plans of WRA were still in a highly fluid state, he went on to indicate that he was deeply concerned about the civil liberties of the evacuated people and about the problem of making effective use of the manpower they represented." Eisenhower outlined five work plans that would utilize the represented manpower:

(1) public works, including such things as the development of raw lands for agricultural production; (2) production of food, both for evacuee subsistence and for sale, on Federally owned project lands; (3) manufacture of goods, such as camouflage nets and cartridge belts, which were vitally needed by the military; (4) private employment; and (5) establishment of self-supporting communities which would be managed by the evacuees themselves rather than by the Federal Government.[41]

By the end of May the agency had created a formula for accounting and allocating work at the relocation centers. A bulletin issued to the evacuees called for "partnership enterprises" between the WRA and members of the work corps. Under this plan the WRA was responsible for providing life's basic essentials and developing work opportunities for the internees.

The members of the corps, for their part, would work toward three main objectives: first, to provide for the living requirements of the whole evacuee community to the greatest possible extent; second, to develop the land under WRA jurisdiction in the vicinity of the centers and improve its productive value; and third, to produce a supply of agricultural and manufactured goods surplus to center needs for sale on the open market.

It was originally proposed that the money from the open market profit be advanced to the internees, but many camps eventually simply paid the workers outright. In spite of demands that internees who refused to work be charged, nothing ever came of those plans.[42]

In addition to making the inductees—citizens deprived of very basic rights—perform as part of the national machinery during the war, the camps served as virtual training centers for bureaucratic work.

On an individual basis, however, the War Relocation Authority probably has done more training of employees for the Federal Government than any other Federal agency in the same period of time. The younger generation of the evacuees were particularly adaptable to stenographic, typing, clerical accounting, nurse's aide, mechanical and other types of positions which were badly needed by each of the centers. On the basis of the individual training that these young people received at the centers, many qualified for civil-service employment by the War Relocation Authority in its other offices as time went on. At one time, nearly 20 percent of the Washington office staff were evacuees who had received their original training at the centers. Now hundreds of them are employed by a large number of Federal agencies throughout the Nation. Just as the relocation centers contributed an outstanding unit to the United States Army in the 442nd Combat Team, so also the relocation centers have contributed a good group of well-trained civilian workers for work in the Federal service.[43]

Training for government bureaucratic work was not the only way that these relocation centers fit the larger social patterns of Taylorite management. The centers became laboratories for government social studies. In an effort to establish better social control in the wake of the strikes and riots at Poston, Tule Lake, and Manzanar, the WRA began to study social relations and the informal governments of the camps. "The community analysis reports . . . will provide a wealth of highly valuable material for social scientists and others interested in studying the social patterns of a displaced minority in government-operated camps."[44] These studies of the social patterns and informal arrangements provided another format for the expanding studies of interests and attitudes.[45]

But the community analysis set-up did mean that the desires, beliefs, and attitudes of the evacuees, so far as they could be determined, were constantly taken into consideration and weighed along with other factors. Although the analysts were not often able to predict specific outbreaks of trouble at the centers, they did render almost invaluable service in analyzing the causes of an outbreak, once it had occurred, and in giving the administrators an insight into the course of remedial action most likely to prove effective.[46]

The examination of the legal status of citizenship as it applied to Japanese Americans performed the significant act of focusing increased attention to the Fourteenth Amendment as the font of basic American citizenship rights— a turn of events that consolidated the already considerable American fixation on the Constitution as the arbiter of American politics. More importantly, for American pluralism it was the internment of Japanese Americans that precipitated the shift in the Supreme Court's role from one in which it acted as a check on national power to one where it acted to protect the basic rights of individuals. This shift was very much a part of the larger social shift in which ethnic differences contributed to the nation, and the state increasingly acted to protect them.

Even as this new division of nationalism into recognized differences occurred, race was increasingly understood to be an artificial identification. Educators deconstructed race as a biological fact. The authority of educators, or experts, and the need of the nation was pitted against race as a biological truth.[47]

At this historical moment, several trends in social thought twisted in an interlocking pattern. Society, like industry, was believed to be a whole constituted of parts, with different positions and functions that were united in one social goal. As this occurred, many of those differences were perceived as arbitrary distinctions, only given life because others so recognized them. For example, race was increasingly denaturalized and biologically refuted, even as racial differences (mostly called cultural) were perceived to be valuable contributors to the national identity. This seeming conflict occurred through the increasing conception of the necessity of outside recognition. People were increasingly removed from systems that had provided value and organization. Value was displayed as a recognition that came from some other part— the social whole most principally—that is, the nation and industrial bureaucracy. Social differences became more significantly valued even as they became more obviously socially imposed.

The anthropologists have now exposed the race myth so that its fallacies can be generally understood. Therefore, it is the responsibility of the school to present the facts about race so that youth will understand that there is no pure race, that no race is superior to another physically, mentally, or socially, that the biological composition of the so-called races is so varied that personalities of many distinct types are found in each.[48]

This effort to undercut race attempted to teach children the differences within racial groupings. There were some social differences, teachers were to teach, but of no greater importance than the differences within groups.

We should show children in the primary grades that individuals of any nationality group in our own country differ among themselves, that all persons of a particular race are not lazy, that all of any nationality are not "dumb," that all of any nationality are not polite. In fact, no single characterization, good or bad, applies to a race or nationality or religious group. . . . When we know people and understand their habits and customs, we are usually more sympathetic to their idiosyncrasies than when we do not know anything about them.[49]

Reading about Americans different from ourselves would teach us to identify with them and to appreciate their particular social habits as well as to reduce the political saliency of these differences.[50] "In the best of our fiction, drama, and poetry, the reader is admitted not only into the working-places and homes of the people but also into their hearts and minds. The printed word builds unity by creating the convincing illusion of identity between the reader and the culturally diverse characters that move upon the page."[51] The reading programs teachers were encouraged to put together were to expand the identifications of students to include those nationals of different backgrounds. Reading curriculums were to teach citizens to value a wide range of difference in the interest of promoting international cooperation as the United States stood to benefit from such cooperation.

To these ends we can work for the creation of an indestructible unity among our own people and among them and the great peoples of Europe, Africa, Asia, and South America who are our allies. World-literature can be a force in welding together here in the United States and throughout the world the notable cultures of the Pan-American, Negro, Chinese, Slavic, and English peoples. Nor must we leave out the great literature of Germany Italy, and Japan now being destroyed by the Axis censors. The world for which we are fighting needs them all.⁵²

American national power began to rely on the recognition of elements perceived to be "interior" to the national identity that corresponded to international identities.

These elements became important because of their contribution to the power of the nation. That actions, beliefs, and identities furthered the nation was one way to assure that they were important and not being wasted.

Discrimination and prejudice are not only incompatible with the democratic belief in the dignity and worth of the common man and the American tradition which welcomed the contribution which each individual could make regardless of his race, color, or creed, but discrimination and prejudice which do not permit a nation to encourage and use the talent and ability of all its people to their fullest extent is criminally wasteful of its human resources.⁵³

Racism interfered with American industrial production. Not only did it interfere with efficient management, organization, and control, but different cultures offered a variety of heritages for America to draw on, both for their marketing possibilities and for their value to secure postwar American hegemony.

The combination of anti-racism and recognized diversity formed the necessary basis for future international action. By nationally recognizing internal difference, America would look more tolerant to the rest of the world and would build bridges through America's own immigrant identities to international influence and markets. Young students were educated in international tolerance.

In the high schools many pupils are preparing for war or for the professions or for industrial pursuits that are directly related to war. In the elementary schools pupils are being prepared for peace. This preparation for peace is a preparation for international interests. The essay lists five areas that middle grades should explore. (1) global relations, (2) ideals and traditions of our country, (3) attitudes toward peoples of different cultures, (4) advances in science, and (5) community problems.⁵⁴

"The term 'United Nations' can become meaningful to the peoples concerned only it there exist mutual trust, understanding, and respect," claimed an article on Asiatic films for use in American education.⁵⁵

An additional element in this pluralism was the value of pluralism for a nation increasingly conceiving of itself as a central player on the world stage. "*Regarding our country as one member of a team—the United Nations—dedicated to the victory over totalitarianism.* Every American citizen should realize that he is a member of a world group of United Nations."⁵⁶ During World War II Americans were increasingly encouraged to turn their national differences into international connections. "Therefore, although we must be loyal to worthy American traditions, we must become increasingly citizens of the world."⁵⁷ America, the education staff at Stanford argued, was uniquely suited to teach the world how to live together. "American political genius has united races, creeds, and classes into a working federal union. We have kept this union intact with blood, sweat, and tears. Now it is our duty to train a citizenry that will cherish such an ideal for the entire world."⁵⁸ The ability to organize differences within concepts of national and industrial division of labor would be the global system of the postwar world, it was widely believed.

This attention to the contributions of various racial and ethnic groups to the United States will, according to the Stanford report, give students pride in their heritage and pride in the United States. This payoff reveals connections between national recognition and valuation. Differences become valued by their contribution to the nation-state. "Pride in their heritage gives youth of all groups a sense of security and belongingness and a deep and abiding knowledge that America is great and strong because of what they and their kinsmen and others have given and are contributing to make America and the world a better place in which to live."⁵⁹

Citizenship became closely connected to identification and the ability to see reflections of other identifications as contributors—not to independent elements, but as contributors to your nationality.

CONCLUSION

Education during World War II fostered a citizenship heavily reliant on notions of valuation, which were received from the external sources of the nation and bureaucracy. This recognition could value a diverse range of differences. This understanding of recognition as an exterior process opened up new ranges of possibilities. Even as the state increasingly attempted to control and organize desire, a place of plurality was demarcated.

Attempts on the part of education testing, as well as military testing, to influence attitudes and opinions revealed a growing sense of the freedom possible even within highly structured social relationships. Concurrently, education's growing approval of particular social attributes, while constrained within the needs of the nation, taught an expanded exceptable difference. That is, the state fostered and gave its value to differences in such a way that they eventually gained the strength to value themselves. This process certainly occurred at the level of group identification, but it also occurred internally. The state fostered a sense of the value of our own individualism, a sense that eventually became strong enough to exist on its own. The strengthened individualism made it increasingly possible to resist the desires for recognition of difference from an outside source—an individualism that would in some ways live outside Hegel's notion of history.

NOTES

1. Stanford University School of Education Faculty, *Education in Wartime and After* (New York: D. Appleton-Century Co., 1943), 163.
2. George F. Zook, "How the Colleges Went to War," *The Annals of the American Academy of Political and Social Science* 231 (January 1944): 1.
3. See Grover G. Huebner, "Americanization of the Immigrant," *The Annals of the American Academy of Political and Social Science* (May 1906): 191–213.
4. Stanford University School of Education Faculty, *Education in Wartime and After*, 54.
5. Ibid.
6. Ibid.
7. Manley Irwin, "Reading Materials That Provide Needed Curriculum Enrichment," in *Adapting Reading Programs to Wartime Needs*, ed. William S. Gray (Chicago: University of Chicago Press, 1943), 47.
8. George Kingsley Zipf, *National Unity and Disunity* (Bloomington, Ind.: Principia, 1941). Quotation is from Frank Hankins, Review of *National Unity and Disunity*, *The Annals of the American Academy of Political and Social Science* 217 (September 1941): 173. Of course, harmony required the idea of silence—to display the noise; national harmony used "blackness" as its silence. "Blacks" were often the negative part that demonstrated the positivity of "whites." The metaphor even influenced studies of harmony. Mary Emma Allen presented a particularly interesting example in her scientific study of harmony. Using the Jacob Kwalwasser Melodic and Harmonic Sensitivity Test, Allen determined that at early elementary school ages "Negro" children had superior harmonic sensitivity but by upper age levels "white" sensitivity was, not surprisingly given the intellectual organization of racism at the time, superior. Mary Emma Allen, "A Comparative Study of Negro and White Children on Melodic and Harmonic Sensitivity," *Journal of Negro Education* 11 (April 1942): 158–64.
9. Horace Kallen, *Americans All* (Washington, D.C.: National Education Association, 1942).
10. Harold B. Hoskins, "American Unity and Our Foreign-Born Citizens," *The Annals of the American Academy of Political and Social Science* (March 1942): 158. It should be remembered that the protagonist of *The Melting-Pot* was himself a composer and violinist who dreamed of writing the great American symphony. The play makes none of the connections with harmony that later became important—stubbornly utilizing chemical and alchemical metaphors of melting and combining.
11. H.M. Kallen, "National Solidarity and the Jewish Minority," *The Annals of the American Academy of Political and Social Science* 223 (September 1942): 17.
12. Thomas J. Quigley, "Conflicting National Cultures in American Schools," *The American School Board Journal* 108, 3 (March 1944): 20.
13. Ibid., 22.

14. Marian Schibsby, "Private Agencies Aiding the Foreign-Born," *The Annals of the American Academy of Political and Social Science* 223 (September 1942): 188.
15. J.P. Shalloo and Donald Young, "Foreword," *The Annals of the American Academy of Political and Social Science* 223 (September 1942): vii.
16. Ibid.
17. "Yes, East and West, and North and South, the palm and the pine, the pole and the equator, the crescent and the cross—how the great Alchemist melts and fuses them with his purging flame! Here shall they all unite to build the Republic of Man and the Kingdom of God. Ah, Vera, what is the glory of Rome and Jerusalem where all nations and races come to worship and look back, compared with the glory of America, where all races and nations come to labour and look forward!" Zangwill's leading character prophecies at the end of the play as the curtain falls and the orchestra gently takes up "My Country, 'tis of Thee." Israel Zangwill, *The Melting-Pot: Drama in Four Acts* (New York: Macmillan, 1909), 199–200.
18. Reed Ueda, "Ethnic Diversity and National Identity in Public School Texts," in Diane Ravitch and Maris Vinovskis, eds., *Learning from the Past* (Baltimore, Md.: Johns Hopkins University Press, 1995), 114.
19. Stanford University School of Education Faculty, *Education in Wartime and After*, 67–68.
20. Ueda, "Ethnic Diversity and National Identity," 14.
21. Ruth Benedict, "Race Problems in America," *The Annals of the American Academy of Political and Social Science* 216 (July 1941): 75. Benedict often wrote in critique of attempts at intercultural studies. She asserted that what most minorities or immigrants really wanted was to be American, and that attempts at encouraging cultural diversity within the United States were often attempts to keep the American identity relatively narrow.
22. Kallen, "National Solidarity and the Jewish Minority," 17
23. Stanford University School of Education Faculty, *Education in Wartime and After*, 77.
24. Grayson Kefauver, "Preface," in Stanford University School of Education Faculty, *Education in Wartime and After* (New York: D. Appleton-Century Co., 1943), v.
25. Stanford University School of Education Faculty, *Education in Wartime and After*, 33.
26. Walter H. Magill, "The War Has Set the Pattern for—the Role of Industrial Education in the Postwar Period," *The American School Board Journal* 108, 6 (June 1944): 18.
27. Planning Commission of the National Council of Teachers of English, "The Role of the Teacher of English in Wartime," *English Journal* (January 1942).
28. Robert John Matthew, *Language and Area Studies in the Armed Services: Their Future Significance* (Washington, D.C.: American Council on Education, 1947), xi.
29. Stanford University School of Education Faculty, *Education in Wartime and After*, 65.
30. See Michael Paul Rogin, "'The Sword Became a Flashing Vision': D.W. Griffith's *The Birth of a Nation*," in Rogin, *Ronald Reagan, the Movie and Other Episodes in Political Demonology* (Berkeley: University of California Press, 1987), 190–235.

31. W.E.B. Du Bois, *The Souls of Black Folk* (New York: A.C. McClurg & Co., 1903; reprint, New York: Penguin Classics, 1989), 5.
32. National Distillers Products Corporation (advertisement), *New Yorker*, June 10, 1939, 81.
33. Sanka Coffee (advertisement), *New Yorker*, June 10, 1939, 63.
34. Christian Peper Tobacco Co. (advertisement), *New Yorker*, June 10, 1939, 45.
35. For an exceptionally clear explanation of the difference between imagined and symbolic identification see Slavoj Zizek, *The Sublime Object of Ideology* (London: Verso, 1989), 105–10.
36. Donald R. Perry, "Aliens in the United States," *The Annals of the American Academy of Political and Social Science* 223 (September 1942): 1.
37. Shotaro Frank Miyamoto, "Immigrants and Citizens of Japanese Origin," *The Annals of the American Academy of Political and Social Science* 223 (September 1942): 112.
38. Everett V. Stonequist, "The Restricted Citizen," *The Annals of the American Academy of Political and Social Science* 223 (September 1942): 153.
39. Otto Klineberg, "Race Prejudice and the War," *The Annals of the American Academy of Political and Social Science* 223 (September 1942): 196.
40. Miyamoto, "Immigrants and Citizens of Japanese Origin," 113.
41. *WRA: A Story of Human Conservation* (Washington, D.C.: U.S. Department of Interior, War Relocation Authroity, 1946), 29.
42. Ibid., 78–79.
43. *Administrative Highlights*, 35.
44. *WRA: A Story of Human Conservation*, 187.
45. At the camp at Poston, Alexander Leighton was stationed as sociological observer from June 1942 to September 1943, "making observations and analyses that would have bearing on general problems of administration and government, particularly in occupied areas." Alexander H. Leighton, *The Governing of Men* (Princeton, N.J.: Princeton University Press, 1945), vii–viii.
46. *WRA: A Story in Human Conservation*, 187.
47. In many ways, however, race, particularly as constructed as a distinction between "black" and "white," retained biological meanings. For example, the Red Cross segregated blood types. See Ernest Williams, pen name for Myra Lesnik, "Blood Is Segregated Too," *Militant*, January 1, 31 and February 7, 1942, in C.L.R. James et al., *Fighting Racism in World War II* (New York: Pathfinder, 1980), 148–49. "This is true despite the fact that every scientist worthy of the name has asserted that there is no difference whatsoever in plasma made from the blood of persons of different races." Walter White, "What the Negro Thinks of the Army," *The Annals of the American Academy of Political and Social Science* 223 (September 1942): 67.
48. Stanford University School of Education Faculty, *Education in Wartime and After*, 69–70.
49. Augusta Jameson, "Guidance of Youth in High Schools and Junior Colleges," in *Adapting Reading Programs to Wartime Needs*, ed. William S. Gray (Chicago: University of Chicago Press, 1943), 34.
50. There was much to read: Ruth Benedict and Mildred Ellis, *Race and Cultural Relations* (Washington, D.C.: National Education Association, 1942); Ira D. Reid, *In a Minor Key: Negro Youth in Fact and Fiction* (Washington, D.C.: American Council on Education, 1940); Carl Wittke, *We Who Built America: The Saga of the*

Immigrant (New York: Prentice-Hall, 1940), 472; Francis Brown and Joseph Roucek, *Our Racial and National Minorities* (New York: Prentice-Hall, 1937). Even *Fortune* magazine got into the action: "The Negro's War," *Fortune* (June 1942).

51. John J. DeBoer, "Current Importance of the Literature of Power and Imagination," in *Adapting Reading Programs to Wartime Needs*, ed. William S. Gray (Chicago: University of Chicago Press, 1943), 136.

52. Stanford University School of Education Faculty, *Education in Wartime and After*, 190.

53. Ibid., 72.

54. Manley Irwin, "Reading Materials for the Middle Grades," in *Adapting Reading Programs to Wartime Needs*, ed. William S. Gray (Chicago: University of Chicago Press, 1943), 45.

55. William H. Hartley, "Films for Asiatic Studies in American Education," *The School Review* 51, 4 (April 1943): 219.

56. Stanford University School of Education Faculty, *Education in Wartime and After*, 34.

57. Ibid., 37.

58. Ibid., 38.

59. Ibid., 78.

Chapter 8

"Harness the Potential": World War II and the Organization of Education

> If this education succeeds, then every virtue of an individual is a public utility and a private disadvantage, measured against the supreme private goal—probably some impoverishment of the spirit and the senses or even a premature decline. Consider from this point of view, one by one, the virtues of obedience, chastity, filial piety, and justice.
> —Friedrich Nietzsche, *The Gay Science*, Book 1, section 21

"Our ideal," Sue Maxwell, chairman of the Ensley High School Victory Corps of Birmingham, Alabama, proclaimed, "is to harness the potential strength of our sixteen hundred pupils for whatever national or community need it can best serve at any given time."[1] Selective service and the draft required that teachers and school buildings perform as public servants and public spaces. The impending war created a reasonably clear goal for education— to be of service to the nation and to industry. And a goal is what the adoption of methods of efficiency required.

Theories of reform in the 1930s and 1940s demanded a goal or reason for education that could unify the perspectives of workers, managers, teachers, and administrators as well as students and teachers. The most often touted goal for education was national and vocational efficiency. This organizing framework substantially replaced the earlier model of divinely inspired progress. Between world wars, education was required to define the goals to which it (and the students) worked. Particularly as business ideas, such as efficiency, exerted greater pressure on education, the meaning or purpose became national and vocational.

GOALS OF EDUCATION

One of the most significant consequences of the influence of Taylorism was the increased demand for a goal by which education's success could be measured. Jesse Sears, a colleague and biographer of Ellwood Patterson Cubberley,[2] wrote of Taylor that his "analysis of actual performance seemed important to me, yet I realized that the product of educational effort is not as tangible and measurable as is that of business or industrial effort. Education works to achieve values that lie beyond learning to spell or add or read or write, the results of which we can now measure."[3] John Dewey expressed the need for education to present students with a clearly articulated goal: "Interest measures—or rather is—the depth of the grip which a foreseen end has upon one in moving one to act for its realization."[4] Edgar W. Knight's *Progress and Educational Perspective* asserted that progress in education was closely linked to change since progress requires a goal that education was unable to support. "It is precisely this lack of definiteness about purposes of life in general and educational purposes in particular which, Knight argues, constitutes America's most serious educational mistake," reported a contemporary review.[5]

Efficiency served as a social goal after the death of earlier social goals, such as the common school movement's goal of redemption.[6] Social and personal efficiency became the organizing trope of education and the goal of education. Not only should education be conducted more efficiently, but education should produce efficient citizens and workers. Efficiency justified education through connections to the state and to industry, and valued knowledge by its connections to the nation-state and by its ability to produce good workers.

Once it was assumed that education should be efficient, it became important to define exactly what it should be efficient at doing. What is the goal to which all this efficient labor would be directed? Earlier education projects in the United States were directed to creating godly citizens. But by the 1930s and 1940s, new goals were required to steer the massive state education project. World War II, of course, succeeded in consolidating the goal of national service; a goal that, along with industrial or bureaucratic success, played a significant role in American education. But these two goals failed to finally direct American education. In fact, education, by expressing the question of the necessity of goals, created a new location for democratic contestation and a suspicion that no goal would ever serve.

THE WORKPLACE

Religion, Greek, and music, like many humanistic pursuits, lost out to disciplines that more clearly prepared students for work and the discipline of the workplace. "An example of inefficiency . . . may be taken from a course in algebra, or French, or carpentry or history, given uniformly to all of the pupils in a high school, when experience goes to show that few of these pupils will ever have occasion to use any or all of these subjects in their life work."[7] Students were to be tracked according to talents to ensure the most productive utilization of their talents and taught employable skills.

Interest was increasingly conceived as valuable when in line with the interests of industrial production and the nation. In conjunction with this organization, workers' interest became conflated with the interests of the nation. "No man is good unless good for something," wrote William Allen. "Goodness in business matters has come to imply performance that is satisfactory, which in the world of business means efficiency."[8] Government, including education, should be good, and that meant being efficient, argued Allen. Robert Moses, New York City Parks Commissioner, complained about "college graduates who handicap government departments by inability to write and speak English."[9] Education should create citizens who efficiently meet the needs of the nation.

The exposure of questions concerning overarching values was made more significant by the increasing attention to problems of desire. Goals were often perceived as necessary to the creation of desire. Without final purpose, it was believed, students would not desire education.

NATIONAL GOAL FOR EDUCATION

During World War II, primary and secondary schools worked in conjunction with the needs and demands of the nation-state. Schools and school workers filled the need for part-time administrative functions and functionaries. Schools aided in military training and conformed to the curriculum demands of wartime: physical training and intercultural nationalism. Therefore, education attuned its possible goals with the production of a nationalism based on the nation-state's recognition of value.

On October 16, 1940, almost 17 million men between the ages of 21 and 35 registered for the draft in their local schools. In New York City, 712 schools were used as registration places; 20,000 people worked at this registration, and more than half of these were teachers, while the remainder were Board of Elections inspectors. About 18,000 teachers and 2,500 firemen were held in reserve to aid at locations that needed extra workers.[10] The New York *Journal and American* reported two days prior to registration that "The entire teaching staffs of all public high schools, except those on the substitute list, have been ordered to report at their regular posts on registration day.

Those not used for regular assignments will be held in reserve in the event of need for additional registars [sic]."[11]

In New York City, only three teachers explicitly refused to aid in registration. Declaring themselves conscientious objectors, these teachers refused to aid the massive draft registration. They lost the day's pay and were marked "absent from duty." Virtually all of the 38,000 teachers and supervisors considered it their duty to register young men for selective service.[12] "It was a long day at Board of Education headquarters, ... yesterday," the *New York Times* reported, "perhaps the longest in school history, as officials assigned to the draft registration detail remained at their posts from 6:30 A.M. to 11:30 P.M., ready to act as 'trouble shooters.'"[13]

Of course, the immediate impact of the war went much further than an extra day of work. High schools became important conduits for the culture of nationalism: posters, songs, flags, and teaching all directed the attention of students to the interests of the nation. For example, Sue Maxwell, chairman of the Ensley High School Victory Corps of Birmingham, Alabama, described her high school: "patriotic posters are met at every step in the halls and classrooms."[14] The service flag, with a star for every former student in the military, joined their "new and beautiful" national flag. "A service flag in the auditorium daily reminds us of lads in the jungles of New Guinea, the sands of North Africa, and the rough waters of the Caribbean."[15] "Air-raid drills have become a part of our existence," disrupting the time spent in class even as musical time organized harmony for the nation, "patriotic songs instill courage in those of us who remain to teach or study and give inspiration to those who are on their way." The national work of education did not end with the day: "The shops are open at night for adult defense workers who need added training; teachers and pupils absent themselves from classes to aid in rationing and registration ... students and teachers hurry to defense classes after school or at night, courses in many instances taught by members of our own faculty."[16]

Education's buildings and faculty became important promoters of national objectives. New courses promoted the national program of war-making. Putting education in closer step with basic training created a high demand for summer school courses. Popular among high school boys seeking to complete their high school careers before military service, these programs enabled students to get some college education to increase the possibility of their selection as officer candidates. "By means of close coordination between the high school and college courses ... it would be possible for some to receive a full year of college, and many to secure one semester's credit before entering the military service."[17] High schools and colleges correlated their courses to speed students into higher level courses, a relationship coordinated with military training needs. "It is believed," reported the Jackson, Mississippi *Citizen-Patriot*, "that such a plan will help to supply the demand for officer material, enable some boys to qualify for further college training in uniform, and assist in stabilizing youth returning from the war because he is more likely to return to college if he has made a beginning prior to his military service."[18] In the service of the nation, high schools and colleges were more coordinated with the military and helped to reintegrate returning soldiers into the American economic system.

High schools prepared students for war. In Baton Rouge, there was a proposal that American Legion instructors train and drill high school students so that they would be physically prepared for the military. "The general idea," according to State of Louisiana Commander Cole, "is to select, from Legion posts in each high school town, members who will take a one-week intensive refresher course at Louisiana State University and thereafter be available to conduct drills on high school campuses."[19]

Reportedly, the plan would give students "a leg or two up" on the military training awaiting them. Dean William Russell of Teachers' College, Columbia University and director of the National Citizenship Educational Program, gave several speeches on the importance of training high school boys. At a speech he gave in Seattle, Russell claimed that the Axis threat required American educators to train high school students. "If," he began, "the United States is to have the great army that it needs to eliminate the Axis threat of world domination it must start training the high school boys for the job right now."[20] Since that great army required special skills, high schools greatly extended specialized training. "And, as nine out of every ten men in a modern army must be skilled specialists, it's obvious that we can take a tremendous burden off the war department if we give the boys as much training as possible before they are inducted."[21] Education shouldered its share of the national war burden.

The October 1, 1942 issue of *Education for Victory*, the official biweekly of the United States Office of Education, announced the creation of the high school Victory Corps. This program had eight specific objectives: guidance of youth into critical services and occupations, wartime citizenship training to ensure understanding of the war, physical fitness, voluntary military drill, study of science and mathematics, pre-flight training, pre-induction training for important occupations, and community service directed toward essential civilian activities.[22] These objectives met the two general directives of the Victory Corps: to provide youth with wartime training and to encourage community participation.[23]

The government also set up a program sometimes called the "air-conditioning" program. This program prepared students for aviation—an objective of exceptional interest. To achieve good attitudes and aptitudes toward air transportation, this program modified studies of science, mathematics, social studies, and geography to encourage and train students for air service.[24] *The California Journal of Secondary Education* wrote that "nothing ever before has happened in secondary education quite like the present all-out effort to make aviation-conscious the high-school youth of America."[25]

The threatened drafting of 18- and 19-year-olds strengthened connections between education and military service. These men were younger, it was argued, and therefore more malleable and physically more efficient.

War won't wait on windy argument. Nor can the highest efficiency of our combat forces. It is essential that 18–19-year-olds be subject to draft. Harsh as that may be, we can't avoid facing the realities. Men in the age group between 18 and 27 furnish the best sinews for an army.... Younger soldiers have the best natural equipment for victory. Their reactions are keener, quicker. Physically they are more resilient and more hardy.[26]

Physical education linked the needs of nationalism, the needs of industrial authority and, obviously, the citizen's body.

The need for physical efficiency, essential in all times, has been increased by the war, which has made it necessary for the biological objectives of physical education to be given greater emphasis. The development and maintenance of organic power, an increase in the qualities of speed, endurance, and strength, and the achieving of neuromuscular skills are as basic to the increase of productivity in the industrial world as they are to survival on the battlefield.[27]

High schools greatly increased work in physical education as the recruits' bodies became valuable for the nation. The focus on students as physical bodies was, significantly, a need for youthful bodies—bodies more easily adapted and modified to the needs of war. "Not only was it necessary to train millions for combat duty," reported the American Council on Education at the end of the war, "but other millions had to be trained for the production line and for volunteer assignments in the civilian defense organization."[28]

When the draft was extended to 18-year-olds, far greater attention was devoted to the educational problems and benefits of the military's interruption of normal education patterns.

In signing the teen-age draft bill, Mr. Roosevelt said he was having a study made to enable those whose education is interrupted to resume their schooling when their service with the armed forces is ended. Though any such planning must be tentative for the present, at least it is worthwhile to keep such a program in mind. Not all these boys may be concerned in the same type of career they had planned. Their experience in the service may open new opportunities to them, or help them finding their real talents. But so far as possible, when it is all over even the youth of this war-time generation should be enabled to complete their education, according to desires.[29]

As high schools were encouraged to aid in the training of recruits, they were also encouraged to increase the "toughness" of their discipline, particularly their physical discipline. Encouragement to physical toughness brought many charges and denials of "softness." High schools began much more rigorous amounts of physical discipline and training. Michigan Director of Physical Fitness Elwood Watson strenuously argued that high school boys had quickly toughened under the twelve weeks his program had been in effect at the time of the newspaper article. "It is obvious to me when I see the muscles on these boys that they have made a definite improvement. Those muscles are proof enough that the boys aren't soft and flabby.... I would like to prove to anyone the benefit derived from our high school program."[30] In 1943, when the War Manpower Commission announced that more than 40 percent of draft registrants were rejected for physical weakness, Leon Kranz, head of Northwestern University's physical education department, saw this "as a reflection of 'coddling' of the Nation's youth by automobiles, movies and the radio."[31]

There had been earlier claims about the enfeebling aspects of American education. This was partially a response to what some educators saw as the increased relativism of various reform movements. W.A. Bagley was one of the important members of this brigade. In "An Essentialist's Platform for the Advancement of American Education," published in the *Educational Administration and Supervision* report from the annual meeting of the American Association of School Administrators on February 26, 1938, Bagley accused American education of being "appallingly weak and ineffective."[32] He further asserted that American education needed a pedagogical theory that was "strong, virile, and positive not feeble, effeminate, and vague."[33] The latter, he claimed, had been the dominate theory of American education. (By this account the physical embodiment of the nation—the recruits—betrayed a spiritual truth concerning the nation.)

Kentucky educators denied that their students were flabby or weak, and argued that their new physical fitness programs had significantly toughened young Kentucky boys. On April 15, 1943, Col. Leonard S. Rowntree, medical director of Selective Service, announced "that high school youths in general are 'soft and flabby.' "

Testifying at Washington in favor of a bill to appropriate $8,484,377 a year for the high school Victory Corps program, Colonel Rowntree told the Senate Education Committee that in the past two years his office has accumulated evidence of an overall lack of health and physical fitness among young Americans.

This lack of fitness was not true for Louisville, "according to the best information available here today." The Louisville *Times* further reported that the Army's chief of athletics and recreation, Col. Banks, testified that more rigorous standards had to be applied to high school training. He "told the National War Fitness Conference [that] physical education through play 'must be discarded and a more rugged program instituted' to prepare high school and college youths for Army or Navy service."[34] The Army and Navy set standards for high school fitness programs.[35] Physical fitness was of particular importance to the Victory Corps: "the basic qualification for admission into the National Victory Corps is participation in some daily form of physical exercise."[36]

As the war continued, the nation-state became more and more willing to direct attention to the female body as well as the male body. If the state and industry needed workers, then women could do the work, but first they needed to be trained. Physical education programs in high schools taught physical endurance, strength and, not surprisingly, physical efficiency through posture and body mechanics.

As the war progresses, more and more women are putting in longer hours of mental and physical labor. Women in industry, in volunteer war work, in the business world, and in the home need more endurance, strength, and efficiency in order to render greater service. Women who have developed neuromuscular control are more valuable in industry because they acquire the specific skills needed more readily than others who are not so trained. Posture and body mechanics, which should be an integral part of any physical education program, aid women not only in conserving their own energy but also in being more adept workers.[37]

The growth in physical education for men and women reflected a greater attention to the efficiency of body movement, extending physical efficiency to the health and hygiene habits of citizens. "Elementary, as well as secondary, schools have seldom met their full responsibility for the physical health of the child or for building essential health habits. During the war, more than ever before, we need to design health experiences that will teach good habits of food selection, recreation, sanitation, and rest."[38]

Physical education played a greater role than simply education in dodgeball and dental floss; it was believed to be a communal endeavor that could challenge racial prejudice as well as gender discrimination. Sports activities were particularly well suited to goals of war. "Athletics is one peacetime activity of our schools that is suited to wartime propose," wrote the managing editor of school activities for Topeka, Kansas, C.R. Van Nice, in his comparison of flight crews and football teams.[39] Athletics, for example, contributed to the well-being of future WACS and WAVES. "Girls Drill Team members have become WACS, WAVES, and SPARS."[40] This contribution, moreover, taught women to work with men and women from a variety of racial and ethnic backgrounds.

That every girl be permitted to be on a team regardless of race has not been questioned in the past, but that she be allowed to take part in social dancing has been. Certainly with the whole world at war, bringing all nations and races closer together geographically, it is of increasing importance that the physical education class be made a laboratory for overcoming racial prejudices. Our fight for democracy will be in vain unless we can practice ideals of brotherhood.[41]

The increased demand for women to join the brotherhood of workers not only troubled gender codes, but also brought much greater numbers of people under the authority of bureaucratic institutions and physical discipline.

This concern over toughness also demonstrated a concern over the creation and extension of adolescence. The invention of the "teenager," a person in between childhood and adulthood, was partially predicated on the demand to attend school for a greater period of time.[42] "It is true we have prolonged boyhood by extending the time spent in school but there has been exaggerated comment on the immaturity of 18- and 19-year-old 'boys,' " reported the Great Falls, Montana *Tribune*. "Now that the 18- to 19-year-old draft measure has passed," the newspaper continued, "it is pertinent to recall that not many decades ago in this country a youth of 18 years of age was considered a grown man and not a boy. They didn't talk of them as babies in the days of the frontier and in the development period following."[43] The growth in the teaching of physical education resulted from a perceived need to toughen future inductees who had possibly been weakened by modern indulgences the deferment of adult life.

Mathematical sciences and physical education were not the only disciplines harnessed to the national cart; humanities contributed. History served a strong role, as outlined by Harry Bard in "High School History After the War."[44] Citizenship concerns became very pronounced in humanistic disciplines.[45] Music even carried its part.[46] English, not surprisingly, was also of central concern in the education of young soldiers and workers. Stanford's School of Education faculty reported that the average percentage among "Negroes" of illiteracy was 16.3, while for native "whites" the percentage was 1.5 and among foreign-born "whites" 9.9. "Obviously," the report concluded, "changes in the English curriculum and in its application are urgently needed as a war necessity. No nation can win a war with an illiterate army. Even a few illiterates are a serious element of weakness."[47] The national goal in education in English promised to strengthen the American military.

COLLEGES

Colleges supplied facilities and training the military needed. In February 1943, the War Manpower Commission listed 281 non-federal schools, colleges, and universities that were to be used by the navy and war departments for specialized training. In World War I there had been a brief attempt at the Student Army Training Corps (SATC) on 525 college campuses. It only lasted a few months. "Its relatively short existence," reported the American Council on Education, "did little to pave the way for the organization of any service by the colleges in World War II."[48] World War II, however, brought extensive use of colleges for the goals of national war-making and set extensive precedent for the national employment of college in the postwar period.

Educators met in Baltimore in January and July 1942 and called for greater coordination between education and the needs of the nation-state. In August, the Committee on the Relationships of Higher Education to the Federal Government recommended the establishment of college training corps. Eventually, on October 15, 1942, the President of the United States wrote a letter to the Secretaries of War and the Navy requesting a study of "the highest utilization of American colleges," and the War and Navy Departments subsequently called upon the American Council on Education for suggestions.[49]

Schools like Tulane became closely tied to the production of engineers for the military. "According to the announcement Tulane University will be utilized in the training of engineers for the navy department." Some examples of the increasingly close relationship between universities and the state include Louisiana State's training of engineers for the War Department and Mississippi State's training of aviation cadets.[50] "This is important, of course," the Baton Rouge *Times* informed readers. "Already, Louisiana State university is making its facilities of use in the war effort. It is capable of doing this to a greater extent, even for certain 'highly specialized' training."[51]

The Army required that every recruit who wanted to pursue college education during the war serve thirteen weeks as a soldier before being assigned to a college. Medical and engineering students were deferred until the end of the current semester, when they also served thirteen weeks.

Every male inducted into the Army could expect to spend the first nine weeks in basic training. After this time, anyone could take a special aptitude test for acceptance into a specialized training program. The Army was interested in training men as technicians, who could later become officers. Since the Army Specialized Training Program (ASTP) had to compete with all the other men in the Army personnel, and since by the time they had completed ASTP the Army's need for officers had substantially been met, and also because the Army had a great need for young physically fit replacements, few of the ASTP trainees became officers.[52] The Navy, on the other hand, put trainees through a course solely to make officers.[53] The 2,000 men assigned by the Army were scheduled to report to the first army contract colleges in March 1943; the second group were scheduled to report on April 1943. The program was expected to train about 250,000 soldier-students.[54] In December 1943, the program reached its highest enrollment: 140,000 soldiers enrolled in approximately 200 institutions.[55] In February of the next year, Gen. Marshall curtailed the program because he believed that too few men were being trained for the infantry.

The Army and Navy approaches to their uses of college facilities differed significantly: the Navy's V-12 program allowed that "the principles that were followed in the preparation of the curricula were largely evolved from practices that were recognized as sound in colleges and universities,"[56] while the Army's ASTP program was described by Herge as "an Army college within each contract institution."⁵⁷ The Navy's V-12 program, like the Army, reached its peak enrollment in the fall of 1943, when 84,379 trainees were pursuing undergraduate studies and 6,667 were engaged in graduate work pursuant to medicine and theology. The V-12 program promised to send students to college as the Navy's expense for twelve terms of sixteen weeks each.⁵⁸ The V-12 program, however, was never as abruptly curtailed as the Army's program.⁵⁹

Several elements of the Army's ASTP program deserve mention. First, the rigid curricula generated a fair amount of discussion. In contrast to typical university instruction, students were given no choice in course selection or organization. There was some criticism of this policy "as unrealistic, as an attempt to put square pegs into round holes. It was attacked as undemocratic and contrary to the traditions of American education."⁶⁰ But Herge concluded, "it was necessary in the Army program to insist upon less wasteful utilization of time even at the cost of requiring trainees weak in necessary subjects to study them."⁶¹ At a school in North Dakota, President Eversull assured the citizens of Fargo that when the Army arrived, their methods of discipline would be instituted. "The army when it sends its young students here for college work, will install a regime of the strictest discipline for those students. Their day will begin at 5:30 A.M. and will end at 10:00 P.M. and it will be a 54 hour week of classroom work and study." In addition to the Army's scheduling power, they would also supervise, study, and organize the topics of instruction. "Studying will be done under supervision and the army will say what subjects are to be taught and the number of hours to be devoted to each subject every day. The text books used will be from a list of about half a dozen approved by the army." Moreover, the Army instituted stringent testing. "There will be periodic screening tests, and those who do not make the grade will be sent back to the army camps."⁶²

Students in both high school and college were increasingly encouraged to develop military habits of time management. "The teacher should suggest that the student map a military time budget," one journal suggested to teachers. Students would be encouraged to internalize the importance of organizing their time and preparing themselves for war.

The student knows that a soldier has to modify his habits. He knows that he must rise at a certain hour, attend military classes, participate in daily physical sessions, engage in drill, perform chores around the post, and study his homework besides seeking the recreation he might desire. The soldier can do all these things only because his time is carefully budgeted.⁶³

The force of interest in the war effort allowed administrators to increase their power to structure what counted as wasteful or productive. The coordinator of one unit reported:

The AST Program had several valuable lessons for the University and its faculty. First among these was perhaps the value of a fixed and intelligently chosen curriculum. This had many advantages over the system of electivism that has run wild in our modern education. The solid content is assured. The faculty (or Army) experience prescribes more widely for students than their own experimentation. Floating, indecision, lost time and choice of courses on extrinsic motives are avoided.[64]

Faculty workloads and schedules came under similar attention. The time the faculty had normally given over to research or rest, summers and long weekends, was increasingly commandeered by the military or deemed wasteful. "College faculties are accustomed to long week-ends and long summers in which to refresh themselves and pursue their private academic interests. They are accustomed to encouragement in research and regard their private study as a professional duty expected of them by their employers."[65] The private expenditure of time by faculty members was an object of public concern.

One-third of all colleges and universities (663) were utilized by the Army or Navy; and about one half of the four-year institutions.[66] Neglected were "nearly all teachers' colleges, colleges for women, small liberal arts colleges, colleges for Negroes, and junior colleges." These schools, wrote the president of the American Council on Education, "had no contracts for Army and Navy units."[67] The funds dispersed to secondary education to prepare for war went mostly to large universities.

National success at war was the main goal toward which education was directed in the war period. To this end, students internalized commitment to the war. That is, they would harmonize their desires with the national goals of war. Schools taught students the goals of the war so that students could easily understand their interest in the goal. Given the widely perceived importance of goals to education, this is not surprising. "Thanks to education," editorialized the *School Board Journal*, "no generation of American fighting men has a clearer notion of the goals for which we fight than the present."[68]

EDUCATION CONCERNING THE WAR EFFORT

Once again, the important idea that knowledge of goals would succeed in forming desires found expression in the issues of education. "A whole-hearted and intelligent consumer response," suggested the Stanford School of Education faculty, slipping the issue of citizenship education into language of the marketplace, "depends on the consumers' having an adequate and convincing understanding of the importance of their actions and accurate reports on the effect their support is having on the war effort."[69] The success of the war effort required citizens (or consumers) to mentally picture a clear goal. The senior class of Bellwood-Antis High School in Bellwood, Pennsylvania presented a pageant play, the first part of which presented "what we are fighting for."⁷⁰ The four scenes that made up this tableau were the "Four Freedoms" Norman Rockwell had painted for the *Saturday Evening Post*. Roosevelt's speech and Rockwell's paintings, two of the most widely distributed attempts to supply personal reasons for participation in national war-making, cast the goals of war in terms of rights.

"Being an American citizen in a time of war is a full-time job," wrote the president of the Union for Democratic Action, New York City, Frank Kingdon, in *The Annals of the American Academy of Political and Social Science*. This full-time work required different approaches for different people, Kingdon concluded, but "there are, however, certain backgrounds of approach or attitude which I think are worth emphasizing."⁷¹ Attitudes, like interests, became the location of modification. Winning the war required proper attitudes, interests, and intellectual context for action. Action removed from the proper attitudes would fail.

The failure of World War I to end war was attributed to the lack of interest in the goals of that war. "World War I was a war to end wars, a war to be followed by new hope for mankind; but it turned out that there were too many people, in our country as well as in others, who were not sufficiently interested in the democratic way of life."⁷² The modification of political interest became central to social control. Citizens, it was believed, needed to understand why the actions that they should pursue were in their interest. "If the people fight the war without understanding, they may lose it. If they try to make peace without understanding, they will lay the basis for future wars. Knowledge of the war and its issues is a social necessity; ignorance can be regarded as a social crime."⁷³ Understanding was believed central to support for the war. Understanding was, much like Dewey's notions of the needs of education, predicated on the importance of having a clear objective, or a common goal.

High schools and colleges instituted many programs to achieve greater synchronism between institutions of education and the military. What all of these programs accomplished was the increased organization of education around the needs of the nation-state. The understanding of what teachers did was increasingly centralized in the nation-state. "Some teachers may seem to be working for two things, salary and quitting time," wrote the president of the San Diego board of education, "but the great majority of teachers who love teaching and who can envision something of the results of their patriotic devotion to duty in the product are the most valuable public servants to be found in any governmental agency."⁷⁴ High school and college curriculums were adjusted to produce graduates adequately prepared for military service. Curriculums were also adjusted to strengthen citizenship. High schools and colleges attempted to quickly get students prepared for military service. The goal of national service and utility became the central goal for education.

"Students once loyal to their schools are now giving expression to a common loyalty, loyalty to their conception of American Democracy, whose liberty they enjoy and in whose war they have a part."[75] "We might well ponder the question—if functionally illiterate men are a drag on military efficiency, is it not also obvious that the same group is, and will be, an increasing drag on our social structure?"[76] Economic social structure and political structure acted as answers to the question of the goal of education—education should remove the drags on national and industrial efficiency. Education also became increasingly tied to the need to create subjects constructed to properly participate in twentieth-century capitalism. The creation of manpower was a significant wartime concern.

The United States Office of Education and the War Department asked every high school in the United States to offer pre-induction courses in physics and shopwork to all boys in grades eleven and twelve. They also sent every high school outlines for five "Pre-Induction Training Courses." "Clearly," a report in *The School Review* explained, "the center of wartime change in the curriculum lies in the fields of physical sciences and mathematics." Moreover, "every secondary-school administrator has responsibility for modifying the curriculum so as to make the greatest possible contribution to manpower both in the armed forces and in industry."[77] The Cooperative Committee on Science Teaching issued a report entitled "High-School Science and Mathematics in Relation to the Manpower Problem." "The report is based on the assumption that all pupils in Grades XI and XII—girls as well as boys—will take courses to equip them for meeting manpower needs either in the armed forces or in industry and the essential civilian occupations."[78] Industrial positioning was a significant element of wartime educational programs, particularly for women. "*More boys and girls have received some form of vocational training in our high school than at any time in our history.* We are reaping the benefits already. More and more girls are seeing the advantages of some vocational training."[79] Women increasingly submitted to industrial authority as men accepted military authority. In this way, World War II significantly extended the social power of industrial authority to groups of people who had fulfilled different roles in the industrial system.

Some colleges reported female-to-male ratios of five women to one man. At schools the Army used as training centers, this was offset by the Army students. Three hundred thousand women served within the armed forces and "were trained for hundreds of duties ranging from hospital work to pilot training, and from clerical work to military command and administration." Women were increasingly put in the direct service to the nation-state. On June 30, 1945, 153,716 women worked in the Army, 121,465 in the Navy, 16,454 cadet nurses had been graduated, and by December 1944 there had been 916 women pilots on duty with WASP.[80] "Outworn prejudices regarding the ability of women were changed by experience, ushering in wider possibilities in the future education of women."[81]

The experiences of women during the war, not only in the women's military services but in all sorts of occupations, have lessened the cultural differences between men and women. This development is of importance in relation to one of the prime objectives of civilian education in a democratic society—the offering to all young men and women of equal opportunities to develop their capacities. As a practical matter, the speed with which civilian education is shaped in accord with that principle, and the extent to which it moves in that direction, will also be influenced and accelerated or retarded, as the case may be, by the rate of evolution of contemporary and future cultural and economic conditions.[82]

Equal opportunity involved an equal education in the discipline of industrial and national organization. Postwar society would develop out of the ability of men and women to develop their individual skills for the nation and the world. After the war, soldiers and workers would have to be realigned to fulfil their roles.

Orton Darnall, president of the San Diego Board of Education, addressed the School Administrators' Conference in Los Angeles in August 1943 on the topic of "Our School in Wartime and After." "One of the greatest" postwar problems, he claimed, "will be the rehabilitation of returning enlisted men, and this will automatically fall in the vocational field."[83]

The war's demand for skills produced strong inducements to vocational education. Students were encouraged to pursue programs of study that would vocationally benefit the nation in an orderly way. One 1942 publication, *Vocations for Boys*, attempted to "dissipate the worship of 'white-collar' work; to present the attractiveness of manual work; to show that all useful work is dignified and worthy of pursuit; to fire youth's imagination in thinking about new types of careers; and finally to contribute to the national welfare by encouraging a more wholesome distribution of workers among the occupations."[84] In spite of the book's attempt to make manual labor glamorous, it titled the one chapter dealing with occupations in the liberal arts "For the Elect Only."

POSTWAR OBJECTIVES

Many predicted that the issue of education's objectives would be particularly salient in the postwar world. "In other words," explained the Dean of the School of Education, University of Texas at Austin, "there is evidence of a reaction in many quarters against the apparent lack of definiteness and consistency in the objectives of American schools. The postwar period will very probably be marked by a concerted drive to define more clearly and in more specific fashion the things that the schools of the nation should endeavor to accomplish."[85]

The wartime experience demonstrated that civilian educational method can be modified so that subject specialties through proper emphasis and through collaboration on the part of instructors can contribute to a meaningful whole. If this be true in wartime, it ought also to be true in the postwar era when the educational pattern will need to be cut to fit the needs of a changing civilian society.[86]

Education programs in the postwar period, it was hoped, would learn some of the lessons taught by the experience of education in the war. These lessons included the integration of knowledge into the whole, time-saving techniques, the need for specific goals, the need for a permanent record, the importance of testing, and the need for self-control. This last need was aided, it was believed, by military service. "Deep-rooted in the military training doctrines of both the Army and Navy," claimed the report by the American Council on Education, "are the basic principles of moral responsibility."[87] The report of the Board of Education to the Governor of the State of Connecticut for 1945 asserted: "We must build a nation of people who can control themselves, for until we can control our selves, we are not safe for freedom, we are not safe for liberty."[88] Self-control, it was widely believed, would extend commitment to industrial authority and discipline.

NOTES

1. Sue Maxwell, "A Birmingham High School Meets the Challenge of War," *The American School Board Journal* 107 (July 1943): 20.

2. Ellwood Patterson Cubberley, San Diego Superintendent of Schools, was invited to participate in the creation of the Stanford University Education program, which he headed. He played a significant role in the professionalization of educational instruction in the United States. Jesse B. Sears and Adin D. Henderson, *Cubberley of Stanford and His Contribution to American Education* (Stanford, Calif.: Stanford University Press, 1957).

3. Jesse Sears, *An Autobiography* (Palo Alto, Calif.: Author, 1959), 102; see also David Tyack and Elisabeth Hansot, *Managers of Virtue: Public School Leadership in America, 1820–1980* (New York: Basic Books, 1982), 158.

4. John Dewey, *Democracy and Education* (New York: Free Press, 1916), 130.

5. Paul C. Reinert, Review of Edgar W. Knight, *Progress and Educational Perspective* (New York: Macmillan, 1942) in *The School Review: A Journal of Secondary Education* 51, 1 (January 1943): 56.

6. Tyack and Hansot, *Managers of Virtue*, 34.

7. J.C. Wright and Charles R. Allen, *Efficiency in Education: A Study of the Applications of the Principles of Efficiency to Educational Administration, Supervision, and Methods of Teaching* (New York: John Wiley & Sons; London: Chapman & Hall, 1929), 4.

8. William Allen, *Efficient Democracy* (New York: Dodd, Mead & Co., 1907), 6.

9. "Ignorant Collegians Assailed by Moses," *New York Times*, January 11, 1939, 3.

10. "Draft Offices Here Swamped by Phone Calls," New York *Sun*, October 14, 1940.

11. "Phone Queries Conscription," New York *Journal and American*, October 14, 1940.
12. "3 City Teachers Refuse to Aid the Draft Today," *New York Times*, October 16, 1940.
13. "Education Board Puts in Busiest Day," *New York Times*, October 17, 1940.
14. Maxwell, "A Birmingham High School," 20.
15. Ibid.
16. Ibid.
17. "Pre-Induction Course Offered," Grand Rapids, Mich. *Herald*, June 6, 1943.
18. "Summer School Authorized to Aid Pre-Inductee Youths," Jackson, Mich. *Citizen-Patriot*, March 9, 1943.
19. "Training for Teen-Ages," New Orleans, La. *Times-Picayune*, November 24, 1942.
20. "Educator Asks Preinduction Youth Training," Seattle, Wash. *Post-Intelligencer*, May 13, 1943.
21. Ibid.
22. *Physical Fitness Through Physical Education for the Victory Corps*, United States Office of Education, Victory Corps Series, Pamphlet No. 2 (Washington, D.C.: U.S. Government Printing Office, 1942).
23. "High School Victory Corps Announced," *Education for Victory* 1, 15 (October 1, 1942). 1. See also *High School Victory Corps*, United States Office of Education, Victory Corps Series, Pamphlet No. 1 (Washington, D.C.: U.S. Government Printing Office, 1942).
24. Stanford University School of Education Faculty, *Education in Wartime and After* (New York: D. Appleton-Century Co., 1943), 158.
25. *The California Journal of Secondary Education* (January 1943).
26. "Pass the Teen-Age Draft," St. Louis, Mo. *Globe-Democrat*, November 1, 1942.
27. Stanford University School of Education Faculty, *Education in Wartime and After*, 277.
28. Alonzo G. Grace, *Educational Lessons from Wartime Training* (Washington, D.C.: American Council on Education, 1948), 9.
29. "For Resuming Education," Baton Rouge, La. *Times*, November 16, 1942.
30. "Jackson High Boys Soft? It Isn't True, Says Watson; Tells of Test in Gym," Jackson, Mich. *Citizen-Patriot*, April 18, 1943.
31. "Draft Rejections Due to Youth 'Coddling,' Educator Asserts," Washington, D.C. *Star*, March 15, 1943.
32. W.C. Bagley, "An Essentialist's Platform for the advancement of American Education," *Educational Administration and Supervision* 24 (1938): 241, in Herbert M. Kliebard, *The Struggle for the American Curriculum, 1893–1958* (New York: Routledge, 1995), 197.
33. Bagley, "An Essentialist's Platform," 256; Kliebard, *The Struggle for the American Curriculum*, 198.
34. "Louisville Schoolboys Declared Generally Fit," Louisville, Ky. *Times*, April 15, 1943.
35. "Swimming Course Planned for Pre-Induction Training at THS," Tucson, Ariz. *Star*, April 20, 1943.
36. Maxwell, "A Birmingham High School," 21.

37. Stanford University School of Education Faculty, *Education in Wartime and After*, 278.
38. Ibid. 160.
39. C.R. Van Nice, "Democracy Aided by Its Educational Frills," *The American School Board Journal* 107, 2 (August 1943): 36.
40. Ibid.
41. Stanford University School of Education Faculty, *Education in Wartime and After*, 277.
42. The *Oxford English Dictionary* dates "teenager" at 1941. *Webster's* dates it at 1939. "Teen-age" is found somewhat earlier, according to the *Oxford English Dictionary*, in 1921.
43. "Young Men," Great Falls, Mont. *Tribune*, November 14, 1942.
44. *Baltimore Bulletin of Education* 19 (April–May–June 1942): 201–7.
45. Franklin Burdette, ed., *Education for Citizen Responsibilities* (Princeton, N.J.: Princeton University Press for the National Foundation for Education in American Citizenship, 1942); Franklin Burdette, "Education for Citizenship," *Public Opinion Quarterly* 6 (Summer 1942): 269–79; William Carr, "Learning Citizenship through Student Activities," *Journal of the National Education Association* 31 (February 1942): 55–56; Max Herzberg, *Situation in Which Citizenship Can Be Taught* (Plainfield, N.J.: New Jersey Secondary School Teachers' Association, 1941); *Improvement in Instruction in the Required Course in Citizenship in California High Schools*, Report of the Subcommittee on United States History and Civics of the General Education Committee, a Joint Committee of the California State Department of Education and the Association of California Secondary School Principals (Sacramento, Calif.: State Department of Education, 1941); Harry Johnson, "Civic Education in Eugene High School," *Harvard Educational Review* 12 (March 1942): 165–70; Grace A. Turkington and Phil Conley, *Your Country and Mine: A Textbook in Democratic Citizenship* (Boston: Ginn & Co., 1943).
46. Lawrence Thomas, "Relation of Music to Social Studies," *Curriculum Journal* 13 (April 1942): 166–69.
47. Stanford University School of Education Faculty, *Education in Wartime and After*, 186.
48. Grace, *Educational Lessons from Wartime Training*, 211.
49. Henry C. Herge, *Wartime College Training Programs of the Armed Services* (Washington, D.C.: American Council on Education, 1948), 9.
50. "WMC Names Four Schools in State," New Orleans, La. *Times-Picayune*, February 7, 1943.
51. "For Resuming Education."
52. Herge, *Wartime College Training Programs*, 17.
53. Ibid., 11.
54. "Wartime Program for Our Colleges," Fort Dodge, Iowa *Messenger & Chronicle*, February 26, 1943; Herge, *Wartime College Training Programs*, 12.
55. Grace, *Educational Lessons from Wartime Training*, 213.
56. Navy Department, Bureau of Naval Personnel, History Project, "History of the Navy College Training Programs" (MS on file in Office of Naval History, Navy Department), 81, in Herge, *Wartime College Training Programs*, 21.
57. Herge, *Wartime College Training Programs*, 20.

58. "Youth and War: What to Plan for, What to Expect," Norfolk, *Virginian-Pilot*, March 14, 1943.
59. Grace, *Educational Lessons from Wartime Training*, 214.
60. Herge, *Wartime College Training Programs*, 37.
61. Ibid.
62. "Lack of Students Makes AC Campus a 'Deserted Village,'" Fargo, N.D. *Forum*, March 18, 1943.
63. Lawrence Gallagher, "A War Pattern for Teachers," *The American School Board Journal* 107, 3 (September 1943): 16.
64. Herge, *Wartime College Training Programs*, 38-39.
65. Ibid., 37.
66. Ibid., 13.
67. George F. Zook, "How the Colleges Went to War," *The Annals of the American Academy of Political and Social Science* 231 (January 1944): 6.
68. "N.E.A. Asks Federal Aid for Wartime Schools," *The American School Board Journal* 107, 2 (August 1943): 44.
69. Stanford University School of Education Faculty, *Education in Wartime and After*, 14.
70. "An Effective Tableau for War Graduation," *The American School Board Journal* 107, 2 (August 1943): 47.
71. Frank Kingdon, "Being an American in Wartime," *The Annals of the American Academy of Political and Social Science* 222 (July 1942): 1.
72. Stanford University School of Education Faculty, *Education in Wartime and After*, 21.
73. Ibid., 34.
74. Orton E. Darnall, "Board of Education Responsibilities in War and Peacetime," *The American School Board Journal* 107, 4 (October 1943): 44.
75. Van Nice, "Democracy Aided by Its Educational Frills," 36.
76. A.C. Flora, "Today's Challenge to American Schools," *The American School Board Journal* 108, 3 (March 1944): 48.
77. Robert J. Havighurst, "Educational News and Editorial Comment," *The School Review* 51, 2 (February 1943): 67.
78. Ibid.
79. Ernest G. Lake, "A Superintendent Plans for the Future in Vocational Education," *The American School Board Journal* 108, 3 (March 1944): 17.
80. Grace, *Educational lessons from Wartime Training*, 174.
81. Ibid., 150.
82. Ibid., 178.
83. Darnall, "Board of Education Responsibilities," 44.
84. Harry Dexter Kitson and Mary Rebecca Lingenfelter, *Vocations for Boys* (New York: Harcourt, Brace & Co., 1942), xii.
85. B.F. Pittenger, "Postwar Educational Controversies," *The American School Board Journal* 107, 5 (November 1943): 18.
86. Herge, *Wartime College Training Programs*, 71.
87. Ibid., 78-79.
88. State of Connecticut, "Report of the Board of Education to the Governor," State of Connecticut Public Document No. 8 (1945), 41, in ibid., 79.

Chapter 9

"Trying to Get Hold of the Mental Process": Education, Mental Hygiene, and Individualism

> Fundamentally, all our actions are altogether incomparably personal, unique, and infinitely individual; there is no doubt of that. But as soon as we translate them into consciousness *they no longer seem to be.*
> —Friedrich Nietzsche, *The Gay Science*,
> Book 5, section 354

"Interest and discipline," John Dewey observed, "are correlative aspects of activity having an aim. Interest means that one is identified with the objects which define the activity and which furnish the means and obstacles to its realization."[1] One of the significant aspects of changes in education was the attempt to get students to desire to learn and to identify with the goals of education. As Taylor planned to modify conceptions of interest so that workers and managers believed they had interests in common, educators attempted to teach students to desire what educators were teaching. Instead of teaching students information, teachers attempted to teach students to desire information. In the same way that the application of Taylorian methods to the physical body removed conceptions of individualism from work and action, the application of management methods to unseen desires, motives, and attitudes made these personal attributes less than private and less than individual. Attention directed to motives and desires fostered a new understanding of individualism: each and every person was seen as inscrutable and unknowable, with even the most similar or common action containing vastly individual meanings. This was yet another contribution of discipline to individualism.

DEWEY AND DESIRE

John Dewey's influential studies of education and social reform directed greater attention to the formulation of interest for education within the student and influenced a generation of educators. During the second decade of the twentieth century, his Hegelian pragmatism became a central feature of social science and reform and contributed to the growing application of systems of industrial management to education. His contributions included the focus on modifying desires, integrating the student into society and the importance of establishing clearly understandable goals for education. Dewey's contributions had their corollaries in industry, especially in methods of industrial management that attempted to manage employees in ways similar to those used by educators. "As will appear from the book itself," he wrote in his preface to *Democracy and Education*, "the philosophy stated in this book connects the growth of democracy with the development of the experimental method in the sciences, evolutionary ideas in the biological sciences, and the industrial reorganization, and is concerned to point out the changes in subject matter and methods of education indicated by these developments."[2] His work, he explained, used methods associated with industrial reorganization to reform education.

In 1899, for example, Dewey argued that if scientific knowledge of education had advanced to the stages of scientific management of industry, then no one would question its application. "If our teachers were trained as architects are trained; if our schools were actually managed on a psychological basis as great factories are run on the basis of chemical and physical science ... we should never dream of discussing this question."[3] For Dewey, education should achieve the ideal of the rational factory, where obedience to the rules of science ensured the production of a socially efficient product.

Dewey's later work combined the value of social efficiency with the value of personal development. Both, he believed, were necessary for personal fulfillment. If a person's "career" was not useful to society, then the individual could scarcely count on their own satisfaction. Education and work needed to be of value to society as well as the individual. "Any individual has missed his calling, farmer, physician, teacher, student, who does not find that the accomplishments of results of value to others is an accompaniment of a process of experience inherently worthwhile."[4] Individual differences and interests would be seen to be valuable when reflected in the light of social order.

Students desired experience that was worthwhile, that is, experience that aimed to benefit the individual and the community. The best way to teach, Dewey maintained, was to do more than simply convey information. Teachers should create within students a desire for education. Fixing the mind of the student firmly on the goal of education, Dewey concluded, created and maintained the student's interest in much the same way that Taylor hoped to teach workers the harmony between their interests and those of management so that the workers would drive themselves without overt force from management. "Interest measures—or rather is—the depth of the grip which a foreseen end has upon one in moving one to act for its realization."[5] Interest and discipline were not antagonistic methods but different aspects of the same force. "Interest and discipline are correlative aspects of activity having an aim."[6] People worked and strove, Dewey believed, for identifiable aims. Educators aided in this work by teaching what made work interesting, not in the artificial sense of advertising, but interesting because it related to the self-interest of the worker.

Discipline as force, Dewey argued, was not counter to developing interest, but was simply another way to produce interest. "Interest and discipline are connected, not opposed," he argued. "Even punishing a child for inattention is one way of trying to make him realize that the matter is *not* a thing of complete unconcern; it is one way of arousing 'interest,' or bringing about a sense of connection."[7] Very direct physical force often produced resistance; so by creating interest, the teacher, like a Taylorian manager, averted resistance and encouraged students to control themselves.

Educators, like managers, expected that new methods would open up greater resources of control. Dewey suggested that a scientific understanding of such things as desire and ethics led to a well-managed social space. "We can anticipate no other outcome than increasing control in the ethical sphere—the nature and extent of which can be best judged by considering the revolution that has taken place in the control of physical nature through a knowledge of her order."[8] Dewey, like Taylor, thought that science offered means of controlling the physical world and would in a matter of time supply the means to control the world of desires. Education would aid social order by directing students to the work they could most efficiently and enjoyably perform. Correct organization of desire also strengthened the social order, where people found their desires actualized in their relationships with others. For example, J. Kadushin described the need to develop an interest within students for mathematics, a discipline particularly suited to the needs of the nation-state as it faced the most technological war ever. "Learning," he argued, "goes on best in the degree that the individual sees and feels the significance to his own felt needs of what he does."[9] Interests that learning could fasten to included bureaucratic promotion.

Schools consolidated an interest in the good through an interest in the efficient by encouraging a belief in hierarchical progress—a belief that by getting an education, workers could eventually occupy positions of management. "Education will count after the war," argued C.C. Henson, principal of the Isidore Newman School, when he addressed the Exchange Club at the St. Charles hotel in New Orleans during a noon luncheon. "Boys," he said, "should be encouraged to complete their studies at least to the extent of obtaining a high school diploma, before entering the armed services."[10] This encouragement ran into the need for excess labor and created unrealistic expectations that everyone could be a leader. "One of the principal problems of secondary education now—and a problem which will, perhaps, be *the* most important problem after the war—is the problem of educating boys and girls so that they may realize their ambitions for better things but, at the same time, teaching them not to expect and desire too much."[11]

By World War II, such accounts of education had become commonplace. More educators than ever before conceived of their job as the creation within students of the proper attitudes to education—it became the dominate theme of education policy. A clear knowledge of shared goals disciplined subjects into approved ways of acting with a small expenditure of force.

The best morale is based on a fine balance between intellectual understanding of issues and the emotional readiness to fight for one's convictions. Common understanding means common acceptance of certain ends in view and a widespread recognition of what means will probably have to be taken to achieve those ends. . . . This kind of morale has been given special stress in the American army in recent years, with the result that foreign observers are amazed at the "effortless discipline" obtained.[12]

Understanding often achieved meaning in distinction to emotional enthusiasm. "It is not explosive, variable, and unsteady. The person who gives vent to explosions of emotion may lower the morale of his group. The hysteric or maniac is not a useful addition to a company bent on purposeful action in unity."[13] True understanding was displayed in restrained ways of behaving.

BEHAVIOR

There was extensive attention to the role of education in the construction of this restrained, citizen whose interests were located in the nation. The correct attitudes produced the proper behavior. For example, a committee at the Passaic, New Jersey school board dodged an attempt to define democracy, finally deciding that democracy could best be defined by the attitude of the citizens. "The committee decided to attempt this definition through a statement of the ways in which persons *behave* in a democracy."[14] As the Superintendent and Assistant Superintendent of Schools for Passaic, the authors pledged:

We believe in and will endeavor to make a democracy in which persons *behave* as follows:

1. They respect the individual personality.
2. They are considerate of others.

3. They cooperate with others.
4. They use their talents for both individual and social profit.
5. They discover and accept their own inadequacies and improve upon them if possible.
6. They lead or follow according to their abilities for the benefit of the group.
7. They assume responsibilities inherent in the freedom of a democracy.
8. They solve their problems by thinking them through, rather than by resorting to force and emotion.
9. They govern themselves for the common good.
10. They accept the rule of the majority while respecting the rights of the minority.
11. They are tolerant.
12. They think, speak and act freely, with due regard for the rights of others.
13. They adapt themselves to changing conditions in a democracy for individual and common good.
14. They are constantly seeking to achieve the most effective democratic way of living.
15. They seek by their own example to lead other persons to live democratically.[15]

Democratic behavior required citizens to use their talents for the social good, adapt themselves to changing conditions, constantly seek the most effective yet democratic way of life, and govern themselves. Citizens were to be internally well-regulated and self-disciplining. "The immediate object of good discipline is, and should be," W.F. Himmelreich, of County High School, Douglas, Wyoming wrote,

> to prepare the child or adult to make an intelligent satisfying adjustment in the many and varied situations that must be met in social living—in fact in the scheme of social being in its entirely—if one is to be a well-poised, cultured, happy individual, and a useful member of society. In effect true, lasting, and effective discipline must be achieved through inner controls.[16]

Social goals required the internalization of social control and regulation. By increasingly seeing their place within society, citizens would learn to value their own attributes that furthered social goals.

MENTAL HYGIENE

The "mental hygiene" movement made up one of the most significant education trends at the eve of the war.[17] "The aims of education and of mental hygiene are theoretically the same," wrote Herbert A. Carroll, Professor of Psychology at University of New Hampshire, in 1947.[18] Or as Clarence Hincks, Director for Mental Hygiene in both the United States and Canada at various times, wrote in 1940, "it is becoming increasingly obvious that mental hygiene and education are related disciplines."[19] This, like much of the application of scientific management in the late 1930s and early 1940s, was an attempt to improve the social order by dealing with attitudes, motives, and personality. David B. Klein, professor of psychology at University of Texas, claimed in 1944 that it was "concerned with the realization and maintenance of the mind's health and efficiency."[20] Scientific management's interest in promoting efficiency by adjusting interests and attitudes became a significant aspect of the relationship between education and psychology. The promotion of mental hygiene as an education movement was, furthermore, often funded by organizations interested in promoting good vocational efficiency and skills. For example, the Mental Hygiene Committee of The Vocational Adjustment Bureau for Girls funded a two-year study of the applicability of mental hygiene methods at the kindergarten level and eventually funded the implementation of those methods.[21]

The mental hygiene movement attempted to prevent mental illness through efficient mental habits. "What might be designated as prophylactic mental hygiene is intended to prevent the development of mental disease or the loss of mental efficiency."[22] The elements of mental hygiene that encouraged prevention of mental illness also focused on efficiency and right-order. "Meliorative mental hygiene, on the other hand, is concerned less with actual disease and more with improving mental efficiency . . . injecting more zest in one's daily living . . . the effect of monotony and bleak routine on housewife or factory worker . . . the place of such emotionalized attitudes as jealousy, envy, and bitter competition in a well-ordered mental household."[23]

The student who successfully disciplined their mental household, cleansing it of bad mental habits, could hope to attain efficiency and happiness. "It is estimated that from thirty to fifty [out of 100 high school students] will fail to reach the maximum efficiency and happiness in life possible for them, because of unwholesome emotional habits and personality traits."[24] "The expression *mental hygiene*," wrote A.J. Rosanoff, "is used to mean the science and practice of the preservation of mental health and efficiency."[25] Horatio M. Pollock wrote, "a great multitude of persons are living happier and more efficient lives because of their knowledge of mental hygiene."[26]

Mental hygiene could help students live well-adjusted and integrated lives. More specifically, mental hygiene would produce good morale. "If one were forced to furnish a one-word definition of mental hygiene, possibly the most adequate and revealing would be the word *morale*," claimed David Klein.[27] Morale and emotion formed the focus of interest for mental hygiene. Herbert A. Carroll explained that this new trend in psychology "has led, especially, to a study of the emotions—their nature, their development, their control."[28] "It is vitally concerned with motives," wrote Carroll.[29] All behavior, mental hygienists reported, stemmed from motives. "Any kind of behavior, no matter how strange it may seem to be, is motivated behavior."[30] This attention to morale, emotions, and desires was a way to deal with social problems before they occurred. "We are no longer content to combat mental illness, crime, and a host of lesser evils through attention to end products alone," wrote Clarence Hicks.[31] Personalities were to be adjusted and desires modified. "Since personality adjustment is not an accident but should be the result of trained direction and assistance under hygienic learning conditions, the major factors of the educative process are discussed in terms of their mental-hygiene components," wrote Lester and Alice Crow, educators in New York City in 1942.[32] "The mental-hygiene point of view, with its emphasis on understanding the motives which underlie conduct and its attempt to effect adjustment to the factors in the situation, is rapidly displacing older ideas of discipline," wrote Percival Symonds.[33]

The application of scientific management to education concentrated on the adjustment of attitudes. Wright and Allen included in *Efficiency in Education* a table comparing "The Manufacturing Process" to "The Educational Process," with point number three comparing the changes that the two processes brought to their product. The manufacturing process "changes the characteristics of the material as to form, shape, physical or chemical properties," while the educational process "changes the characteristics of the learner as to attitudes, ideals, and possession of skills."[34]

Mental hygiene directed educators to build students with desires well integrated to the needs of society. Mental hygiene created "a systemic effort to aid children to develop a well-adjusted personality."[35] The prevention of mental and emotional problems was aimed at the creation of good morale and well-adjusted personality. Or, as Sherman explained, "from the mental hygiene standpoint, education implies direction and redirection of attitudes."[36] Norman Fenton introduced his book *Mental Hygiene in School Practice* by explaining that "the major purpose of this book is to suggest practical ways of making schools more effective with respect to the development of personality in pupils."[37] "The modern definition of the total field of hygiene," Fenton wrote in 1943, "is the preservation, inculcation, and promotion of those conditions of influences that lead to the most effective development of the personality of the individual and his most interesting, wholesome, and useful life in society."[38] The influence of the school, wrote L.F. Shaffer, "should be an integrating and adjusting one."[39]

The conception of students in terms of product fostered the appropriation of elements and terms of scientific management. One survey of education's results explained the complexity of the problem in industrial terms of product. "Confronted with the complexity of the problem of surveying the products of our schools and of predicting the possible outcomes of education . . . the school's interest in outcomes is centered in the personalities of pupils and the development of their character."[40] Mental hygiene accounted for the work of the school in a language of production borrowed from industry and focused on emotional adjustment and integration. "In this adjustment to the environment the parts of the reacting mechanism must work in such cooperation that the individual throws himself whole-heartedly into whatever activities he engages in and does not worry when at times he fails because his responses have been inadequate."[41] The well-adjusted individual must work well as part of the machinery of society. Individual motives, interests, desires, and intellectual states must be in tune with the rest of the social organism.

World War II increased interest in mental hygiene. In defining exactly what mental hygiene was, Norman Fenton, Professor of Education at Stanford University, explained the special need during the war:

What constitutes good mental health is especially difficult to define at a time of great change, when a nation enters a war or when it returns again to the life of peacetime. On both of these occasions the need for mental hygiene is acute in order to facilitate the adjustment of citizens, young and old, to the change in the conditions of their lives; yet there might be differences in the implications of the term in the two situations.[42]

Wartime aggravated social maladjustment, making the methods of social harmony more important. "During and since the recent world war," wrote psychiatrist Herbert A. Carroll, "there has been a marked increase in the interest in the problem of mental health."[43] Mental hygiene's attention to morale and emotional accommodation became very salient during the war. "The morale of our people at present is good.... However, whether the war is long or short, the principles of hygienic adjustment and control must function if we are to maintain emotional stability and the democratic way of life."[44]

Instruction of soldiers in the educational facilities of the military evidenced a great deal of concern over the students' desire to learn. A book of readings called *The Fight for Freedom: College Readings in Wartime* was specifically prepared for college students headed for the military. Included along with "The Declaration of Independence," "Huck Finn and Jim," and "The New Nationalism" by Theodore Roosevelt was an anonymous article, "Psychology for the Fighting Man." This brief article, intended to prepare soldiers for military service, included information concerning study skills.

Having set the stage as well as possible for most effective study, you should next develop an absorbing interest in the material to be mastered. It is not necessary to resort to self-delivered mental pep-talks. Enthusiasm grows naturally out of the realization that a study is important in reaching a desirable goal, that it will satisfy your curiosity or that it will give you a chance to exercise some special talent. The task is to arouse interest.[45]

Students, it was increasingly believed, had to be interested in what they were studying in order to learn. Interest came, it was widely believed, from a clearly set goal and from attention to the modification of interest. "We once taught *subjects*; then, happily, we began to teach *boys and girls*. Now we also teach *groups of boys and girls*—each child against the background of a social situation," announced C.R. Van Nice, Managing Editor of School Activities for Topeka, Kansas.[46] This attention to the development of interest had its critics, who believed that "old-fashioned" discipline was being replaced by overly indulgent encouragement.

"The pressure is also being exerted to have the schools return to older curricula and to take on more of the form of military organization."[47] Often referred to as softening, new educational methods presented a challenge to the military's demand for discipline and masculinity. The new educational methods, on the other hand, attempted to reach a citizen's thoughts, desires, and attitudes. The softening of education referred to attempts on the part of educators to produce interest. This attention to the modification of students' interests, critics charged, pandered to students. The critics asserted that the authority of bureaucratic officials should drive education and, moreover, students should do as they were told.

Students and workers (and soldiers) were increasingly expected to identify with the goals of those who claimed bureaucratic authority—teachers, managers, superintendents, or generals. This widespread social conception of authority and human interest opened up an attention to intellectual organization. People not properly conceiving of their interests and the sites of those interests were perceived as a social liability that produced social confusion.

This was one of the larger strategies to create interest in education and the workplace. Social mobility, social efficiency, and individual recognition became the goals for education. Social efficiency and personal economic achievement were central aims toward which scientific management directed workers' attention.

This attention to the creation and modification of interests was a significant aspect in the disciplines of the early-twentieth-century reformers, an interest displayed in Frederick W. Taylor's writings. Harlow Person, in his preface to a collection of Taylor's writings, argued that the central power of scientific management was its unification of perspectives. "Therefore, true Scientific Management calls for a unifying point of view and a unity of interests and of efforts seldom present in a particular establishment." The effort of teaching workers this perspective was one of the most important functions of management. "And especially must management be skilled in aiding workers to understand the purpose and meaning of Scientific Management and in maintaining their confidence in the purpose and in the management."[48]

Central to the maintenance of Taylor's system was the explanation of shared interest.

It is safe to say that no system or scheme of management should be considered which does not in the long run give satisfaction to both employer and employee, which does not make it apparent that their best interests are mutual, and which does not bring about such thorough and hearty cooperation that they can pull together instead of apart.

Workers and management must work together with the knowledge that their shared interests will be promoted by efficient work. The most significant element in this equation is consolidation of interests. Workers must understand their interests as furthered by the new organization of work and authority. "It cannot be said that this condition has as yet been at all generally recognized as the necessary foundation for good management."[49] By convincing workers that managerial control of planning and production was in their best interests, managers could expect greater production. This sort of work would also improve the worker. "These conditions not only serve the best interests of the employer, but they tend to raise each workman to the highest level which he is fitted to attain by making him use his best faculties forcing him to become and remain ambitious and energetic, and giving him sufficient pay to live better than in the past."[50]

By pushing workers to this level, managers created conditions by which workers increasingly came to perceive their work as an individual procedure that required bureaucratic recognition. Education in the early part of the twentieth century experimented with Taylor's methods of scientific management. Most significantly, Taylorism contributed to concern over goals and desire. Taylorism's interest in the "one best way" drove a concentration on purpose.

The social attention to a well-ordered mind had several repercussions. Education came to require a goal—most often the needs of the nation and industry. In order to meet these needs, the minds of students had to be well ordered, which meant that the desires of the students could be expressed in the demands of the nation—that is, that their desires had productive goals. This reduced the intrinsic value of action and thought. If actions and thoughts had to be evaluated in light of their contribution to superior objectives or communities, they were actually insufficiently valuable in their own right. Programs such as mental hygiene attempted to ensure that thoughts and motives of students were well in line with the needs of the state. Even as industrial standardization of work reduced the avenues of individualism through work, the ordering of the mind made dreams, desires, motives, and morale standardized, reducing the individualism of thought.

The rippling of elements associated with scientific management throughout American society began by turning work and action into highly standardized, almost mechanical, procedures. Standardizing physical movement and academic progress drove historical conceptions of individualism from those places. As movement, action, mental adjustment, and intellectual desire and elements of managerial control all became standardized, the ability to believe in "expressing" the self through action dissipated. The randomness and unpredictability associated with individualism adhered to an internal and invisible location. Motives, attitudes, and desires had to be correctly ordered. They became the sites of increased interest in control as they collected the understanding that betrayed a lack of control. Attempts to modify and control internal desires, never wholly successful, did succeed in illustrating the standardization of highly personal internal dimensions.

CONCLUSION

The effects that the elaboration of Taylorite theories had on education and the military was very similar to some accounts of language and desire elaborated in philosophical writing during this period. For example, Ludwig Wittgenstein's account of the role of language in human consciousness also explores the ways that language and accounts of intellectual activity apply overly general ideas to individual experiences. Attempts by educators to standardize intellectual activity—to create mentally well-adjusted students—required re-elaboration of the meanings of individualism if thought and desire were to remain an activity of distinct individualism. This was similar to the way that Taylor attempted to adjust physical movement to what was most efficient by challenging the ability of workers to express their individuality through their work. The attempt by educators to make intellectual activity function in the most efficient manner threatened to drain intellectual activity of much of its individualism. Here, Wittgenstein offers clues to the reformulations that came about: first, human individualism was made an almost hidden element in every human action, even the very common; second, the individual became more complex and mysterious—even the most common of people became reservoirs of mystery and indeterminacy.

Wittgenstein's passages on understanding begin with a demonstration of the ways we use the word "understanding," and then go on to demonstrate how we have failed to say anything about how people understand things, finally concluding that we cannot say anything general or transcendental about it. The claim in Section 153 of *Philosophical Investigations* makes just this point. "We are trying to get hold of the mental process of understanding which seems to be hidden behind those coarser and therefore more readily visible accompaniments. But," the section reminds us, "we do not succeed; or rather, it does not get as far as a real attempt." Wittgenstein continued: "For even supposing I had found something that happened in all those cases of understanding,—why should *it* be the understanding?"[51]

Wittgenstein found it confusing that a person could be said to understand their own meaning. "What does this act of meaning (the pain, or the piano-tuning) consist in? No answer comes—for the answers which at first sight suggest themselves are of no use.—'And yet at the time I meant the one thing and not the other.' Yes,—now you have only repeated with emphasis something which no one has contradicted anyway."⁵² "But can you doubt that you meant *this*?—No; but neither can I be certain of it, know it."⁵³ The word "know," Wittgenstein asserted, does not function as metaphysical proof. He attempted to demonstrate the inability of people to linguistically understand their own actions and desires and to illustrate the ways that words such as "know" do not perfectly fit an individual.

Wittgenstein's description of the relationship between language and the individual is very similar to the account that Nietzsche offers of language and consciousness, in which he surmises that the languages we use to communicate are social creations and, therefore, fail to communicate what is most personal or individual. "My idea," Nietzsche wrote, "is, as you see, that consciousness does not really belong to man's individual existence but rather to his social or herd nature; that, as follows from this, it has developed subtlety only insofar as this is required by social or herd utility."⁵⁴ In Nietzsche's and Wittgenstein's account of language, and attempts to use language to communicate the self of the individual, language is a social machinery that because of its ability to communicate what is most common fails to communicate what is most personal. Wittgenstein continued, "A *picture* held us captive. And we could not get outside it, for it lay in our language and language seemed to repeat it to us inexorably."⁵⁵ Language appeared to refer to common experiences with words like "know," "understand," and "mean," yet the experiences described by those words could be radically diverse. "The propositions describing this world-picture might be part of a kind of mythology. And their role is like that of rules of a game; and the game can be learned purely practically, without learning any explicit rules."⁵⁶ The words function in a language that does not have a perfect or solid connection to what is individual about humans.

"The difficulty," Wittgenstein claimed, "is to realize the groundlessness of our believing."⁵⁷ Our belief in the accuracy of language is built on territory that is taken by faith. Language does not describe objects exterior to itself but reveals its own scaffolding in facts that appear to be beyond doubt. Language, for Wittgenstein, much like Nietzsche, is a social phenomenon that does not quite get to what is distinct and individual about people. For Wittgenstein, much of the publicness of language is worked out in his discussions of the impossibility of a private language. Wittgenstein's account of language as rules drains language of some of its individual content. Once the use of language becomes a matter of following rules, it becomes less a matter of the elaboration of a distinct self. " 'All the steps are really already taken' means: I no longer have any choice. The rule, once stamped with a particular meaning, traces the lines along which it is to be followed through the whole of space.—But if something of this sort really were the case, how would it help?" Or as he says even more clearly, "When I obey a rule, I do not choose. I obey the rule *blindly*."⁵⁸ Wittgenstein's account of language as rule following seems designed to remove individuals from their use of language in much the same way that the increasing scientific and managerial attention to motives and desires depersonalized the most personal experiences.

Neither Nietzsche nor Wittgenstein, however, allow individualism to disappear into an unreachable self. Both suggest that what is individual travels along language, action, and behavior almost effortlessly. "Fundamentally," Nietzsche continued in section 354 of *The Gay Science*, "all our actions are altogether incomparably personal, unique, and infinitely individual; there is no doubt of that. But as soon as we translate them into consciousness *they no longer seem to be.*" The things we do and the things we say remain incomprehensibly individual, even as they utilize highly social means. As Wittgenstein concluded the *Tractatus Logico-Philosophicus*: "What we cannot speak about we must pass over in silence."[59] But in other places Wittgenstein suggests that what we can speak about travels in what we say. "And this is how it is:" Wittgenstein wrote to a friend, "if only you do not try to utter what is unutterable then *nothing* gets lost. But the unutterable will be—unutterably—*contained* in what has been uttered!"[60]

In *Philosophical Investigations*, Wittgenstein examined the different experiences of looking at a vase: "But *this* does not happen in all cases in which I 'mean the shape', and no more does any other one characteristic process occur in all these cases."[61] The mental experience referred to by directing your attention alternately to the shape then the color of a vase is not always the same. Wittgenstein makes the individual's use of language rather mysterious. "Imagine a person whose memory could not retain *what* the word 'pain' meant—so that he constantly called different things by that name—but nevertheless used the word in a way fitting in with the usual symptoms and presuppositions of pain," Wittgenstein requests in a quotation, to which he adds the comment, "in short he uses it as we all do."[62] "The essential thing about private experience is really not that each person possesses his own exemplar," Wittgenstein went on to claim, "but that nobody knows whether other people also have *this* or something else. The assumption would thus be possible—though unverifiable—that one section of mankind had one sensation of red and another section another."[63]

These accounts of the complex relationship between individuals and the social accounts of their internal desires and understandings resemble the understandings that state institutions produced for American citizens. The application of Taylor's methods to physical labor removed much of the ability for workers to find in their work their own individual voice. As similar methods were applied to the human mind in order to create efficient mental action and well-adjusted attitudes, many of the very personal intellectual processes, such as thought, desire, and motive, were also drained of much of their individualism. Attention directed to motives and desires opened up a substantially new way of understanding individualism: Each and every person was seen as inscrutable and unknowable; even the most similar or common action could contain vastly individual meanings. Discipline applied to mental functions expounded important philosophical changes for vast numbers of students brought through America's education system, and in this way education promoted an individualism for millions of students.

NOTES

1. John Dewey, *Democracy and Education* (New York: Free Press, 1916), 137.
2. Ibid., iii.
3. John Dewey, "Psychology and Social Practice" (1899), in *John Dewey: The Middle Works, 1899–1924*, 15 vols. (Carbondale: Southern Illinois University Press, 1976–1983), 1:149–50.
4. Ibid., 1:122.
5. Ibid., 1:130.
6. Ibid., 1:137.
7. Ibid., 1:129.
8. John Dewey, "Significance of the Problem of Knowledge" (1897), in *John Dewey: The Early Works, 1882–1898*, 5 vols. (Carbondale: Southern Illinois University Press, 1967–1972), 5:21–22.
9. J. Kadushin, "Mathematics in Present-Day Industry," *The Mathematics Teacher* 35 (October 1942): 260–64.
10. "Value of Education After War Is Cited," New Orleans, La. *Times-Picayune*, December 16, 1942.
11. Robert Havighurst, "Educational News and Editorial Comment," *The School Review* 51, 2 (February 1943): 71.
12. Stanford University School of Education Faculty, *Education in Wartime and After* (New York: D. Appleton-Century Co., 1943), 84.
13. Ibid., 85.
14. Willard B. Spalding and William C. Kvaraceus, "What Do We Mean by Democracy?" *The American School Board Journal* 108, 2 (February 1944): 50.
15. Ibid.
16. W.F. Himmelreich, "Patters of Discipline," *The American School Board Journal* 108, 3 (March 1944): 25.
17. The term dates from Adolph Meyer and Clifford Beers, who in 1908 set up a state committee of mental hygiene in Connecticut. This early mental hygiene work was mostly a psychiatric field of interest; it was really in the 1930s that mental hygiene became associated with public education. See Lester D. Crow and Alice Crow, *Mental Hygiene in School and Home Life for Teachers, Supervisors, and Parents* (New York: McGraw-Hill Book Co., 1942), 3. Most commentators credited Clifford Beers's book *A Mind That Found Itself, an Autobiography* (rev. ed.; Garden City, N.Y.: Doubleday, 1923) with being the founding text of the mental hygiene movement, a book for which William James wrote the introduction. See also Central Hanover Bank and Trust Company, *The Mental Hygiene Movement: From the Philanthropic Standpoint* (New York: Department of Philanthropic Information, 1939), 35; and William Welch, address delivered at the 20th Anniversary Meeting of the National Committee for Mental Hygiene, 1929, in *Mental Hygiene* 14 (1930): 196.
18. Herbert Carroll, *Mental Hygiene: The Dynamics of Adjustment* (New York: Prentice-Hall, 1947), 8.

19. Clarence M. Hincks, foreword to John D.M. Griffin, S.R. Laycock, and W. Line, *Mental Hygiene: A Manual for Teachers* (New York: American Book Co., 1940), vii.
20. David B. Klein, *Mental Hygiene: The Psychology of Personal Adjustments* (New York: Henry Holt and Co., 1944), 3.
21. Mental Hygiene Committee of the Vocational Adjustment Bureau for Girls, *Mental Hygiene Project at Kindergarten Level, 1937–1939*, Report to the Board of Education, City of New York (New York: Mental Hygiene Committee, 1939). This study concluded with a statement of the interest of mental hygiene in adjusting attitudes: "We conclude that conferences with individual teachers regarding their children, though time-consuming, are the most effective means of influencing their attitudes and methods" (180). In this case the teachers' attitudes were to be changed in order to adjust the attitudes of the students, since the teachers were understood to be the primary influence on the attitudes of students.
22. Klein, *Mental Hygiene*, 16.
23. Ibid.
24. Griffin, Laycock, and Line, *Mental Hygiene*, 5.
25. A.J. Rosanoff, *Manual of Psychiatry and Mental Hygiene* (New York: John Wiley & Sons, 1938), 749.
26. Horatio M. Pollock, "What May Be Hoped for in the Prevention of Mental Disease," *The Psychiatric Quarterly* 4 (1930): 234.
27. Klein, *Mental Hygiene*, 19.
28. Carroll, *Mental Hygiene*, 1.
29. Ibid., 18.
30. Ibid., 19.
31. Hincks, foreword to Griffin, Laycock, and Line, *Mental Hygiene*, vii.
32. Crow and Crow, *Mental Hygiene in School and Home Life*, vi.
33. Perceval M. Symonds, *Mental Hygiene of the School Child* (New York: Macmillan, 1934), x.
34. J.C. Wright and Charles R. Allen, *Efficiency in Education: A Study of the Applications of the Principles of Efficiency to Educational Administration, Supervision, and Methods of Teaching* (New York: John Wiley & Sons; London: Chapman & Hall, 1929), 5.
35. Mandel Sherman, *Mental Hygiene and Education* (New York: Longmans, Green and Co., 1934), vii.
36. Ibid., 99.
37. Norman Fenton, *Mental Hygiene in School Practice* (Stanford, Calif.: Stanford University Press, 1943), vii.
38. Ibid., 4.
39. L.F. Shaffer, *The Psychology of Adjustment* (New York: Houghton Mifflin Co., 1936), 501.
40. Griffin, Laycock, and Line, *Mental Hygiene*, 2–3.
41. Symonds, *Mental Hygiene of the School Child*, 4.
42. Fenton, *Mental Hygiene in School Practice*, 3.
43. Carroll, *Mental Hygiene*, iii.
44. Crow and Crow, *Mental Hygiene in School and Home Life*, 21.
45. Anonymous, "Psychology for the Fighting Man," from National Research Council, *Psychology for the Fighting Man*, published by *The Infantry Journal* (1943)

in Roger Sherman Loomis and Gabriel M. Liegey, *The Fight for Freedom: College Readings in Wartime* (New York: Farrar & Rinehart, 1943), 307.

46. C.R. Van Nice, "Democracy Aided by Its Educational Frills," *The American School Board Journal* 107, 2 (August 1943): 36.

47. Stanford University School of Education Faculty, *Education in Wartime and After*, 134.

48. Harlow Person, foreword to Frederick Winslow Taylor, *Scientific Management* (New York: Harper & Row, 1947), xiv–xv.

49. Frederick Winslow Taylor, *Shop Management*, in *Scientific Management* (New York: Frederick Taylor, 1911; reprint, New York: Harper & Row, 1947), 21–22.

50. Ibid., 29.

51. Ludwig Wittgenstein, *Philosophical Investigations*, trans. G.E.M. Anscombe (New York: Macmillan, 1989), part I, section 153.

52. Ibid., part I, section 678.

53. Ibid., part I, section 679.

54. Friedrich Nietzsche, *The Gay Science*, trans. Walter Kaufmann (New York: Vintage, 1974), Book 5, section 354.

55. Wittgenstein, *Philosophical Investigations*, part I, section 115.

56. Ludwig Wittgenstein, *On Certainty*, ed. G.E.M. Anscombe and G.H. von Wright, trans. Denis Paul and G.E.M. Anscombe (New York: Harper and Row, 1972), section 95.

57. Ibid., section 166.

58. Wittgenstein, *Philosophical Investigations*, part I, section 219.

59. Wittgenstein, *Tractatus Logico-Philosophicus*, trans. D.F. Pears and B.F. McGuinness (London: Routledge and Kegan Paul, 1961), section 7, p. 74.

60. Ray Monk, *Ludwig Wittgenstein: The Duty of Genius* (New York: Free Press, 1990), 151.

61. Wittgenstein, *Philosophical Investigations*, part I, section 35.

62. Ibid., part I, section 271.

63. Ibid., part I, section 272.

Part IV

Conclusion

Chapter 10

Discipline and Citizen

> For the love of the newly discovered ego is much more powerful now than the love of the old, used-up "fatherland," which has been touted to death; and the need to achieve some security from the terrifying ups and down of fortune opens even nobler hands as soon as anyone who is powerful and rich shows that he is ready to pour gold into them.
> —Friedrich Nietzsche, *The Gay Science*,
> Book 1, section 23

Institutions (in this case state institutions) order and control citizens, but such institutions also produce aspects of subjectivity that can be said to free citizens. The individualisms explored in this examination include the reduction in the power of racial and ethnic identities, new locations of individualism (that is, new conceptions of the citizen's relation to themselves), and the reduction in the need for systems of meaning to give value to individual actions. In these three ways I would suggest that state institutions in the late twentieth century contributed to important possibilities of human freedom, individualism, and ethics. This account of the production of independence by state institutions should not hide the fact that these institutions very clearly acted with a tremendous amount of coercive power. My interest is not in defending this domination, but in discovering elements of that domination that may weaken it.

The first contribution of state institutions to individualism is the creation of identity, by which I mean the creation of a greater awareness of the action of identification. In a socially pervasive way, communities like race and religion came to be seen as identities, not as human truths. Quite simply, the state influenced a change in identification among those who attended schools and fought in the war. They began to identify with a new community—one that highlighted national affiliation—as soldiers and students were removed from the rituals and behaviors of other communities in such a manner that these behaviors came to be understood as identifications. Karl Marx explained that it was this sort of discipline that would eventually bring the final destruction of the very means of discipline (capitalism). In *The Communist Manifesto,* Marx explained that capitalism destroyed all the old relationships that must be destroyed in order for Communism to exist.

All fixed, fast-frozen relations, with their train of ancient and venerable prejudices and opinions, are swept away, all new-formed ones become antiquated before they can ossify. All that is solid melts into air, all that is holy is profaned, and man is at last compelled to face with sober senses, his real conditions of life, and his relations with his kind.[1]

In order to avoid the fundamentalism in Marx's claim (i.e., that this process reveals the "real conditions of life"), other writers have explored similar procedures in different languages and from different directions. For example, in *The Gay Science*, Friedrich Nietzsche claimed that "whenever a human being begins to discover how he is playing a role and how he *can* be an actor, he *becomes* an actor."[2] In terms of identity, military discipline and regimentation taught soldiers that identities were roles.

Even the tremendously powerful American distinction between the invented terms "white" and "black" lost some of their reality through military service. A white platoon sergeant from South Carolina reported concerning black soldiers, "When I heard about it, I said I'd be damned if I'd wear the same shoulder patch they did. After that first day when we saw how they fought, I changed my mind. They're just like any of the other boys to us."[3] World War II also produced a symbol of the change occurring in American conceptions of identity with the racial segregation of industry with Executive Order 8802. On June 25, 1941, President Franklin D. Roosevelt commanded the "full and equitable participation of all workers in defense industries, without discrimination because of race, creed, color, or national origin" in response to the March-on-Washington Movement, led by A. Philip Randolph.[4]

Religious differences also lost force. One Research Branch questionnaire introduced a series of questions with the following pronouncement:

America is made up of a great many different kinds and groups of people. There are city people and country people. There are Northerners and Southerners and Westerners. There are Catholics, Jews, and Protestants. There are Poles, Italians, Mexicans, Scotch, and many other nationalities. There are people whose skin color is white, black, yellow, brown, and red. There are big business and little business men, factory workers, clerks, and farmers. There are business leaders, labor leaders, government leaders, farm leaders. There are Republicans, Democrats, Communists, Socialists, and Independents. Some of these different groups always get along well together; others sometimes don't get along so well.[5]

After this nationalization of ethnic, religious, class, and regional identities, soldiers were asked to name the groups they thought most likely to come into conflict after the war and the groups they personally disliked. Education, like military service, reduced the power of racial conceptions. "If we are dealing with folk beliefs," concluded one government study, "such as in the innate inferiority of the Negro, we are likely to find the better educated much more liberal than the less educated."[6] Education and military service transformed social facts into identifications and citizens into actors.

Significantly, by the World War II period identities were conceptually organized to support national power in much the same manner as industrial divisions of labor relied on differences to consolidate a whole. In Honolulu, the *Nippu Jiji* newspaper, read largely by Americans of Japanese decent, sponsored a war slogan contest three months after the bombing of Pearl Harbor. One of the honorable mention slogans indicated the connections between unity, difference, and work. Masaru Koike proposed, "Unity Through Words but Victory Through Work."[7] In this example unity became linguistic, and victory would be achieved if each citizen contributed their work. The pairing suggests that work is somewhat other than unity (i.e., each worker performs a different job). Another somewhat outstanding example was Native American code talkers. The Navajo code talkers exemplified the military utility that brought together cultural differences in the interest of the nation. That is, cultural characteristics distinct to the Navajos became nationally important when it was discovered that their language presented almost insurmountable challenges to enemy codebreakers.[8] Ernie Pyle also reported the Navajo war dances that Navajo marines performed before the invasion of Okinawa. "The rituals for victory were acceptable especially if they helped the whites too," reported one recent history.[9] The Indians concluded their pre-invasion chant by singing the Marine Corps Hymn in Navajo.[10] Like the differences within an industrial division of labor, differences became valuable as they contributed to the nation.

The second element of human independence that came out of the disciplines of World War II included the reformulation of the location of the individual's distinct self. That is, where earlier generations could find "individualism" in their work and in their way of doing work, this generation reformulated their understanding of "individualism." The standardization of physical action in military discipline removed individualism from physical movement. Furthermore, the standardization of educative desires in education abandoned "character" and even "desire" to social experience. This standardization, the direct result of the application of Taylorized divisions of labor to national civic life, required the reformulation of the individual. Rituals supported by time schedules, desk rows, playgrounds, lunch hours, role calls, and hall monitors, as well as curriculums, played a role in the construction of a political citizenship or subjectivity predicated on a powerful individualism in which even the most personal of experiences (interests and attitudes) became much more public. This transformation made the individual much more mysterious and more independent of outside recognition. Individualism was discovered less in physical action and, as Taylorism increasingly functioned as a model for intellectual discipline, less in articulated desires and attitudes. "The school's interest in outcomes is centered in the personalities of pupils and the development of their character," wrote John Griffin in a mental hygiene manual for teachers.[11] Character, personality, and desire were perceived as standardized experiences, a perspective that forced the redeployment of individualism similar to Nietzsche's in the late nineteenth century. "Fundamentally, all our actions are altogether incomparably personal, unique, and infinitely individual; there is no doubt of that. But as soon as we translate them into consciousness *they no longer seem to be*," offered Nietzsche in an account of the socialness of consciousness.[12]

For Nietzsche, furthermore, language and consciousness are social experiences. What is most individual can scarcely exist in the expression and consciousness of the self.

The problem of consciousness (more precisely, of becoming conscious of something) confronts us only when we begin to comprehend how we could dispense with it; and now physiology and the history of animals place us at the beginning of such comprehension.... For we could think, feel, will, and remember, and we could also "act" in every sense of that word, and yet none of all this would have to "enter our consciousness" (as one says metaphorically). The whole of life would be possible without, as it were, seeing itself in a mirror. Even now, for that matter, by far the greatest portion of our life actually takes place without this mirror effect; and this is true even of our thinking, feeling, and willing life, however offensive this may sound to older philosophers.[13]

"Usually, one takes consciousness itself as the general sensorium and supreme court," Nietzsche wrote in his notebooks in late 1887 or early 1888. "Nonetheless, it is only as means of communication: it is evolved through social intercourse and with a view to the interests of social intercourse."[14] The individual appears as a twinkle in the eye and freedom is never quite the condition of the self.

The third element of individualism that developed out of state discipline exists mostly as a freedom made possible by the two changes already described. The deconstruction of non-national identity created problems for all identities. That is, the reduction in the truth of other identities contributed to critiques of national identity. The problem of national identity became more significant as citizens perceived themselves as more significantly alienated from their fellow citizens. This paired movement opened up the possibility of an individualism not based on a national (or other) form of recognition. The demand for recognition has been one of the difficulties of individualism; as people are removed from systems of tradition that supplied ways for them to understand their place within the world, the demand to have others (or Others) recognize their ways of living as valuable has often frustrated a bountiful individualism.[15]

In Book 1, section 23 of the *Gay Science*, Nietzsche explored the growth of human independence from the need for recognition of value, even from the nation-state.

For the love of the newly discovered ego is much more powerful now than the love of the old, used-up "fatherland," which has been touted to death; and the need to achieve some security from the terrifying ups and downs of fortune opens even nobler hands as soon as anyone who is powerful and rich shows that he is ready to pour gold into them.

What Nietzsche called the *"signs of corruption"* included the evaporation of the Machiavellian demand that the state protect itself from Fortune's wheel and extend itself through time. Identities and recognitions come in much smaller doses: "There is hardly any secure future left; one lives for today, and this state of the soul makes the game easy for all seducers, for one allows oneself to be seduced and bribed only 'for today' while reserving the future and one's virtue."[16] The short-term seduction of the subject conveys the limitations of identity, as the self can commit to identities and communities that are already revealed as acts that can be undone. "To say it briefly (for a long time people will still keep silent about it)," Nietzsche proclaimed in Book 5, section 356, "what will not be built anymore henceforth, and *cannot* be built anymore, is—a society in the old sense of that word; to build that, everything is lacking, above all the material. *All of us are no longer material for a society*; this is a truth for which the time has come."[17] To proclaim this truth is not to forbid identification; subjects are still seduced into community but seduced temporarily and with cognizance of other possible lovers. For Nietzsche, the desire for recognition of individual value by large systems of meaning actually betrayed the subject's (or citizen's) own lack of value (or belief in their own value).

The strongest account of Nietzsche's resistence to the demands for recognition is his "thought experiment" of the eternal return. He contrived this story to develop a model for self-valuation. The eternal return attempted to place the power of valuation more securely in the individual. Lives and actions were not to be valued for their contributions to nations, religions, humanity, or even temporary individual successes, but were to be valued through a willingness to live every detail of a person's life for eternity. "Or how well disposed would you have to become to yourself and to life," he asked in *The Gay Science*, "*to crave nothing more fervently* than this ultimate eternal confirmation and seal?"[18] For Nietzsche, willing your own life became the only source of value. "Becoming must be explained without recourse to final intentions; becoming must appear justified at every moment (or incapable of being evaluated; which amounts to the same thing); the present must absolutely not be justified by reference to a future, nor the past by reference to the present."[19]

Nietzsche supplemented this revision of recognition with an account concerning the necessity of discipline. "One thing is needful," claimed Nietzsche. "To 'give style' to one's character—a great and rare art! It is practiced by those who survey all the strengths and weaknesses of their nature and then fit them into an artistic plan until every one of them appears as art and reason and even weaknesses delight the eye."[20] Style requires the artistic disciplining of the self. "It is the strong and domineering natures that enjoy their finest gaiety in such constraint and perfection under a law of their own . . . even when they have to build palaces and design gardens they demur at giving nature freedom."[21] Michel Foucault's conception of the discipline was significantly influenced by Nietzsche. Foucault conceived of this discipline in several ways. In *Discipline and Punish*, he demonstrated that changes in eighteenth- and nineteenth-century methods of discipline were connected to changes in understandings of human consciousness and subjectivity; more specifically, he examined the role of prisons in the formation of a new series of understandings concerning the subject—understandings with attendant notions of freedom and individualism, or what he called the soul.

Rather than seeing this soul as the reactivated remnants of an ideology, one could see it as the present correlative of a certain technology of power over the body. It would be wrong to say that the soul is an illusion, or an ideological effect. On the contrary, it exists, it has a reality, it is produced permanently around, on, within the body by the functioning of a power that is exercised on those punished—and, in a more general way, on those one supervises, trains and corrects, over madmen, children at home and at school, the colonized, over those who are stuck at a machine and supervised for the rest of their lives. This is the historical reality of this soul, which, unlike the soul represented by Christian theology, is not born in sin and subject to punishment, but is born rather out of methods of punishment, supervision and constraint.[22]

The soul or human freedom is birthed in punishment and discipline. "Discipline 'makes' individuals," Foucault claimed later in the same book. "It is the specific technique of a power that regards individuals both as objects and as instruments of its exercise."[23] In his later work, Foucault kept the schema in which discipline constituted individuals but offered alternatives to the highly coercive non-reciprocal power of the state.

"We, however," Nietzsche wrote, in an account distanced from state power, "*want to become those we are*—human beings who are new, unique, incomparable, who give themselves laws, who create themselves."[24] Foucault's account of care of the self, also highly influenced by Nietzsche, involved the creation of a self as a work of art though rigorous discipline. "It is remarkable," wrote Foucault of the authors who he believed sketched out this account of discipline, "that with rare exceptions, this desire for rigor expressed by the moralists did not take the form of a demand for intervention on the part of public authority."

"One would not find in the writings of the philosophers any proposal for a general and coercive legislation of sexual behaviors. They urge individuals to be more austere if they wish to lead a life different from that of 'the throngs'; they do not try to determine which measures or punishments might constrain everyone in a uniform manner."[25] Even though directed against herd behavior in the individual, the ethic involved in care of the self is a social ethic, Foucault carefully points out. "Around the care of the self, there developed an entire activity of speaking and writing in which the work of oneself on oneself and communication with others were linked together. Here we touch on one of the most important aspects of this activity devoted to oneself: it constituted, not an exercise in solitude, but a true social practice."[26] The practitioner talks to friends and advisors concerning the state of her soul and the rigorous discipline she takes to create that self as a work of art. The self in this scheme is to be crafted like a work of art in which much work is required but over which there are no absolute normalizing standards. Elsewhere Foucault explained: "What strikes me is the fact that, in our society, art has become something that is related only to objects and not to individuals or to life. . . . But couldn't everyone's life become a work of art?"[27] With this conception Foucault was able to break out of problems of normalization and recognition. To create the self with style, Nietzsche wrote, "is practiced by those who survey all the strengths and weaknesses of their nature and then fit them into an artistic plan until every one of them appears as art and reason and even weaknesses delight the eye." Nietzsche, the artist, continued: "Here a large mass of second nature has been added; there a piece of original nature has been removed—both times through long practice and daily work at it. Here the ugly that could not be removed is concealed; there it has been reinterpreted and made sublime."[28]

While the Taylor-made subject was particularly obedient to many elements of the late-twentieth-century social order, it did not create a subject so well taylored that it fit that order perfectly. In this lack of fit Americans found subjectivity and individualism, even against extensive ordering powers of the late twentieth century, and were increasingly able to make themselves fit themselves.

NOTES

1. Karl Marx, *The Communist Manifesto* (New York: W.W. Norton, 1988), 58.
2. Friedrich Nietzsche, *The Gay Science*, trans. Walter Kaufmann (New York: Vintage Books, 1974), Book 5, section 356.
3. Samuel Stouffer, Edward Suchman, Leland DeVinney, Shirley Star, and Robin Williams, Jr., *The American Soldier, Vol. 1: Adjustment During Army Life* (Princeton, N.J.: Princeton University Press, 1949), 592.
4. "The March-on-Washington Movement," New York *Amsterdam Star-News*, June 28, 1941, in Herbert Aptheker, ed., *A Documentary History of the Negro People in the United States, Vol. 4: 1933–1945* (New York: Citadel Press, 1992), 405–6.
5. Samuel Stouffer, Edward Suchman, Leland DeVinney, Shirley Star, and Robin Williams, Jr., *The American Soldier, Vol. 2: Combat and Its Aftermath* (Princeton, N.J.: Princeton University Press, 1949), 584.
6. Ibid., 617.
7. Lawrence R. Samuel, *Pledging Allegiance: American Identity and the Bond Drive of World War II* (Washington, D.C.: Smithsonian Institution Press, 1997), 105.
8. Margaret T. Bixler, *Winds of Freedom: The Story of the Navajo Code Talkers of World War II* (Darien, Conn.: Two Bytes, 1992); Alison R. Bernstein, *American Indians and World War II: Toward a New Era in Indian Affairs* (Norman: University of Oklahoma Press, 1991); Lynn Escue, "Coded Contradictions: Navajo Talkers and the Pacific War," *History Today* 41 (July 1991); Laurence M. Hauptman, *The Iroquois Struggle for Survival: World War II to Red Power* (Syracuse, N.Y.: Syracuse University Press, 1985); Doris Paul, *The Navajo Code Talkers* (Philadelphia, Pa.: Dorrance, 1973); Broderick H. Johnson, ed., *Navajos and World War II* (Tsaile, Ariz.: Navajo Community College Press, 1977).
9. Bernstein, *American Indians and World War II*, 57; Ernie Pyle, "Ceremonial Dances in the Pacific," in U.S. Bureau of Indian Affairs, *Indians in the War* (Chicago: U.S. Department of Interior, Office of Indian Affairs, 1946), pp. 12–14.
10. Philip Johnson, "Marine Corps Hymn in Navajo," *Master Key* (September 1945): 153. Johnson, a child of Christian missionaries to the Navajos, originally proposed that Navajos be used as code talkers to Major General Clayton Vogel, Commanding General of the U.S. Marine Corps., Amphibious Corps, Pacific Fleet. Vogel granted permission to organize the 382nd Marine Platoon for the code talkers. The success of this platoon extended the permission for the code talker program to an unlimited number of recruits; 420 Navaho would participate in the program in the course of the war.
11. John D.M. Griffin, S.R. Laycock, and W. Line, *Mental Hygiene: A Manual for Teachers* (New York: American Book Co., 1940), 3.
12. Nietzsche, *The Gay Science*, Book 5, section 354.
13. Ibid.
14. Friedrich Nietzsche, *The Will to Power*, trans. Walter Kaufmann (New York: Vintage Books, 1968), Book 3, section 524.
15. Charles Taylor suggests quite plausibly that recognition becomes an issue with the "collapse of social hierarchies." Charles Taylor, "The Politics of Recognition," in *Multiculturalism*, ed. Amy Guttmann (Princeton, N.J.: Princeton University Press, 1994), 26.

16. Nietzsche, *The Gay Science*, Book 1, section 23.
17. Ibid., Book 5, section 356.
18. Ibid., Book 4, section 341.
19. Nietzsche, *The Will to Power*, Book 3, section 708.
20. Nietzsche, *The Gay Science*, Book 4, section 290.
21. Ibid.
22. Michel Foucault, *Discipline and Punish* (New York: Vintage Books, 1979), 29.
23. Ibid., 170.
24. Nietzsche, *The Gay Science*, Book 5, section 336.
25. Michel Foucault, *The Care of the Self* (New York: Vintage Books, 1988), 40.
26. Ibid., 51.
27. Michel Foucault, "On the Genealogy of Ethics," in *Ethics: Subjectivity and Truth*, ed. Paul Rabinow (New York: The New Press, 1997), 261.
28. Nietzsche, *The Gay Science*, Book 4, section 290.

Bibliography

"Absence of Draft Cards Bars Boys from Joints." Topeka, Kans. *Capital*, February 20, 1943.
"Absenteeism to Bring Draft Reclassification." Washington, D.C. *Star*, March 9, 1943.
"Acting on 'Work or Fight' Order." Allentown, Pa. *Morning Call*, March 4, 1943.
Adams, Michael C.C. *The Best War Ever: America and World War II*. Baltimore: Johns Hopkins University Press, 1994.
Aitken, Hugh G.J. *Scientific Management in Action: Taylorism at Watertown Arsenal, 1908–1915*. Princeton, N.J.: Princeton University Press, 1985.
Akin, William. *Technocracy and the American Dream: The Technocrat Movement, 1900–1941*. Berkeley: University of California Press, 1977.
"Alabama Draft Chief Orders 500 Strikers Reclassified." Washington, D.C. *Star*, March 20, 1943.
Alchon, Guy. *The Invisible Hand of Planning: Capitalism, Social Science, and the State in the 1920s*. Princeton, N.J.: Princeton University Press, 1985.
Allen, Charles. *Efficiency in Education: A Study of the Applications of the Principles of Efficiency to Educational Administration, Supervision, and Methods of Teaching*. New York: John Wiley & Sons, 1929.
Allen, Mary Emma. "A Comparative Study of Negro and White Children on Melodic and Harmonic Sensitivity." *Journal of Negro Education* 11 (April 1942): 158–64.
Allen, William. *Efficient Democracy*. New York: Dodd, Mead and Co., 1907.
Allswang, John M. *The New Deal and American Politics*. New York: John Wiley, 1978.

Alperin, Robert J. "Organization in the Communist Party, U.S.A., 1931–1938." Ph.D. diss., Northwestern University, 1959.

Althusser, Louis. *Lenin and Philosophy*, trans. Ben Brewster. New York: Monthly Review Press, 1971.

Anderson, Benedict. *Imagined Communities*, 2nd rev. ed. New York: Verso, 1993.

Anderson, Troyer S. "Munitions for the Army—A Five Year Report on the Procurement of Munitions by the War Department Under the Direction of the Under Secretary of War (9 April 1946)," U.S. Army, Office of the Chief of Military History, 2–3.

Anonymous. "Informal Social Organization in the Army." *The American Journal of Sociology* 51, 5 (March 1946): 365.

———. "Jim Crow in the Army Camps." *The Crisis* 47, 12 (December 1940). In Herbert Aptheker, ed., *A Documentary History of the Negro People in the United States, Vol. 4: 1933–1945*. New York: Citadel Press, 1992, 397.

———. "Psychology for the Fighting Man." From National Research Council, *Psychology for the Fighting Man*. Published by *The Infantry Journal* (1943). In Roger Sherman Loomis and Gabriel M. Liegey, *The Fight for Freedom: College Readings in Wartime*. New York: Farrar & Rinehart, 1943.

Apple, Michael W. *Education and Power*. New York: Routledge, 1995.

Aptheker, Herbert, ed. *A Documentary History of the Negro People in the United States, Vol. 4: 1933–1945*. New York: Citadel Press, 1992.

Arendt, Hannah. *On Revolution*. New York: Viking Compass, 1965.

Aristotle. *The Politics*, trans. T.A. Sinclair. New York: Penguin, 1987.

———. *The Politics*, trans. Ernest Barker. Oxford: Oxford University Press, 1995.

———. *The Politics*, trans. Trevor Saunders. Oxford: Clarendon Press, 1995.

Armstrong, E.T. "Is Our Present High School System Inefficient?" *American School Board Journal* 42 (February 1911): 3–4.

"Army Accepts Diseased Men." San Francisco *News*, April 21, 1943.

"Army Call Shows Democracy Isn't Soft, Dykstra Asserts." Buffalo, N.Y. *News*, October 17, 1940.

"Army Deserter Is Caught by Police." Clinton, Iowa *Herald*, March 13, 1943.

Arndt, H.W. *The Economic Lessons of the Nineteen-Thirties*. New York: Augustus M. Kelley, 1965.

Associated Press. "16,000,000 in Nation Sign Up for Duty in Draft Army." Buffalo, N.Y. *Courier-Express*, October 17, 1940.

Attack on Hidden Waste. Army Pictorial Service, National Archives, Record Group 111, Series M, Item 1073, 1944.

Auerbach, Jerold S. "The Influence of the New Deal." *Current History* 48, 286 (June 1956): 334–65.

———. "The La Follette Committee: Labor and Civil Liberties in the New Deal." *Journal of American History* 51, 3 (December 1964): 435–59.

———. *Labor and Liberty: The La Follette Committee and the New Deal*. New York: Bobbs-Merrill, 1966.

———. "New Deal, Old Deal, or Raw Deal: Some Thoughts on New Left Historiography." *Journal of Southern History* 35 (February 1969): 18–30.

———. "Southern Tenant Farmers: Socialist Criticism of the New Deal." *Labor History* 7, 1 (Winter 1966): 3–18.

Babcock, George De Albert. *The Taylor System in Franklin Management.* New York: The Engineering Magazine Co., 1917.
Bagley, W.C. "An Essentialist's Platform for the Advancement of American Education." *Educational Administration and Supervision* 24 (1938): 241. In Herbert M. Kliebard, *The Struggle for the American Curriculum, 1893-1958.* New York: Routledge, 1995, 197.
Bailey, Pearce, Frankwood Williams, and Paul Komora. *The Medical Department of the United States Army in the World War, Vol. X: Neuropsychiatry.* Washington, D.C.: Government Printing Office, 1929.
Balibar, Etienne, and Immanuel Wallerstein. *Race, Nation, Class: Ambiguous Identities.* New York: Verso, 1991.
Baltimore Bulletin of Education 19 (April–May–June 1942): 201–7.
Banta, Martha. *Taylored Lives: Narrative Productions in the Age of Taylor, Veblen, and Ford.* Chicago: University of Chicago Press, 1993.
Beers, Clifford. *A Mind That Found Itself, An Autobiography*, rev. ed. Garden City, N.Y.: Doubleday, 1923.
Beiner, Ronald, ed. *Theorizing Citizenship.* Albany: State University of New York Press, 1995.
"Bellaire Draft Officials Receive New Regulation." Wheeling, W.Va. *Intelligencer*, May 28, 1943.
Bellush, Bernard. *The Failure of the NRA.* New York: W.W. Norton, 1975.
Bendix, Reinhard. *Nation-Building and Citizenship: Studies of Our Changing Social Order.* Berkeley: University of California Press, 1977.
———. *Work and Authority in Industry: Ideologies of Management in the Course of Industrialization.* Berkeley: University of California Press, 1974.
Benedict, Ruth. "Race Problems in America." *The Annals of the American Academy of Political and Social Science* 216 (July 1941): 75.
Benedict, Ruth, and Mildred Ellis. *Race and Cultural Relations.* Washington, D.C.: National Education Association, 1942.
Beniger, James R. *The Control Revolution: Technological and Economic Origins of the Information Society.* Cambridge, Mass.: Harvard University Press, 1986.
Benjamin, Walter. *Reflections.* New York: Schocken Books, 1978.
———. "The Work of Art in the Age of Mechanical Reproduction." In Benjamin, *Illuminations*, trans. Harry Zohn. New York: Schocken Books, 1968.
Bennett, David H. *Demagogues in the Depression: American Radicals and the Union Party, 1932–1936.* New Brunswick, N.J.: Rutgers University Press, 1969.
Bennett, William. *American Education: Making Work.* Washington, D.C.: U.S. Department of Education, 1988.
Bercovitch, Sacvan. *The Office of the Scarlet Letter.* Baltimore: Johns Hopkins University Press, 1991.
Bermann, R.B. "2 'Witnesses' Found Guilty in Draft Case." Seattle, Wash. *Post-Intelligencer*, June 2, 1943.
Bernstein, Alison R. *American Indians and World War II: Toward a New Era in Indian Affairs.* Norman: University of Oklahoma Press, 1991.
Bernstein, Irving. "The End of the Turbulent Years." In *The New Deal: The Critical Issues*, ed. Otis L. Graham, Jr. Boston: Little, Brown, 1971.
———. *The Lean Years.* Boston: Houghton Mifflin, 1972.

———. *The New Deal Collective Bargaining Policy.* New York: Da Capo Press, 1975.
———. *Turbulent Years.* Boston: Houghton Mifflin, 1969.
Berube, Allan. *Coming Out Under Fire: The History of Gay Men and Women in World War Two.* New York: The Free Press, 1990.
Bicha, Karel Denis. "Liberalism Frustrated: The League for Independent Political Action, 1928–1933." *Mid-America* 48, 1 (January 1966): 19–28.
Bixler, Margaret T. *Winds of Freedom: The Story of the Navajo Code Talkers of World War II.* Darien, Conn.: Two Bytes, 1992.
"Blind and Ladle of 1918 Sought for Draft Draw." New York *Herald Tribune*, October 18, 1940.
Block, Fred. "Beyond Relative Autonomy: State Managers as Historic Subjects." *Socialist Register* 17 (1980): 227–42.
———. *The Origins of International Economic Disorder.* Berkeley: University of California Press, 1977.
———. "The Ruling Class Does Not Rule: Notes on the Marxist Theory of the State." *Socialist Revolution* 33 (May–June 1977): 6–28.
Bloom, Allan. *The Closing of the American Mind.* New York: Simon and Schuster, 1987.
Blum, Albert A. "Labor and the Federal Government, 1850–1933." *Current History* 48, 286 (June 1965): 328–33.
Blumberg, Barbara. *The New Deal and the Unemployed: The View from New York City.* Lewisberg, Pa.: Bucknell University Press, 1979.
Board of Education, City of New York. *Report on Training in the Armed Services with Implications for Postwar Education in New York City.* New York: Board of Education, 1946.
"Boards Expose Racket in Sale of Draft Cards." Philadelphia, Pa. *Inquirer*, June 10, 1943.
Bobbitt, John Franklin. *The Curriculum of Modern Education.* New York: McGraw-Hill Book Co., 1941.
———. "The Elimination of Waste in Education." *The Elementary School Journal* 12, 6 (February 1912): 259–71.
———. "Harvard Reaffirms the Academic Tradition." *The School Review* 54 (1946): 326–33.
———. *The Supervision of City Schools: Some General Principles of Management Applied to the Problems of City-School Systems.* "Twelfth Yearbook of the National Society for the Study of Education." Part I. Bloomington, Ind.: Public School Publishing Co., 1913, 11–15.
Bodnar, John. "Immigration, Kinship, and the Rise of Working Class Realism in Industrial America." *Journal of Social History* 14, 1 (Fall 1980): 45–65.
———. *Remaking America.* Princeton, N.J.: Princeton University Press, 1991.
Bonn, M.J. *The Crisis of Capitalism in America.* New York: John Day, 1932.
Boorstin, Daniel. *The Americans: The Democratic Experience.* New York: Random House, 1973.
Borges, Jorge Luis. *Labyrinths.* New York: New Directions Publishing, 1962.
Bowles, Samuel and Herbert Gintis. "The Crisis of Liberal Democratic Capitalism: The Case of the United States." *Politics and Society* 11, 1 (1982): 51–93.

Bowman, K.M. "Psychiatry at War." *The American Mercury* 59, 249 (September 1944).
Braeman, John. "The New Deal and the 'Broker State': A Review of the Recent Scholarly Literature." *Business History Review* 46, 4 (Winter 1972): 409–29.
Braeman, John, Robert H. Bremner, and David Brody, eds. *The New Deal: The National Level*. Columbus: Ohio State University Press, 1975.
Braeman, John, Robert H. Bremner, and Everett Walters, eds. *Change and Continuity in Twentieth Century America*. Columbus: Ohio State University Press, 1975.
Brandeis, Louis. *"Half Brother, Half Son": The Letters of Louis D. Brandeis to Felix Frankfurter*, ed. Melvin I. Urofsky and David W. Levy. Norman: University of Oklahoma Press, 1991.
Brandes, Stuart. *American Welfare Capitalism, 1880–1940*. Chicago: University of Chicago Press, 1976.
Bridges, Amy. "Nicos Poulantzas and the Marxist Theory of the State." *Politics and Society* 4, 2 (1974): 161–90.
Brockie, Melvin D. "Theories of the 1937–1938 Crisis and Depression." *Economics Journal* 60, 238 (June 1950): 292–310.
Brody, David. "Labor and the Great Depression: The Interpretive Prospects." *Labor History* 13, 2 (Spring 1972): 231–44.
———. "The New Deal and World War II." In *The New Deal: The National Level*, ed. John Braeman, Robert H. Bremner, and David Brody. Columbus: Ohio State University Press, 1975.
———. "Radicalism and the American Labor Movement: From Party History to Social History." In *Political Power and Social Theory*, Vol. 4, ed. Maurice Zeitlin and Howard Kimeldorf. Greenwich, Conn.: JAI Press, 1984.
Brotz, H., and E. Wilson. "Characteristics of Military Society." *American Journal of Sociology* 51 (1946).
Brown, Francis, and Joseph Roucek. *Our Racial and National Minorities*. New York: Prentice-Hall, 1937.
Brown, Linda. "Challenge and Response: The American Business Community and the New Deal, 1932–1934." Ph.D. diss., University of Pennsylvania, 1972.
Burawoy, Michael. "Terrains of Contest: Factory and State under Capitalism." *Socialist Review* 58 (July–August 1981): 83–124.
Burdette, Franklin. "Education for Citizenship." *Public Opinion Quarterly* 6 (Summer 1942): 269–79.
Burdette, Franklin, ed. *Education for Citizen Responsibilities*. Princeton, N.J.: Princeton University Press for the National Foundation for Education in American Citizenship, 1942.
Burns, Helen. *The American Banking Community and New Deal Banking Reforms, 1933–1935*. Westport, Conn.: Greenwood Press, 1974.
Butler, Judith. *Bodies That Matter: On the Discursive Limits of "Sex."* New York: Routledge, 1993.
———. *Gender Trouble: Feminism and the Subversion of Identity*. New York: Routledge, 1990.
Callahan, Raymond. *Education and the Cult of Efficiency*. Chicago: University of Chicago Press, 1962.

Cannon, James P. *The Left Opposition in the U.S., 1928–1931*. New York: Monad, 1981.
Carlo, Antonio. "The Crisis of the State in the Thirties." *Telos* 46 (Winter 1980–1981): 62–80.
Carmichael, Leonard. "College Faculties in Government Service." *The Annals of the American Academy of Political and Social Science* 231 (January 1944): 42–46.
Carr, William. "Learning Citizenship Through Student Activities." *Journal of the National Education Association* 31 (February 1942): 55–56.
Carroll, Herbert. *Mental Hygiene: The Dynamics of Adjustment*. New York: Prentice-Hall, 1947.
Case, Roscoe David. *The Platoon School in America*. Stanford, Calif.: Stanford University Press, 1931.
Castells, Manuel. *The Economic Crisis and American Society*. Princeton, N.J.: Princeton University Press, 1980.
"Cave Hideout Fails to Save Draft Evader." Louisville, Ky. *Courier-Journal*, February 6, 1943.
Central Hanover Bank and Trust Company. *The Mental Hygiene Movement: From the Philanthropic Standpoint*. New York: Department of Philanthropic Information, 1939.
Chambers, M.M. *Opinions on Gains for American Education from Wartime Armed Services Training*. Washington, D.C.: American Council on Education, 1946.
Chandler, Alfred D., Jr. "The Structure of American Industry in the Twentieth Century: A Historical Overview." *Business History Review* 43, 3 (Autumn 1969): 255–97.
———. *The Visible Hand: The Managerial Revolution in American Business*. Cambridge, Mass.: Harvard University Press, 1977.
Chandler, Lester. *America's Greatest Depression, 1929–1941*. New York: Harper & Row, 1970.
Chase, Stuart. *A New Deal*. New York: Macmillan, 1932.
Christian Peper Tobacco Co. (advertisement). *New Yorker*, June 10, 1939, 45.
Churchill, Winston. *The Second World War*, Vol. 2. Boston: Houghton Mifflin, 1985.
Clarke, Simon. "Marxism, Sociology and Poulantzas' Theory of the State." *Capital and Class* 2 (Summer 1977): 1–31.
Classification of Enlisted Men, Personnel Placement in the Army. Office of War Information, Bureau of Motion Pictures. National Archives, Record Group 111, Series TF/.0578, 1942.
Clothier, Robert C. "The War Training Program and Postwar Education," *Educational Record* 24 (July 1943): 273–305.
Cochran, Thomas C. *American Business in the Twentieth Century*. Cambridge, Mass.: Harvard University Press, 1957.
———. *The American Business System: A Historical Perspective, 1900–1955*. Cambridge, Mass.: Harvard University Press, 1957.
———. *Business in American Life*. New York: McGraw-Hill Book Co., 1972.
Cohen, Lizabeth. *Making a New Deal: Industrial Workers in Chicago, 1919–1939*. New York: Cambridge University Press, 1990.
Cohen, Robert. "Mental Hygiene for the Trainee: A Method for Fortifying the Army's Manpower." *The American Journal of Psychiatry* 100, 1 (July 1943).

Cohen, Ronald. "Schooling Uncle Sam's Children: Education in the USA, 1941–1945." In *Education and the Second World War: Studies in Schooling and Social Change*, ed. Roy Lowe. Washington, D.C.: The Falmer Press, 1992, pp. 46–58.
Cohen, Stanley, and Andrew Scull, eds. *Social Control and the State*. Oxford: Blackwell, 1983.
"College Course for 17-Year-Olds Urged by Regent." New Orleans, La. *Times-Picayune*, December 13, 1942.
Compton, Karl T. "Organization of American Scientists for the War." *Science* 98 (July 23, 1943): 71–76; 98 (July 30, 1943): 93–98.
Conkin, Paul K. *The New Deal*. New York: Thomas Y. Crowell, 1967.
Connolly, William. *The Ethos of Pluralization*. Minneapolis: University of Minnesota Press, 1995.
Connolly, William, ed. *Legitimacy and the State*. New York: New York University Press, 1984.
Cooke, Morris Llewellyn. "Scientific Management of the Public Business." *American Political Science Review* 9 (August 1915): 488–95.
———. "Some Factors in Municipal Engineering." *Mechanical Engineering* 37 (February 1915): 82.
———. "Who Is Boss in Your Shop? Individual vs. Group Leadership, and Their Relation to Consent and the Ideals of Democracy." *Bulletin of the Taylor Society* 3, 4 (August 1917): 3.
Cooke, Morris Llewellyn, and Philip Murray. *Organized Labor and Production*. New York: Harper & Brothers, 1940.
Copley, Frank Barkley. *Frederick W. Taylor, Father of Scientific Management*. 2 vols. London: Routledge/Thoemmes Press, 1993.
Corey, Lewis. *The Decline of American Capitalism*. New York: Covici, Freide, 1934.
"Courage They Have." Minneapolis, Minn. *Star Journal*, February 5, 1943.
Craig, George. Letter to Lewis Hershey, August 26, 1941. National Archives, Record Group 147, Stack Area 17W4, Row 11, Compartment 02, Entry 2, Records of the Selective Service System, Box 33.
Crow, Lester D., and Alice Crow. *Mental Hygiene in School and Home Life for Teachers, Supervisors, and Parents*. New York: McGraw-Hill Book Co., 1942.
Cubberley, Ellwood. Foreword to Roscoe David Case, *The Platoon School in America*. Stanford, Calif.: Stanford University Press, 1931.
Cuff, Robert D. "Business, the State, and World War I: The American Experience." In *War and Society in North America*, ed. J.L. Granatstein and R.D. Cuff. Toronto: Thomas Nelson and Sons, 1971.
Darnall, Orton. "Board of Education Responsibilities in War and Peacetime." *The American School Board Journal* 107, 4 (October 1943): 42–44.
Davis, Joseph S. *The World Between the Wars, 1919–34: An Economist's View*. Baltimore: Johns Hopkins University Press, 1975.
Davis, Kenneth. *FDR: The Beckoning of Destiny, 1882–1928*. New York: G.P. Putnam's Sons, 1971.
Dawson, Nelson, ed. *Brandeis and America*. Lexington: University Press of Kentucky, 1989.
De Grazia, Victoria. *The Culture of Consent*. Cambridge: Cambridge University Press, 1981.

DeBoer, John. "Current Importance of the Literature of Power and Imagination." In *Adapting Reading Programs to Wartime Needs,* ed. William S. Gray. Chicago: University of Chicago Press, 1943.

Degler, Carl N. "The Third Revolution." In *The New Deal: The Critical Issues,* ed. Otis L. Graham, Jr. Boston: Little, Brown, 1971.

Deleuze, Gilles, and Felix Guattari. *A Thousand Plateaus: Capitalism and Schizophrenia.* Minneapolis: University of Minnesota Press, 1987.

Derber, Milton. *The American Idea of Industrial Democracy, 1865–1965.* Urbana: University of Illinois Press, 1970.

Derber, Milton, and Edwin Young. *Labor and the New Deal.* Madison: University of Wisconsin Press, 1957.

Devinat, Paul. *Scientific Management in Europe.* Geneva: International Labour Office, 1927.

Dewey, John. *Democracy and Education.* New York: The Free Press, 1916.

———. "Psychology and Social Practice" (1899). In *John Dewey: The Middle Works, 1899–1924.* 15 vols. Carbondale: Southern Illinois University Press, 1976–1983, 1:149–50.

———. "Significance of the Problem of Knowledge" (1897). In *John Dewey: The Early Works, 1882–1898.* 5 vols. Carbondale: Southern Illinois University Press, 1967–1972, 5:21–22.

Divine, Robert A. *American Immigration Policy, 1924–1952.* New Haven, Conn.: Yale University Press, 1957.

Dorfman, Joseph. *The Economic Mind in American Civilization.* New York: Viking, 1959.

"Draft Objector Starved Out." Sacramento, Calif. *Union,* June 30, 1943.

"Draft Offices Here Swamped by Phone Calls." New York *Sun,* October 14, 1940.

"Draft Rejections Due to Youth 'Coddling,' Expert Asserts." Washington, D.C. *Star,* March 15, 1943.

"Draft Threat Reduces Absenteeism in Plant." Washington, D.C. *Star,* March 7, 1943.

Draft Welfare Committee, United Office and Professional Workers of America, New York. Letter to President F.D. Roosevelt, June 9, 1941. National Archives, Record Group 147, Stack Area 17W4, Row 11, Compartment 02, Entry 2, Records of the Selective Service System, Box 33.

"Draftees Asked to Bring Evidence of Graduation." Charleston, W.Va. *Gazette,* May 27, 1943.

Du Bois, W.E.B. *The Souls of Black Folk.* New York: A.C. McClurg, 1903; reprint, New York: Penguin Classics, 1989.

DuBridge, L.A. "Science and National Policy," *American Scientist* 34 (April 1946): 226–38.

Durkheim, Emile. *The Division of Labor in Society,* trans. W.D. Halls. New York: The Free Press, 1984.

———. *The Elementary Forms of the Religious Life,* trans. Joseph Ward Swain. New York: The Free Press, 1915.

———. *The Rules of the Sociological Method,* trans. W.D. Halls. New York: The Free Press, 1982.

———. *Suicide,* trans. John A. Spaulding and George Simpson. New York: The Free Press, 1951.

"Education Board Puts in Busiest Day." *New York Times*, October 17, 1940.
Educational Advisory Committee of the New York State Economic Council. *Niagara Falls Report*. New York: New York State Economic Council, February 1, 1935.
"Educator Asks Preinduction Youth Training." Seattle, Wash. *Post-Intelligencer*, May 13, 1943.
Eells, Walter Crosby. *Surveys of American Higher Education*. New York: The Carnegie Foundation for the Advancement of Teaching, 1937.
"An Effective Tableau for War Graduation." *The American School Board Journal* 107, 2 (August 1943): 47.
Efficiency in High Schools: Studies, 1911–14, in the Application of the Principles of Scientific Management to High School Problems. A collection of bulletins of the High School Teachers Association of New York City.
Elkin, Henry. "Aggressive and Erotic Tendencies in Army Life." *The American Journal of Sociology* 51 (March 1946): 5.
Elliott, William Y. *The Pragmatic Revolt in Politics: Syndicalism, Fascism and the Constitutional State*. New York: Howard Fertig, 1968.
Ellis, John. *The Sharp End: The Fighting Man in World War II*. New York: Charles Scribner's Sons, 1980.
Enough and on Time. War Department, Signal Corps, National Archives, Record Group 111, Series TF/2094, 1942.
Evans, George, by command of Lt. Gen. Brehon B. Somervell. "Mental Induction Standards and Procedures," 11 May 1943. National Archives, Record Group 337, AGF 353, Entry 55, Box 677.
Evans, Holden A. "An Analysis of Machine-Shop Methods: The Government Has No Monopoly of Inefficient Shops." *American Machinist* 31 (1910): 568–73.
———. *Cost Keeping and Scientific Management*. New York: McGraw-Hill Book Co., 1911.
———. *One Man's Fight for a Better Navy*. New York: Dodd, Mead and Co., 1940.
———. "Reduction in Cost of Navy Yard Work." *American Machinist* 31 (June 30, 1910): 1200–1202.
Fass, Paula. *Outside In: Minorities and the Transformation of American Education*. New York: Oxford University Press, 1989.
Feiss, Richard. "Personal Relationship as a Basis of Scientific Management." Paper read before the Society to Promote the Science of Management, Philadelphia, Pa., October 23, 1915. Printed in *Bulletin of the Society to Promote the Science of Management* 1, 6 (November 1915): 5–15.
Fenton, Norman. *Mental Hygiene in School Practice*. Stanford, Calif.: Stanford University Press, 1943.
Fenton, Norman, and Dean A. Worcester. *An Introduction to Educational Measurements*. New York: Ginn & Co., 1928.
Field Psychiatry for the General Medical Officer. PMF 5011. Adapted from a British Training Film by the Army Pictorial Services Signal Corps. National Archives, Record Group 111, Series M/1167, 1945.
Fighting Men, Baptism of Fire. War Department, Signal Corps. National Archives, Record Group 111, Series TF/2014, 1943.
Flicker, David, and Paul Weiss. "Nostalgia and Its Military Implications." *War Medicine* 4, 4 (October 1943).

Flora, A.C. "Today's Challenge to American Schools." *The American School Board Journal* 108, 3 (March 1944): 48.
"For Resuming Education." Baton Rouge, La. *Times*, November 16, 1942.
Foucault, Michel. *The Care of the Self*. New York: Vintage Books, 1988.
———. *Discipline and Punish*. New York: Vintage Books, 1979.
———. "On the Genealogy of Ethics." In *Ethics: Subjectivity and Truth*, ed. Paul Rabinow. New York: The New Press, 1997.
"Four Years Given Draft Evader Pair." Clinton, Iowa *Herald*, April 7, 1943.
Freedman, Harry. "The Services of the Military Mental Hygiene Unit." *American Journal of Psychiatry* 100, 1 (July 1943): 34.
Freidel, Frank. *Franklin D. Roosevelt: The Apprenticeship*. Boston: Little, Brown, 1952.
Fusfeld, Daniel. *The Economic Thought of Franklin D. Roosevelt and the Origins of the New Deal*. New York: Columbia University Press, 1956; reprint, New York: AMS Press, 1970.
Gallagher, Lawrence. "A War Pattern for Teachers." *The American School Board Journal* 107, 3 (September 1943): 16.
Gallup, George. *The Gallup Poll, Public Opinion 1935-1971*. New York: Random House, 1972.
George, David Lloyd. *War Memoirs of David Lloyd George*. 2 vols. London: Odhams Press, 1942.
Giedion, Siefried. *Mechanization Takes Command: A Contribution to Anonymous History*. New York: Oxford University Press, 1969.
Gies, Joseph. "Automating the Worker." *American Heritage of Invention and Technology* 6, 3 (Winter 1991): 56–63.
Gilbert, James B. *Designing the Industrial State: The Intellectual Pursuit of Collectivism in America, 1880–1940*. Chicago: Quadrangle Books, 1972.
Grace, Alonzo G. *Educational Lessons from Wartime Training*. Washington, D.C.: American Council on Education, 1948.
Graebner, William. *The Engineering of Consent: Democracy and Authority in Twentieth-Century America*. Madison: University of Wisconsin Press, 1987.
Gray, William S., ed. *Adapting Reading Programs to Wartime Needs*. Chicago: University of Chicago Press, 1943.
Greenfield, Kent Roberts, Robert R. Palmer, and Bell I. Wiley. "Ground Forces in the Army: A Statistical Study." In *The Organization of Ground Combat Troops*. Washington, D.C.: Historical Division, Department of the Army, 1947.
Griffin, John D.M., S.R. Laycock, and W. Line. *Mental Hygiene: A Manual for Teachers*. New York: American Book Co., 1940.
Haber, Samuel. *Efficiency and Uplift: Scientific Management in the Progressive Era, 1890–1920*. Chicago: University of Chicago Press, 1964.
Halder, F. "Gutachten zu Field Service Regulations." *U.S. Army Historical Division Study*, No. P133. Bonn, 1953.
Hankins, Frank. Review of *National Unity and Disunity*. *The Annals of the American Academy of Political and Social Science* 217 (September 1941): 173.
Harrison, Forrest. "Psychiatry in the Navy." *War Medicine* 3, 2 (February 1943).
Hartley, William. "Films for Asiatic Studies in American Education." *The School Review* 51, 4 (April 1943): 219.

Hartung, Maurice. "Educational News and Editorial Comment." *The School Review* 51, 5 (May 1943): 259.
Hauptman, Laurence M. *The Iroquois Struggle for Survival: World War II to Red Power.* Syracuse, N.Y.: Syracuse University Press, 1985.
Havighurst, Robert. "Educational News and Editorial Comment." *The School Review* 51, 2 (February 1943): 67–71.
Headquarters Army Ground Forces, Army War College, 24 November 1943. To: Commanding General, Tank Destroyer Replacement Training Center, North Camp Hood, Texas. By Command of Lt. Gen. Leslie J. McNair. National Archives, Record Group 337, AGF 341, Entry 55, Box 587, Binder 7.
Headquarters, IRTC, Fort McClellan, Alabama. To: Commanding General, Replacement and School Command, Birmingham, Alabama, 21 September 1943. National Archives, Record Group 337, AGF 353.01, Entry 55, Box 715.
Headquarters Third Army, Fort Sam Houston, Texas. "Enlisted Personnel for Quartermaster Troop Transport Companies." To: Commanding General, Army Ground Forces, Army War College, Washington, D.C., 13 September 1943. National Archives, Record Group 337, AGF 353, Entry 55, Box 665.
Heeres Dienstvorschrift 300. *Truppenfuhrung.* Berlin, 1936.
Hegel, G.W.F. *Reason in History.* New York: Macmillan, 1953.
Herge, Henry C. *Wartime College Training Programs of the Armed Services.* With chapters on special phases by Sidney L. Pressey, Harold Sprout, Gordon K. Chalmers, Raymond J. Connolly, and Edward C. Elliott, for the Commission on Implications of Armed Services Educational Programs. Washington, D.C.: American Council on Education, 1948.
Herzberg, Max. *Situation in Which Citizenship Can Be Taught.* Plainfield: New Jersey Secondary School Teachers' Association, 1941.
"High School Draft Card Ring Smashed by G-Men." Oakland, Calif. *Post Enquirer,* June 19, 1943.
High School Victory Corps. United States Office of Education, Victory Corps Series, Pamphlet No. 1. Washington, D.C.: Government Printing Office, 1942.
"High School Victory Corps Announced." *Education for Victory* 1, 15 (October 1, 1942).
Himmelreich, W.F. "Patterns of Discipline." *The American School Board Journal* 108, 3 (March 1944): 25.
"History of the Navy College Training Programs." Manuscript on file in Office of Naval History, Navy Department, Navy Department, Bureau of Naval Personnel, History Project, 81.
Hollingshead, A.B. "Adjustment to Military Life." *American Journal of Sociology* 51 (1946).
Hong, Nelson. "Draft Dodger Spends 15 Months in Woods." Tacoma, Wash. *News-Tribune,* May 7, 1943.
Hoskins, Harold B. "American Unity and Our Foreign-Born Citizens." *The Annals of the American Academy of Political and Social Science* 220 (March 1942): 158.
Hovland, Carl I., Arthur Lumsdaine, and Fred Sheffield. *The American Soldier, Vol. 3: Experiments on Mass Communication.* Princeton, N.J.: Princeton University Press, 1949.

Hoxie, Robert Franklin. *Scientific Management and Labor*. N.p., 1915; reprint, New York: Augustus M. Kelley, 1966.
Huebner, Grover G. "Americanization of the Immigrant." *The Annals of the American Academy of Political and Social Science* (May 1906): 191–213.
Hughes, Thomas P. *American Genesis: A Century of Invention and Technological Enthusiasm, 1870–1970*. New York: Penguin Books, 1989.
———. *Networks of Power: Electrification in Western Society, 1880–1930*. Baltimore: Johns Hopkins University Press, 1983.
Hunt, Edward Eyre, ed. *Scientific Management since Taylor: A Collection of Authoritative Papers*. New York: McGraw-Hill Book Co., 1924.
Huntington, Samuel. *The Soldier and the State*. New York: Vintage Books, 1964.
"Ignorant Collegians Assailed by Moses." *New York Times*, January 11, 1939, 3.
Improvement in Instruction in the Required Course in Citizenship in California High Schools. Report of the Subcommittee on United States History and Civics of the General Education Committee. A Joint Committee of the California State Department of Education and the Association of California Secondary School Principals. Sacramento, Calif.: State Department of Education, 1941.
"Indian Chief Defies Draft, Move to Arrest Him Fails." Buffalo, N.Y. *Courier-Express*, October 17, 1940.
Instruction of the Soldier, Dismounted, Without Arms, Positions and Facings. War Department, Army Signal Corps. National Archives, Record Group 111, Series TF/0248, 1941.
Introduction to the Army. War Department, Army Signal Corps. National Archives, Record Group 111, Series TF/2067.
Irigaray, Luce. *Speculum of the Other Woman*, trans. Gillian Gill. Ithaca, N.Y.: Cornell University Press, 1985.
Irwin, Manley. "Reading Materials for the Middle Grades." In *Adapting Reading Programs to Wartime Needs*, ed. William S. Gray. Chicago: University of Chicago Press, 1943, 45.
"Jackson High Boys Soft? It Isn't So, Says Watson: Tells of Test in Gym." Jackson, Mich. *Citizen-Patriot*, April 18, 1943.
Jaffe, Louis L. *Judicial Control of Administrative Action*. Boston: Little, Brown, 1965.
James, C.L.R. et al. *Fighting Racism in World War II*. New York: Pathfinder, 1980.
Jameson, Augusta. "Guidance of Youth in High Schools and Junior Colleges." In *Adapting Reading Programs to Wartime Needs*, ed. William S. Gray. Chicago: University of Chicago Press, 1943, 34.
Jameson, Fredric. *The Political Unconscious: Narrative as a Socially Symbolic Act*. Ithaca, N.Y.: Cornell University Press, 1981.
"Jefferies, Former Boxing Champion, Writes Views as Conscientious Objector." Syracuse, N.Y. *Herald-Journal*, October 18, 1940.
"Johns Hopkins Research Staff to Aid Government, Industry." *Washington Post*, June 20, 1946.
Johnson, Brig. Gen. Hugh. Notes of Lecture Delivered at the Army War College, Washington, D.C., October 20, 1939. National Archives, Record Group 147, Stack Area 17W4, Row 11, Compartment 02, Entry 2, Records of the Selective Service System, Box 33.

———. "Selective Service—Now." Radio Address by Gen. Hugh S. Johnson over Station WJSV, Columbia Broadcasting Service, Washington, D.C., August 23, 1940. National Archives, Record Group 147, Stack Area 17W4, Row 11, Compartment 02, Entry 2, Records of the Selective Service System, Box 33.

Johnson, Broderick, ed. *Navajos and World War II*. Tsaile, Ariz.: Navajo Community College Press, 1977.

Johnson, Eldon L. "Lessons from Military-Sponsored College Training." *Journal of Higher Education* 16 (March 1945): 113–20.

Johnson, Harry. "Civic Education in Eugene High School." *Harvard Educational Review* 12 (March 1942) 165–70.

Johnson, Philip. "Marine Corps Hymn in Navajo." *Master Key* (September 1945): 153.

Joint Board on Scientific Information Policy for Office of Scientific Research and Development, War Department, and Navy Department. *Electronics Warfare: A Report on Radar Countermeasures*. Washington, D.C.: Joint Board on Scientific Information Policy, November 29, 1945.

"Judge Denies Soldier's Plea as Objector." Little Rock, *Arkansas Democrat*, March 4, 1943.

"Jury Adjourns Draftees' Case," New York *Sun*, October 17, 1940.

Kadushin, J. "Mathematics in Present-Day Industry." *The Mathematics Teacher* 35 (October 1942): 260–64.

Kallen, H.M. *Americans All*. Washington, D.C.: National Education Association, 1942.

———. "National Solidarity and the Jewish Minority." *The Annals of the American Academy of Political and Social Science* 223 (September 1942): 17.

Kasson, John. *Civilizing the Machine: Technology and Republican Values in America, 1875–1920*. New York: Grossman, 1976.

Kefauver, Grayson. "Preface." In Stanford University School of Education Faculty, *Education in Wartime and After*. New York: D. Appleton-Century Co., 1943.

Kelly, George Armstrong. "Who Needs a Theory of Citizenship?" In *Theorizing Citizenship*, ed. Ronald Beiner. Albany: State University of New York Press, 1995.

Kennedy, David. *Over Here: The First World War and Economic Society*. New York: Oxford University Press, 1980.

Kennett, Lee B. *G. I.: The American Soldier in World War II*. Norman: University of Oklahoma Press, 1997.

Kerber, Linda K. *Women of the Republic: Intellect and Ideology in Revolutionary America*. New York: Norton, 1980.

Kingdon, Frank. "Being an American in Wartime." *The Annals of the American Academy of Political and Social Science* 222 (July 1942): 1.

Kitson, Harry Dexter, and Mary Rebecca Lindenfelter. *Vocations for Boys*. New York: Harcourt, Brace and Co., 1942.

Klein, David. *Mental Hygiene: The Psychology of Personal Adjustments*. New York: Henry Holt and Co., 1944.

Kliebard, Herbert M. *The Struggle for the American Curriculum*. New York: Routledge, 1995.

Klineberg, Otto. "Race Prejudice and the War." *The Annals of the American Academy of Political and Social Science* 223 (September 1942): 190-98.

Kymlicka, Will, and Wayne Norman. "Return of the Citizen: A Survey of Recent Work on Citizenship Theory." In *Theorizing Citizenship*, ed. Ronald Beiner. Albany: State University of New York Press, 1995.

"Lack of Students Makes AC Campus a 'Deserted Village.'" Fargo, N.D. *Forum*, March 18, 1943.

Lake, Ernest G. "A Superintendent Plans for the Future in Vocational Education." *The American School Board Journal* 108, 3 (March 1944): 17.

Leighton, Alexander H. *The Governing of Men*. Princeton, N.J.: Princeton University Press, 1945.

Leiserson, William M. *Adjusting Immigrant and Industry*. New York: Harper, 1924.

Levine, Rhonda F. *Class Struggle and the New Deal: Industrial Labor, Industrial Capital, and the State*. Lawrence: University Press of Kansas, 1988.

Lipsitz, George. *Rainbow at Midnight: Labor and Culture in the 1940s*. Urbana: University of Illinois Press, 1994.

Loomis, Roger Sherman, and Gabriel M. Liegey. *The Fight for Freedom: College Readings in Wartime*. New York: Farrar & Rinehart, 1943.

Lowi, Theodore J. *The End of Liberalism: The Second Republic of the United States*, 2nd ed. New York: Norton, 1979.

Magill, Walter. "The War Has Set the Pattern for—The Role of Industrial Education in the Postwar Period." *The American School Board Journal* 108, 6 (June 1944): 18.

Maier, Charles S. "Between Taylorism and Technocracy: European Ideologies and the Vision of Industrial Productivity in the 1920s." *Journal of Contemporary History* 5 (1970): 27-61.

"Man Refuses Army Service, Gets Three Years in Prison." Seattle, Wash. *Times*, March 2, 1943.

Marx, Karl. *The Communist Manifesto*. New York: W.W. Norton, 1988.

———. *Selected Writings*, ed. Lawrence H. Simon. Indianapolis: Hackett Publishing Co., 1994.

Matthew, Robert John. *Language and Area Studies in the Armed Services: Their Future Significance*. Washington, D.C.: American Council on Education, 1947.

Maxwell, Sue. "A Birmingham High School Meets the Challenge of War." *The American School Board Journal* 107 (July 1943): 20.

McAndrew, William. "The Danger of Running a Fool Factory." *Ladies' Home Journal* 29 (September 1912).

McCall, William Anderson. *How to Measure in Education*. New York: Macmillan, 1922.

McConnell, T.R., and Malcolm M. Willey, eds. Foreword to the issue on "Higher Education and the War." *The Annals of the American Academy of Political and Social Science* 231 (January 1944): vii.

McPherson, James M. *Battle Cry of Freedom*. New York: Oxford University Press, 1988.

Mearns, William Hughes. "Our Medieval High Schools—Shall We Educate Children for the Twelfth or the Twentieth Century?" *Saturday Evening Post* 184 (March 2, 1912): 18-19.

Mental Hygiene Committee of the Vocational Adjustment Bureau for Girls. *Mental Hygiene Project at Kindergarten Level, 1937–1939*. Report to the Board of Education, City of New York. New York: Mental Hygiene Committee, 1939.
Merriam, Charles. *The Making of Citizens*. Chicago: University of Chicago Press, 1931; reprint, New York: Teachers College Press, 1966.
Method of Directing the Work of Government Employees. Hearing before the Committee on Labor, House of Representatives, Sixty-Fourth Congress, First Session, on H.R. 8665, A Bill to Regulate the Method of Directing the Work of Government Employees; March 30, 31, April 1, 4, 1916. Washington, D.C.: Government Printing Office, 1916, H-147-9, 133.
Miller, Toby. *The Well-Tempered Self: Citizenship, Culture, and the Postmodern Subject*. Baltimore: Johns Hopkins University Press, 1993.
Millett, John D. *The Organization and Role of the Army Service Forces*. Washington, D.C.: Office of the Chief of Military History, Department of the Army, 1954.
Millis, Walter. *Arms and Men*. New York: Putnam, 1956.
Mitchell, Theodore C. "Loss of Efficiency in the Recitation." *Educational Review* 45 (January 1913): 27–28.
Miyamoto, Shotaro Frank. "Immigrants and Citizens of Japanese Origin." *The Annals of the American Academy of Political and Social Science* 223 (September 1942): 107–13.
Monk, Ray. *Ludwig Wittgenstein: The Duty of Genius*. New York: The Free Press, 1990.
Moutet, Aimee. "Les origines du systeme de Taylor en France: Le point de vue patronal (1907–1914)." *Le Mouvement Social* 93 (October–December 1975): 15–49.
Munroe, James Phinney. *New Demands in Education*. Garden City, N.Y.: Doubleday, Page & Co., 1912.
Munsterberg, Hugo. "Psychology and the Navy." *The North American Review* 197 (February 1913): 159–80.
Nash, Gerald D. *The Great Depression and World War II: Organizing America, 1933–1945*. New York: St. Martin's Press, 1979.
National Distillers Products Corporation (advertisement). *New Yorker*, June 10, 1939, 81.
Nauheim, F. *Behold the Upright*. New York: Apollo Books, 1970.
"The Navy V-12 Program." *Journal of the American Association of Collegiate Registrars* 19 (January 1944): 161–69.
"N.E.A. Asks Federal Aid for Wartime Schools." *The American School Board Journal* 107, 2 (August 1943): 44.
"The Negro's War." *Fortune* (June 1942).
Nelson, Daniel. *Frederick W. Taylor and the Rise of Scientific Management*. Madison: University of Wisconsin Press, 1980.
———. *Managers and Workers: Origins of the New Factory System in the United States, 1880–1920*. Madison: University of Wisconsin Press, 1975.
Nelson, Daniel, and Stuart Campbell. "Taylorism Versus Welfare Work in American Industry: H.L. Gantt and the Bancrofts." *Business History Review* 46 (Spring 1972): 1–16.

Nietzsche, Friedrich. *The Gay Science*, trans. Walter Kaufmann. New York: Vintage Books, 1974.
———. *The Will to Power*, trans. Walter Kaufmann. New York: Vintage Books, 1968.
Nix, B.G. Headquarters, Tank Destroyer Replacement Training Center, North Camp Hood, Texas, 10 November 1943. "Request for Reassignment of Non-English Enlisted Men." To: Commanding General, Replacement and School Command, AGF, Birmingham 3, Alabama. National Archives, Record Group 337, AGF 341, Entry 55, Box 587, Binder 7.
Northwest Scientific Association. "An Experiment in Education: Wartime Activities and Programs in Northwest Educational Institutions." *Northwest Science* 18 (February, May, August, and November 1944): 25–32, 52–56, 65–75, 90–103; 19 (February, May, August, and November 1945): 13–27, 34–51, 70–75, 103–7.
Novick, David, Melvin Anshen, and W.C. Truppner. *Wartime Production Controls*. New York: Columbia University Press, 1949.
"Objector to Draft Tells F.B.I. of Many Hardships in Hiding." Little Rock, Ark. *Gazette*, January 3, 1943.
Office of the Surgeon General. Memo of (3 October 1943) GNGAP-I, 3d Ind., Headquarters Army Ground Forces, Army War College, Washington, D.C. To: Commanding General, XIII Corps, Fort DuPont, Delaware. National Archives, Record Group 337, Box 584, AGF 341 (c), Binder No. 4, Quotation from paragraph 2, Circular Letter No. 114, 22 June 1943.
Osborn, Frederick. "Foreword." To Samuel Stouffer, Edward Suchman, Leland DeVinney, Shirley Star, and Robin Williams, Jr., *The American Soldier, Vol. 1: Adjustment During Army Life*. Princeton, N.J.: Princeton University Press, 1949.
Palmer, Robert R. "Mobilization of the Ground Army." *The Organization of Ground Combat Troops*. Washington, D.C.: Historical Division Department of the Army, 1947.
"Pass the Teen-Age Draft." St. Louis, Mo. *Globe-Democrat*, November 1, 1942.
"Paterson Shows Way to Get Health Records of Rejected Men." Patterson, N.J. *Call*, March 3, 1943.
Patten, Simon. "An Economic Measure of School Efficiency." *Educational Review* 41 (May 1911): 467–69.
Patterson, Robert P. "Responsibility for Military Procurement Before the Senate Special Committee Investigating the National Defense Program." 77th Congress, 2nd Session, 16 December 1942. In *The Organization and Role of The Army Service Forces*, ed. John Millett. Washington, D.C.: Office of the Chief of Military History, Department of the Army, 1954, Appendix H.
Paul, Doris. *The Navajo Code Talkers*. Philadelphia, Pa.: Dorrance, 1973.
Payne Educational Sociology Foundation. "Our Changing Armed Forces." *The Journal of Educational Sociology* 16 (May 1943): 533–90. Special Issue, ed. Francis J. Brown.
Perry, Donald R. "Aliens in the United States." *The Annals of the American Academy of Political and Social Science* 223 (September 1942): 1.
Person, Harlow. Foreword to Frederick Winslow Taylor, *Scientific Management*. New York: Harper & Row, 1947.

———. *Industrial Education: A System of Training for Men Entering Upon Trade and Commerce.* New York: Houghton, Mifflin and Co., 1907.
"Phone Queries Conscription." New York *Journal & American*, October 14, 1940.
Physical Fitness Through Physical Education for the Victory Corps. United States Office of Education, Victory Corps Series, Pamphlet No. 2. Washington, D.C.: Government Printing Office, 1942.
Pittenger, B.F. "Postwar Educational Controversies." *The American School Board Journal* 107, 5 (November 1943): 18.
Planning Commission of the National Council of Teachers of English. "The Role of the Teacher of English in Wartime." *English Journal* (January 1942).
Plato. *The Republic*, trans. Francis Cornford. New York: Oxford University Press, 1945.
Pocock, J.G.A. "The Ideal of Citizenship Since Classical Times." *Queens Quarterly* 99, 1 (Spring 1992). In *Theorizing Citizenship*, ed. Ronald Beiner. Albany: State University of New York Press, 1995.
Polenberg, Richard. *War and Society: The United States, 1941–1945.* New York: J.B. Lippincott, 1972.
Pollock, Horatio. "What May Be Hoped for in the Prevention of Mental Disease." *The Psychiatric Quarterly* 4 (1930).
Porter, Ray E. "Memorandum for the Commanding Generals, Army Air Forces, Army Ground Forces, Army Service Forces," 24 August 1943. National Archives, Record Group 337, AGF 353.01, Entry 55, Box 715.
Porter, Theodore M. *The Rise of Statistical Thinking, 1820–1900.* Princeton, N.J.: Princeton University Press, 1986.
Posnock, Ross. "Henry James, Veblen and Adorno: The Crisis of the Modern Self." *Journal of American Studies* 21 (1987): 31–54.
"Pre-Induction Course Offered." Grand Rapids, Mich. *Herald*, June 6, 1943.
President's Research Committee on Social Trends. *Recent Social Trends in the United States*, Vols. I and II. New York: McGraw-Hill Book Co., 1933.
"Procedure Smooth." *New York Times*, October 17, 1940.
"Process of Draft Is Given in Detail." *New York Times*, October 13, 1940.
Purcell, Edward A., Jr. *The Crisis of Democratic Theory: Scientific Naturalism and the Problem of Value.* Lexington: University Press of Kentucky, 1973.
Pursell, Carroll. "The American Ideal of a Democratic Technology." In *The Technological Imagination: Theories and Fictions*, ed. Teresa de Lauretis, Andreas Huysen, and Kathleen Woodward. Madison, Wis.: Coda Press, 1980.
———. *The Machine in America: A Social History of Technology.* Baltimore: Johns Hopkins University Press, 1995.
Pyle, Ernie. "Ceremonial Dances in the Pacific." In U.S. Bureau of Indian Affairs, *Indians in the War.* Chicago: U.S. Department of Interior, Office of Indian Affairs, 1946.
"The Questionnaire Which Selective Service Registrants Will Fill Out After Oct. 16." Buffalo, N.Y. *Evening News*, October 12, 1940.
Quigley, Thomas J. "Conflicting National Cultures in American Schools." *The American School Board Journal* 108, 3 (March 1944): 22.
Rabinbach, Anson. *The Human Motor: Energy, Fatigue, and the Origins of Modernity.* Berkeley: University of California Press, 1991.

Railey, Hilton. "Morale in the U.S. Army: An Appreciation." Written for the *New York Times*, September 29, 1941. Typescript in USAMHI Library.
Read, Cecil. "Efficiency of Methods in Solving Algebraic Equations." *Bulletin, Municipal University of Wichita* (University Studies Bulletin No. 3, Wichita, Kans.) 12, 11 (1937): 29.
"Registration of Youths to Open Today." Little Rock, Ark. *Gazette*, December 11, 1942.
Reid, Ira D. *In a Minor Key: Negro Youth in Fact and Fiction.* Washington, D.C.: American Council on Education, 1940.
Reilly, Philip. *The Surgical Solution: A History of Involuntary Sterilization in the United States.* Baltimore: Johns Hopkins University Press, 1991.
Reinert, Paul C. Review of Edgar W. Knight, *Progress and Educational Perspective* (New York: Macmillan, 1942). In *The School Review: A Journal of Secondary Education* 51, 1 (January 1943): 56.
Reports of the Chief of Ordnance, 1911, 1912, 1913, and 1914. Washington, D.C.: Government Printing Office.
Robinson, Glen O. *American Bureaucracy: Public Choice and Public Law.* Ann Arbor: University of Michigan Press, 1991.
Rogin, Michael Paul. " 'The Sword Became a Flashing Vision': D.W. Griffith's *The Birth of a Nation.*" In Rogin, *Ronald Reagan, the Movie and Other Episodes in Political Demonology.* Berkeley: University of California Press, 1987, 190–235.
Roosevelt, Franklin, and Felix Frankfurter. *Roosevelt and Frankfurter: Their Correspondence.* Annotated by Max Freedman. Boston: Atlantic Monthly Press, 1967.
Rosanoff, A.J. *Manual of Psychiatry and Mental Hygiene.* New York: John Wiley & Sons, 1938.
Rose, Arnold. "The Social Structure of the Army." *The American Journal of Sociology* 51, 5 (March 1946): 364.
Ross, Dorothy. *The Origins of American Social Science.* New York: Cambridge University Press, 1991.
Ross, Katherine Bogart. Letter to Gen. Lewis Hershey, October 14, 1941, Erie, Pennsylvania. National Archives, Record Group 147, Stack Area 17W4, Row 11, Compartment 02, Entry 2, Records of the Selective Service System, Box 33.
Ruch, Giles M., and George D. Stoddard. *Tests and Measurements in High School Instruction.* Yonkers, N.Y. and Chicago: World Book Co., 1927.
Ruggles, Arthur. "A Symposium on Psychiatry in the Armed Forces." *The American Journal of Psychiatry* 100, 1 (July 1943): 11.
Russell, John Dale, ed. *Higher Education under War Conditions.* Proceedings of the Institute for Administrative Officers of Higher Institutions, Vol. XV. Chicago: University of Chicago Press, 1943.
Samuel, Lawrence R. *Pledging Allegiance: American Identity and the Bond Drive of World War II.* Washington, D.C.: Smithsonian Institution Press, 1997.
Sanka Coffee (advertisement). *New Yorker*, June 10, 1939.
Savage, Howard J. Foreword to Walter Crosby Eells, *Surveys of American Higher Education.* New York: The Carnegie Foundation for the Advancement of Teaching, 1937.

"Scatter-Brained! No Wonder He Never Accomplishes Anything Worthwhile!" *System: The Magazine of Business* 51 (January 1927): 119.
Schibsby, Marian. "Private Agencies Aiding the Foreign-Born." *The Annals of the American Academy of Political and Social Science* 223 (September 1942): 182–89.
"Scholarship Winner Refuses to Register." Utica, N.Y. *Observer-Dispatch*, October 18, 1940.
Schultz, Frank. "Basic Research Needed for Postwar Educational Planning." *The American School Board Journal* 108, 6 (June 1944).
"Scientific Management." *Life and Labor* 2 (December 1912): 368–69.
Sears, Jesse. *An Autobiography*. Palo Alto, Calif.: Author, 1959.
———. *Public School Administration*. New York: The Ronald Press, 1947.
Sears, Jesse B., and Adin D. Henderson. *Cubberley of Stanford and His Contribution to American Education*. Standford, Calif.: Stanford University Press, 1957.
Segal, Howard P. *Technological Utopianism in American Culture*. Chicago: University of Chicago Press, 1985.
"The Selective Draft Now and in 1917." Schenectady, N.Y. *Union-Star*, October 17, 1940.
Selective Service Regulations, First Edition, September 23, 1940 to February 1, 1942. Washington, D.C.: Government Printing Office, 1944. National Archives, MR 1-9, Section VII, 31, Record Group 147, Stack Area 17W4, Row 12, Compartment 12, Entry 37, Records of the Selective Service System, Box 1.
Seltzer, Mark. *Bodies and Machines*. New York: Routledge, 1992.
Sennett, Richard. *Authority*. New York: Knopf, 1980.
"S.F. Draft Card Ring: School Boys Held." *San Francisco News*, June 19, 1943.
Shaffer, L.F. *The Psychology of Adjustment*. New York: Houghton Mifflin Co., 1936.
Shalloo, J.P., and Donald Young. "Foreword." *The Annals of the American Academy of Political and Social Science* 223 (September 1942): vii.
Sherman, Mandel. *Mental Hygiene and Education*. New York: Longmans, Green and Co., 1934.
Silk, Leonard, and David Vogel. *Ethics and Profits: The Crisis of Confidence in American Business*. New York: Simon and Schuster, 1976.
Skocpol, Theda. *States & Social Revolutions*. New York: Cambridge University Press, 1979.
Smith, R. Eberton. *The Army and Economic Mobilization*. Washington, D.C.: Office of the Chief of Military History, 1959.
Snedden, David. "Combining Efficiency and Democracy in Educational Administration." *The American School Board Journal* 42, 1 (January 1911).
"Soldier to Seek Release from Army." Little Rock, Ark. *Gazette*, March 4, 1943.
Sollors, Werner. *Beyond Ethnicity: Consent and Descent in American Culture*. New York: Oxford University Press, 1986.
Spalding, Willard D., and William C. Kvaraceus. "What Do We Mean by Democracy?" *The American School Board Journal* 108, 2 (February 1944): 50.
Spaulding, Frank E. *Measuring Textbooks*. New York: Newson and Co., 1922.
———. *School Superintendent in Action in Five Cities*. Rindge, N.H.: R.R. Smith, 1955.
Speier, Hans. "The Effect of War on the Social Order." *The Annals of the American Academy of Political and Social Science* 218 (November 1941): 87–96.

Spruyt, Hendrik. *The Sovereign State and Its Competitors*. Princeton, N.J.: Princeton University Press, 1994.

Stabile, Donald. *Prophets of Order*. Boston: South End Press, 1984.

Stanford University School of Education Faculty. *Education in Wartime and After*. New York: D. Appleton-Century Co., 1943.

Starr, Paul. *The Social Transformation of American Medicine: The Rise of a Sovereign Profession and the Making of a Vast Industry*. New York: Basic Books, 1982.

Stigler, Stephen M. *The History of Statistics: The Measurement of Uncertainty before 1900*. Cambridge, Mass.: Harvard University Press, 1986.

Stilgoe, John. "Privacy and Energy-Efficient Residential Site Design: An Example of Conduct." *Journal of Architectural Education* 37, 3–4 (Spring–Summer 1984): 20–25.

Stimpson, George. "Some Absenteeism Cures Hold Harsh Note." Cedar Rapids, Iowa *Gazette*, March 14, 1943.

Stonequist, Everett V. "The Restricted Citizen." *The Annals of the American Academy of Political and Social Science* 223 (September 1942): 149–56.

Stouffer, Samuel, Edward Suchman, Leland DeVinney, Shirley Star, and Robin Williams, Jr. *The American Soldier, Vol. 1: Adjustment During Army Life*. Princeton, N.J.: Princeton University Press, 1949.

———. *The American Soldier, Vol. 2: Combat and Its Aftermath*. Princeton, N.J.: Princeton University Press, 1949.

Sullivan, Harry Stack. "Psychiatry and the National Defense." *Psychiatry* 4 (May 1941).

Sullivan, Louis. "Kindergarten Chats." *Kindergarten Chats and Other Writings*. Rev. ed. 1918; reprint, New York: Writtenborn, 1965.

"Summer School Authorized to Aid Pre-Inductee Youths." Jackson, Mich. *Citizen-Patriot*, March 9, 1943.

"Swimming Course Planned for Pre-Induction Training at THS." Tucson, Ariz. *Star*, April 20, 1943.

Symonds, Perceval. *Mental Hygiene of the Social Child*. New York: Macmillan, 1934.

Taylor, Charles. "The Politics of Recognition." In *Multiculturalism*, ed. Amy Guttman. Princeton, N.J.: Princeton University Press, 1994.

———. *Sources of the Self*. Cambridge, Mass.: Harvard University Press, 1989.

Taylor, Frederick Winslow. "Government Efficiency." *Bulletin of the Taylor Society* 2, 5 (December 1916): 9.

———. "Personal History: Some Interesting Facts and Comments About His Early Training and Later Pastimes, by the Founder of Scientific Management, A Personal Letter." *Bulletin of the Taylor Society* 2, 5 (December 1916): 5–7.

———. *The Principles of Scientific Management*. In *Scientific Management*. New York: Frederick Taylor, 1911; reprint, New York: Harper & Row, 1947.

———. *Shop Management*. In *Scientific Management*. New York: Frederick Taylor, 1911; reprint, New York: Harper & Row, 1947.

———. *Testimony Before the Special House Committee. Hearings Before Special Committee of the House of Representatives to Investigate the Taylor and Other Systems of Shop Management Under Authority of H. Res. 90; Vol. III, pp. 1377–1508*. New York: Frederick Taylor, 1911; reprint, New York: Harper & Row, 1947.

Taylor Society. *Scientific Management in American Industry*, ed. H.S. Person. New York: Harper & Brothers, 1929.
"The Taylor System in Government Shops: The Report of the House Committee to Investigate Various Systems of Shop Management Is in General Adverse." *The Iron Age* 89 (March 21, 1912): 746.
"10 Who Refused to Register Face U.S. Grand Jury Quiz." Utica, N.Y. *Observer-Dispatch*, October 17, 1940.
Terman, L.M. *The Measurement of Intelligence*. Boston: Houghton Mifflin, 1916.
Thomas, Lawrence. "Relation of Music to Social Studies." *Curriculum Journal* 13 (April 1942): 166–69.
Thompson, C. Bertrand. *The Theory and Practice of Scientific Management*. Boston: Houghton Mifflin, 1917.
"3 City Teachers Refuse to Aid the Draft Today." *New York Times*, October 16, 1940.
Tichi, Cecelia. *Shifting Gears: Technology, Literature, Culture in Modernist America*. Chapel Hill: University of North Carolina Press, 1987.
Tilly, Charles. *Coercion, Capital and European States*. Cambridge: Basil Blackwell, 1990.
"Training for Teen-Ages." New Orleans, La. *Times-Picayune*, November 24, 1942.
Traub, Rainer. "Lenin and Taylor: The Fate of 'Scientific Management' in the (Early) Soviet Union." *Telos* 37 (Fall 1978): 82–92.
Truscott, L.K., Jr. Letter to Lt. Gen. Leslie McNair, 21 December 1942. Headquarters, First Provisional Brigade, Western Task Force. National Archives, Record Group 337, AGF 353, Entry 55, Box 678.
Tugwell, Rexford G. "The Principle of Planning and the Institution of Laissez Faire." *American Economic Review* 22, 1 (March 1932, Supplement): 75–92.
Turkington, Grace A., and Phil Conley. *Your Country and Mine: A Textbook in Democratic Citizenship*. Boston: Ginn & Co., 1943.
"Two Brothers Sentenced on Draft Charges." Little Rock, *Arkansas Democrat*, April 7, 1943.
Tyack, David, and Elisabeth Hansot. *Managers of Virtue: Public School Leadership in America, 1820–1980*. New York: Basic Books, 1982.
Ueda, Reed. "Ethnic Diversity and National Identity in Public School Texts." In *Learning from the Past*, ed. Diane Ravitch and Maris Vinovski. Baltimore: Johns Hopkins University Press, 1995.
Urwick, Lyndall, ed. *The Golden Book of Management: A Historical Record of the Life and Work of Seventy Pioneers*. London: N. Neame, 1956.
U.S. Bureau of Labor. "Intensity of Labor." In *Report on Condition of Women and Child Wage-Earners in the United States*. Vol. 9, *History of Women Workers in the United States*. Washington, D.C., 1911.
U.S. Congress. House of Representatives. *Methods of Directing the Work of Government Employees*. A Bill to Regulate the Methods of Directing the Work of Government Employees. 64th Cong., 1st sess., H.R. 8665, H-147-9. *Congressional Record* (March 31, 1916).
U.S. Congress. House of Representatives. Committee on Education. *Effect of Certain War Activities upon Colleges and Universities*. Report from the Committee on Education, pursuant to H. Res. 63. 79th Cong., 1st sess. Washington, D.C.: Government Printing Office, 1945.

U.S. Congress. Senate. *The Government's Wartime Research and Development, 1940–44*. Report from the Subcommittee on War Mobilization to the Committee on Military Affairs, pursuant to S. Res. 107. Part I, Survey of Government Agencies. Washington, D.C.: Government Printing Office, 1945.

———. *The Government's Wartime Research and Development, 1940–44*. Report from the Subcommittee on War Mobilization to the Committee on Military Affairs, pursuant to S. Res. 107 and S. Res. 146. Part II, Findings and Recommendations. Washington, D.C.: Government Printing Office, 1945.

———. *National Science Foundation*. Preliminary Report on Science Legislation from the Subcommittee on War Mobilization to the Committee on Military Affairs, pursuant to S. Res. 107 and S. Res. 146. Washington, D.C.: Government Printing Office, 1945.

———. *The Social Impact of Science: A Select Bibliography with a Section on Atomic Power*. Subcommittee on War Mobilization of the Committee on Military Affairs, pursuant to S. Res. 107 and S. Res. 146. Washington, D.C.: Government Printing Office, 1945.

U.S. Congress. Senate. National Affairs Committee. *Efficiency of Naval Militia*. 63rd Cong., 2nd sess., January 22, 1914. Senate Report 167, 1:6552.

U.S. War Department. Army Service Forces. Army Specialized Training Division. *Essential Facts About the Army Specialized Training Program* (Mimeographed). Washington, D.C.: Government Printing Office, 1943.

———. *Training Unit Contract Instructions for University and College Authorities Offering Training Facilities for Army Trainees*. Army Service Forces Manual M-102 (Mimeographed). Washington, D.C.: Government Printing Office, 1943.

U.S. War Department. Office of Chief of Staff. *Fifty Questions and Answers on Army Specialized Training Program*. Washington, D.C.: Government Printing Office, 1943.

"Value of Education After War Is Cited." New Orleans, La. *Times-Picayune*, December 16, 1942.

Van Creveld, Martin. *Fighting Power: German and U.S. Army Performance, 1939–1945*. Westport, Conn.: Greenwood Press, 1982.

Van Kleeck, Mary. "The Social Meaning of Good Management." In *Classics in Scientific Management: A Book of Readings*, ed. Donald Del Mar and Rodger D. Collons. University: University of Alabama Press, 1976.

Van Nice, C.R. "Democracy Aided by Its Educational Frills." *The American School Board Journal* 107, 2 (August 1943): 36.

Veblen, Thorstein. *The Engineers and the Price System*. New York: B.W. Huebsch, 1921.

———. *The Place of Science in Modern Civilization, and Other Essays*. New Brunswick, N.J.: Transaction Publishers, 1990.

"Victims of Absenteeism." Macon, Ga. *Telegraph*, March 2, 1943.

Wald, Priscilla. *Constituting Americans*. Durham, N.C.: Duke University Press, 1995.

Waldo, Dwight. *Democracy, Bureaucracy and Hypocrisy*. Berkeley: University of California Press, 1977.

Walzer, Michael. *Spheres of Justice: A Defense of Pluralism and Equality*. New York: Basic Books, 1983.

War Department Memo. "Strike at American Chain and Cable Company, Nonessen, Pennsylvania," September 10, 1941. National Archives, Record Group 147, Stack Area 17W4, Row 11, Compartment 02, Entry 2, Records of the Selective Service System, Box 33.

Ward, Geoffrey C. *A First-Class Temperament: The Emergence of Franklin Roosevelt.* New York: Harper & Row, 1989.

Ward, Lester. *Applied Sociology: A Treatise on the Conscious Improvement of Society by Society.* Boston, 1906.

Waring, Stephen. *Taylorism Transformed: Scientific Management Theory Since 1945.* Chapel Hill: University of North Carolina Press, 1991.

Warren, Maude Radford. "The Case of Seventeen Million Children—Is Our Public-School System Proving an Utter Failure?" *Ladies' Home Journal* 29 (August 1912).

———. "Medieval Methods for Modern Children." *Saturday Evening Post* 182 (March 12, 1912).

"Wartime Program for Our Colleges." Fort Dodge, Iowa *Messenger & Chronicle*, February 26, 1943.

Weber, Max. *Economy and Society*, ed. Guenther Roth and Claus Wittich. 2 vols. Berkeley: University of California Press, 1978.

———. "Legitimacy, Politics and the State." In *Legitimacy and the State*, ed. William Connolly. New York: New York University Press, 1984.

———. "The Nation." In *From Max Weber: Essays in Sociology*, trans. and ed. H.H. Gerth and C. Wright Mills. London: Routledge & Kegan Paul, 1948.

———. *The Protestant Ethic and the Spirit of Capitalism*, trans. Talcott Parsons. New York: Charles Scribner's Sons, 1958.

Weekly Bulletin. Headquarters Army Ground Forces, D.C. Number 3, 24 November 1942. Quotation from War Department letter AG 320.2 (11-4-42) OB-I-A, 9 November 1942. National Archives, Record Group 337, AGF 341, Box 586, Binder 5.

Weibe, Robert. *Self-Rule: A Cultural History of American Democracy.* Chicago: University of Chicago Press, 1995.

Weisberger, Bernard. *The New Industrial Society.* New York: Wiley, 1968.

Welch, William. Address delivered at the 20th Anniversary Meeting of the National Committee for Mental Hygiene, 1929. *Mental Hygiene* 14 (1930): 196.

West, Thomas. *The Competent Life: A Treatise on the Judicious Development, Direction and Employment of Man's Inherited Ability to Aid in the Betterment of Labor.* Cleveland, Ohio: The Cleveland Printing & Publishing Co., 1905.

Wheeler, C.B. "Questionnaire—Scientific Management." National Archives, Record Group 156, Box 266, File 213, Schedule 1-3, Section 1, p. 11.

White, Walter. "What the Negro Thinks of the Army." *The Annals of the American Academy of Political and Social Science* 223 (September 1942): 67.

Wilson, Richard Guy, Dianne H. Pilgrim, and Dickran Tashjian, eds. *The Machine Age in America, 1918–1941.* New York: Brooklyn Museum in Association with Abrams, 1986.

Wilson, Woodrow. *Congressional Government: A Study in American Politics.* 1885; reprint, Baltimore: Johns Hopkins University Press, 1981.

Wittgenstein, Ludwig. *On Certainty*, ed. G.E.M. Anscombe and G.H. von Wright,

trans. Denis Paul and G.E.M. Anscombe. New York: Harper and Row, 1972.
———. *Philosophical Investigation*, trans. G.E.M. Anscombe. New York: Macmillan, 1989.
———. *Tractatus Logico-Philosophicus*, trans. D.F. Pears and B.F. McGuinness. London: Routledge and Kegan Paul, 1961.
Wittke, Carl. *We Who Built America: The Saga of the Immigrant.* New York: Prentice-Hall, 1940.
Wittson, C.L., H. Harris, and W.A. Hunt. "Cryptic Nostalgia." *War Medicine* 3 (January 1943): 58–59.
———. "Detection of the Neuropsychiatrically Unfit." *U.S. Naval Military Bulletin* 40 (April 1942): 340–346.
"WMC Names Four Schools in State." New Orleans, La. *Times-Picayune*, February 7, 1943.
Wood, Leonard. "Heat Up the Melting Pot." Philadelphia, Pa. *Independent*, July 3, 1916, 15.
"'Work or Fight' Bill May Be Approved by Committee Today." Washington, D.C. *Star*, March 12, 1943.
W.R.A.: A Story of Human Conservation. Washington, D.C.: U.S. Department of Interior, War Relocation Authority, 1946.
Wrege, Charles, and Ronald Greenwood. *Frederick W. Taylor: The Father of Scientific Management.* Homewood, Ill.: Business One Irwin, 1991.
Wren, Daniel A. "Industrial Sociology: A Revised View of Its Antecedents." *Journal of the History of the Behavioral Sciences* 21, 4 (October 1985): 311–20.
Wright, Gordon. *The Ordeal of Total War: 1939–1945.* New York: Harper & Row, 1968.
Wright, Gwendolyn. *Moralism and the Model Home: Domestic Architecture and Cultural Conflict in Chicago, 1873–1913.* Chicago: University of Chicago Press, 1980.
Wright, J.C., and Charles R. Allen. *Efficiency in Education: A Study of the Applications of the Principles of Efficiency to Educational Administration, Supervision, and Methods of Teaching.* New York: John Wiley & Sons; London: Chapman & Hall, 1929.
"Young Men." Great Falls, Mont. *Tribune*, November 14, 1942.
"Youth and War: What to Plan for, What to Expect." Norfolk *Virginian-Pilot*, March 14, 1943.
Zangwill, Israel. *The Melting-Pot: Drama in Four Acts.* New York: Macmillan, 1909.
Zelinsky, Wilbur. *Exploring the Beloved Country: Geographic Forays into American Society and Culture.* Iowa City: University of Iowa Press, 1994.
Zipf, George Kingsley. *National Unity and Disunity.* Bloomington, Ind.: Principia, 1941.
Zizek, Slavoj. *The Sublime Object of Ideology.* London: Verso, 1989.
Zook, George F. "How the Colleges Went to War." *The Annals of the American Academy of Political and Social Science* 231 (January 1944): 6.
Zunz, Oliver. *Making America Corporate, 1870–1920.* Chicago: University of Chicago Press, 1990.

Index

A-I status, 53
Adams, Michael C.C., 57 n.7, 66
Adapting Reading Programs to Wartime Needs, 129 n.49, 130 n.54
Administration, 4; mass, 5; methods of, 30, 51
Administrative power, 5, 47
Administrative work, 53, 87, 103
Advisory Commission to the Council of National Defense, 51
Aitken, Hugh G.J., 34, 39 n.21, 40 n.24, 47 n.9
Akin, William, 14, 16
Alchon, Guy, 30, 38 n.2
Alien Registration Act, 120
Aliens in the United States, 129 n.36
Allen, Mary Emma, 127 n.8
Allen, William, 104, 110 n.5, 111 n.25, 133, 146 n.8
American Association of School Administrators, 137
American Chain and Cable Company, 55, 60 n.65

American Council on Education, 114, 136, 140, 146
American Expeditionary Force, 34, 45
American Legion, 135
American Psychiatric Association, 72
American Society of Mechanical Engineers, 15, 18, 36
The American Soldier, Vol. 3: Experiments on Mass Communication, 95 n.50
Americanization, 86, 114, 115
"Americanization of the Immigrant," 127 n.3
Americans All, 127 n.9
Anderson, Benedict, 7
The Annals of American Academy of Political and Social Science, 99–100, 116, 127 n.2, 128 n.15, 129 n.36, 143, 149 n.67
Aptitudes, 73
Arendt, Hannah, 7, 58 n.35
Army, 9, 34, 50, 51, 52, 55, 67, 89, 91; administration, 87; contract colleges,

140; discipline, 81; ground forces, 44, 45, 87; Information and Education Division, 75; Research Branch, 74; structure, 44
Army General Classification Test (AGCT), 70, 71, 73
Army Service Forces (ASF), 45, 46, 47, 52, 87
Army Specialized Training Program (ASTP), 140, 141, 142
Army Surgeon General, 73
Assembly line, 51
Assimilation, 5
Atomization, 14
Attack on Hidden Waste, 47
Attitudes, 73, 75, 81, 85, 92, 126, 135, 143, 151, 154, 156, 157, 159, 161, 163
Authority, 10, 19, 159; administrative, 6, 8, 99, 108; bureaucratic, 5, 9, 13, 93; centralization, 103; managerial, 14, 43; national, 93
Automobiles, 137
Aviation, 135
Axis threat, 135

Bagley, W.A., 137
Ballantine, Arthur, 33
Baltimore and Ohio Railroad, 15
Barth, Carl, 34, 57 n.9
Basic training, 72, 83, 85, 89, 140
Becht, J. George, 101
Becker, F.W., 32
Benedict, Ruth, 116, 128 n.21, 129 n.50
Benjamin, Walter, 7
Berube, Allan, 78 nn.39, 41
The Best War Ever, 57 n.7, 66
Bethlehem, Pennsylvania, 18
Bethlehem Steel, 30
Binet, Alfred, 104
Blankenburg, Rudolph, 18
Block Counting Test, 69
Board of Education to the Governor of the State of Connecticut, 146
Bobbitt, John Franklin, 102, 103, 107–8, 110 n.17, 111 nn.36, 38, 43
Body: destruction, 90; social, 13

Booklover Library, 18
Boorstin, Daniel, 48, 58 n.28
Booz, Frey, Allen and Hamilton, 46, 58 n.19
Bosnia-Herzegovina, 4
Bowman, K.M., 75, 79 n.59
Brandeis, Louis, 15
Brotz, H., 84
Burdette, Franklin, 148 n.45
Bureaucracy, 9, 19, 45, 74; industrial, 124; officials, 159; power, 48
Bureaucratic structure, 9, 13, 19; authority, 30, 92; systems, 53; work, 53, 122
Bureaucratization: authority, 55; warfare, 43
Burke-Wadsworth bill, 64
Bush, George, 11
Business, 43

California Journal of Secondary Education, 135
Callahan, Raymond, 103, 110 n.4, 111 n.22
Capitalism, 11
Capps, Admiral Washington, 31
Career, 152
Carnegie Foundation for the Advancement of Teaching, 105
Carroll, Herbert, 155, 156, 158
Case, Roscoe, 107, 111 n.40
Central Foundry Company, 53
Charlestown Navy Yard, 33
"Chicken," 85–86
Christian Peper Tobacco Co., 120, 129 n.34
Churchill, Winston, 44, 56 n.3
Citizen, 6, 8, 9, 13, 16, 29, 38, 44, 56, 63, 72, 74, 86, 122, 136, 143, 155, 163; soldier, 55, 86
Citizenship, 4, 6, 8, 16, 19, 20, 37, 44, 123, 126, 172; education, 107, 142
Civilian industrial production, 44
Classification, 64
Classification of Enlisted Men, Personnel Placement in the Army, 70, 78 n.34
Cleveland, Ohio, 35

Clothcraft Shops, The Joseph & Feiss Co., 17
Cohen, Robert, 72
College Training Corps, 140
Combat, 90
"Combining Efficiency and Democracy," 110 n.13
Coming Out Under Fire, 78 n.39
Committee on the Relationships of Higher Education to the Federal Government, 140
Common Council for American Unity in New York City, 115
The Communist Manifesto, 170
Community, 6, 19, 84, 152; imagined, 6
"Comparative Study of Negro and White Children on Melodic and Harmonic Sensitivity," 127 n.8
Concentration camps, 121
Concrete Directions Test, 69
Conduct, efficient, 35
Congress, U.S., 34
Congress of Industrial Organizations (CIO), 18, 19, 54
Congressional Committee, 16
Connally bill, 54
Consciousness, 16, 84, 172
Consent, 3, 5
Conservatives, 11
Conversion, 85
Cooke, Morris, 17, 18, 19, 38; Administrator of the Rural Electrification Administration 17; Philadelphia Director of Public Works, 17; "Who Is Boss in Your Shop?" 41 n.37
Cooney, Joseph, 35
Cooperative Committee on Science Teaching, 144
Copley, Frank, 17
Courtis, S.A., 103
Craig, George, 54
Creveld, Martin Van, 49, 58 n.32
Crozier, William (Chief of Army Ordnance), 34
Crow, Alice and Lester, 157
"Cryptic nostalgia," 88–89
Cubberley, Ellwood, 107, 132, 146 n.2

Cuff, Robert, 38; "Business, the State, and World War I," 41 n.40
Culture, 20
Curriculum, 113, 124, 143, 159
Curriculum of Modern Education, 110 n.17, 111 n.38

Darnall, Orton, 145, 149 n.74
Davis, Kenneth S., *FDR: The Beckoning of Destiny*, 39 n.19
DeBoer, John, 130 n.51
Declaration of Independence, 158
Deleuze, Gilles, 90
Democracy, 5, 11, 54, 68, 108, 117, 118, 144, 154–55, 158
"Democracy Aided by Its Educational Frills," 148 n.39
Democracy and Education, 152
Democrats, 4
Department of the Superintendence of the National Education Association, 101
Desire, 108, 151, 153, 160, 161, 163, 171
"Detection of the Neuropsychiatrically Unfit," 94 n.28
Dewey, John, 107, 132, 143, 151, 152, 153; *Democracy and Education*, 146 n.4
DeWitt, Lt. Gen. J.L., 121
Dictionary of Occupational Titles, 71
Differences, 63, 113, 118, 123, 126; religious, 170
Discipline, 3, 6, 9, 11, 19, 65, 81, 82, 92, 157, 159, 169; business, 9; capitalism, 170; drill, 82; education, 12, 141; effortless, 154; freedom, 174; individualism, 152, 162–63, 174, 175; industry, 117, 145; institutional, 8; mental, 163; military, 10, 81, 84, 159, 170; physical, 13, 81, 82, 84, 136; social, 12; time, 83, 84, 140
Diversity, 20, 62, 114, 117
Division, 9; of labor, 63, 75, 113, 172
Domination, 5, 19
Dorfman, Joseph, 37; *The Economic Mind in American Civilization*, 40 n.35

Dorr, Goldthwaite, 46
Draft, 131, 136
Draft boards, 53, 54, 61, 65, 76 nn.5, 6, 7, 8, 86
Draft dodgers, 65
"Draft Offices Here Swamped by Phone Calls," 146 n.10
"Draft Rejections Due to Youth 'Coddling'," 147 n.31
Draft Welfare Committee, 54
Draftees, 82
Du Bois, W.E.B., 119, 128 n.31
Dykstra, Clarence, 68

Eastern Rate Case, 15
"Economic Measure of School Efficiency," 110 n.3
Economic specialization, 11
Economic structure, 7
Economy: national, 54; peacetime, 50
Education, 6, 10, 11, 12, 70, 99, 135, 136, 140, 151, 152; administration, 102; capitalism, 144; citizenship, 142, 171; college faculty, 142; colleges used by Army and Navy, 140; coordination, 134, 143; desire, 151, 154; discipline, 19, 107; efficiency, 99, 101, 131; goals, 132, 133, 142, 151, 159; institutions, 11; interest, 152, 153; language, 133; management, 102, 153; manufacturing, compared to, 157; mental hygiene, 156; methods, 113, 116, 145–46; organization, 131; physical, 136, 137, 138; programs, 12, 146; public, 4; reform, 131, 132; surveys, 99, 105, 106; systems, 5, 99; testing, 99; vocational, 133, 144; war, 158; women, 144, 145
Education and the Cult of Efficiency, 103, 110 n.4, 111 n.22
"Education and the National Defense," 114
Education for Citizen Responsibilities, 148 n.45
Education for Victory, 135, 147 n.23
Education in Wartime and After, 117, 147 n.24

Educational Lessons from Wartime Training, 147 n.28
Eells, Walter Crosby, 105, 111 n.33
Efficiency, 12, 20, 29, 35, 36, 37, 52, 64, 72, 83, 100–126, 132; education, 100, 106, 131–32, 153; management, 125; mental, 156; national, 36, 116; physical, 136; social, 109, 152, 159; student test, 104; time organization, 107; work, 160
Efficiency in Education, 146 n.7, 157
"Efficiency in the High Schools through the Application of the Principles of Scientific Management," 101, 110 n.8
"Efficiency of Methods in Solving Algebraic Equations," 111 n.21
Efficiency of Naval Militia (U.S. Congress, Senate, National Affairs Committee), 40 n.27
Efficient Democracy, 110 n.5, 111 n.25, 146 n.8
Efficient production, 38, 52
Eisenhower, Milton, 121–22
Elections, 4
"The Elimination of Waste in Education," 111 n.43
Eliot, Charles, 50
Ellis, John, *The Sharp End*, 56 n.6
Employees, government, 17
Engels, Friedrich, 89
Enough and On Time, 55, 60 n.66
"An Essentialist's Platform for the Advancement of American Education," 137, 147 n.32
Eternal return, 173
Ethnic: difference, 115; identity, 115; roots, 115
Ethnic Federation, 115
Ethnicity, 6, 9
Europe, 50
Evans, Holden, 31, 32, 33, 36, 37; "An Analysis of Machine-Shop Methods," 39 n.12, 40 nn.31–32; *One Man's Fight for a Better Navy*, 39 n.6; *Cost Keeping and Scientific Management*, 39 n.7
Examination, 61, 76; physical, 82

Exchange Club, 153
Executive Order 8802, 170
Executive Order 9102, 121

Family, 6
Feiss, Richard, 17, 35, 36
Fenton, Norman, 157, 158, 165 n.37
Field Psychiatry for the General Medical Officer, 79 n.43
Fight for Freedom: College Readings in Wartime, 158
Fighting Men: Baptism of Fire, 88, 94 n.26
Film, Asian, 125, 130 n.55
Flicker, David, 89, 94 n.31
Flora, A.C., 149 n.76
Ford, Henry II, 64
Fortune, 173
Foucault, Michel, 8, 9, 10, 174, 175; *Care of the Self*, 177 n.25; *Discipline and Punish*, 177 n.22; "On the Genealogy of Ethics," 177 n.27
"Four Freedoms," 143
Fourteenth Amendment, 121
Frankfurter, Felix, 15, 33, 39 n.18
Freedman, Harry, 94 n.17
Freedman, Max, *Roosevelt and Frankfurter*, 39 n.18
Freedom, 11, 169
Freidel, Frank, *Franklin D. Roosevelt: The Apprenticeship*, 39 n.19
Fullerton, C.A., 101
Fusfeld, Daniel, *The Economic Thought of Franklin D. Roosevelt and the Origins of the New Deal*, 39 n.9

Gallagher, Lawrence, 149 n.63
Gallup, George, 75, 79 n.57
Gang Process Charts, 47
Garfield, Harry, 50
Gary Plan, 107, 108
Gender, 138
General Education in a Free Society, 107
General Staff, 51
God and Country, 87
Goddard, Henry, 104
Goodrich, Admiral Casper F., 33

Governing of Men, 129 n.45
Grace, Alonzo, 94 n.19, 109; *Educational Lessons from Wartime Training*, 111 n.45, 147 n.28, 149 n.59
Graf, Edward, 85
Greenfield, Kent Roberts et al., *The Organization of Ground Combat Troops*, 56 n.4, 57 n.8
Greenwood, Ronald, 38 n.3
Griffin, John, 165 n.24, 172, 176 n.11

Hall, G. Stanley, 103
Halsey Premium, 34
Hansot, Elisabeth, 102
Harbord, James G., 45
Harrison, Forrest, 95 n.47
Hart, H. Martyn, 101
Hartley, William, 130 n.55
"Harvard Reaffirms the Academic Tradition," 111 n.36
Harvard University, 14
Havighurst, Robert, 149 n.77
Hegel, G.W.F., 127, 152
Henson, C.C., 153
Herge, Henry, 140, 141, 148 n.49, 149 n.60
Hershey, Gen. Lewis (Director of Selective Service), 54, 68
Hicks, Clarence, 157, 165 n.19
Hierarchical systems, 53
"High School Victory Corps Announced," 147 n.23
"Higher Education and the War," 110 n.1
"High-School Science and Mathematics in Relation to the Manpower Problem," 144
Himmelreich, W.F., 155
Hincks, Clarence, 155
Hitler, Adolf, 53
Hollingshead, A.B., "Adjustment to Military Life," 93 n.8
Holt Foundry, 54
Hoskins, Harold, 115, 127 n.10
House Committee on Labor, 36
House Naval Committee, 53
House of Representatives, U.S., 16, 40–41 nn.28, 30, 33, 36, 54

Hovland, Carl I., 95 n.50
"How the Colleges Went to War," 127 n.2, 149 n.67
Huebner, Grover, 127 n.3

Identification, 38, 55, 120, 129 n.35
Identity, 4, 5, 20, 21, 36, 119, 169, 170, 171, 172, 173; gender, 144; Japanese, 171; national, 44, 119; Native American, 171
"Ignorant Collegians Assailed by Moses," 146 n.9
Independence, 19
Individual, 9, 10, 16, 88, 131, 151, 152, 162
Individualism, 3, 6, 8, 10, 12, 19, 20, 21, 81–82, 83, 86, 151, 154–55, 160, 161, 163, 169, 171, 172, 173, 174, 175
Induction, 63–66, 70, 72, 76 n.16, 82, 133, 140; World War I, 61
Industrial: discipline, 53; power, 54; production, 55, 125; recognition, 53; systems of control, 53
Industrial Mobilization Plan (IMP), 51, 52
Industrialization, 5, 47
Industry, 4, 19
Information, 12, 61, 62, 74, 105
Information and Education Division, 91
Institutions: state, 3, 8, 169; studies of, 7
Instruction of the Soldier, 93 n.4
Intercultural education, 12, 113, 116–19
Interests, 38, 44, 143, 153, 159, 160
International Association of Machinists, 37
Interstate Commerce Commission (I.C.C.), 15
Introduction to the Army, 67, 70, 82, 86, 93 n.3, 94 n.23
The Invisible Hand of Planning, 38 n.2
IQ Test, 70
Irwin, Manley, 127 n.7, 130 n.54

"Is Our Present High School System Inefficient?" 110 n.2

Jameson, Augusta, 129 n.49
Japanese internment, 121–23
Johnson, Brig. Gen. Hugh, 61, 64, 69, 76 n.1
Johnson, Lyndon, 53
Justice Department, 121

Kadushin, J., 153
Kaiser, Henry J., 52
Kallen, Horace, 115; "American Unity and Our Foreign-Born Citizens," 127 n.10; *Americans All*, 127 n.9; "National Solidarity and the Jewish Minority," 127 n.11, 128 n.22
Kefauver, Grayson, 117
Kennedy, David, *Over Here*, 59 n.42, 94 n.22
Kennett, Lee, *G. I.: The American Soldier in World War II*, 76 n.10, 93 n.1
Kingdon, Frank, 143
Kitson, Harry, 149 n.84
Klein, David, 156, 165 n.20
Kliebard, Herbert, 109, 111 n.37, 147 n.32
Klineberg, Everett, 129 n.39
Knight, Edgar, 132, 146 n.5
Knolle, Henry, 31
Knowledge, 13, 31, 74; social order, 114
Koike, Masaru, 171
Ku Klux Klan, 116
Kwalwasser Melodic and Harmonic Sensitivity Test, 127 n.8

Labor: forced, 54; managed, 163; unskilled, 52
Labor Management War Production Committee, 53
Ladies' Home Journal, 101
Lake, Ernest, 149 n.79
Language, 13, 86, 118, 128 n.28, 139, 161, 171; Greek, 102–3; Navajo,

171; reading, 124, 144; rule following, 162, 163; self, 162, 172
Lee, Frederick P., 66
Legitimacy, 30; state, 8
Lehigh University, 17
Leighton, Alexander, 129 n.45
Leiserson, William, *Adjusting Immigrant and Industry*, 40 n.34
Leisure, 15
Lewis, John L., 18
Liberals, 11
Liberty ships, 52, 53
Lingenfelter, Mary, 149 n.84
Lloyd George, David, 51, 59 n.44
Los Angeles, California, 4

M Day (Mobilization Day), 51
Magill, Walter, 117, 128 n.26
Management, 4, 44, 47, 75, 153; control, 31, 33, 160; efficient, 38; industrial, 19; methods, 8, 13, 151; power, 30; pressure, 14; school, 100; scientific knowledge, 75; systems, 29; theories, 13; time, 141; workers, 18
Managerial: authority, 46, 90; bureaucracy, 43, 44
Managers, 29, 48, 66, 107
Managers of Virtue, 110 n.14
Manhood, 68, 77 n.28
March-on-Washington Movement, 170, 176 n.4
Mare Island, 31, 32, 33
Marine Corps Hymn, 171
Maritime Commission, 50
Marx, Karl, 7, 170, 176 n.1
Masculinity, 137, 159
Mass production, 51
Maxwell, Sue, 131; "A Birmingham High School Meets the Challenge of War," 146 n.1, 147 n.14
Meaning, 161
Medical Circular No. 1, 73
The Medical Department of the United States Army in the World War, Vol. X: Neuropsychiatry, 79 n.53
Meet Private Pete, 86

Melting pot, 115, 116, 127 n.10, 128 n.17
Mental health, 158
Mental hygiene, 72, 151, 155, 156, 157, 158, 160, 172
Mental Hygiene: A Manual for Teachers, 176 n.11
Mental Hygiene: The Psychology of Personal Adjustments, 165 n.20
Mental Hygiene and Education, 165 n.35
Mental Hygiene Committee of The Vocational Adjustment Bureau for Girls, 156
"Mental Hygiene for the Trainee," 79 n.44
Mental Hygiene in School Practice, 157
Mental Hygiene Project at Kindergarten Level, 1937–1939, 165 n.21
Mental illness, 157
"Mental Induction Standards and Procedures," 79 n.51
Mental process, 151
Mental Qualification Test, 69, 77 n.30
Merchants Association of New York, 36
Merriam, Charles, 10
Merrick, Dwight, 34, 35
Methods of Directing the Work of Government Employees (U.S. Congress, House of Representatives, Committee on Labor), 40 n.33, 40–41 n.36
Meyer, George von L., 33
Midvale Steel Works, 14
Military, 4, 5, 9, 12, 13, 19, 30, 35, 36, 37, 38, 45, 50, 51, 52, 69, 73; institutions, 13; intelligence, 81; life, 64; production, 52; psychiatrists, 91; service, 4, 5, 53, 171; training, 82, 84
Millett, John D., 57 n.11
Mitchell, Theodore, 106
Miyamoto, Shotaro Frank, 121, 129 n.37
Mobility, social, 159
Modernity, 48

Modification: desires, 152; moral, 16
Monk, Ray, 166 n.60
Monroe, James Phinney, 100; *New Demands in Education*, 100, 110 n.6
Monroe Calculating Machine Company, 53
Morale, 92, 156, 158
Moses, Robert, 133
Motives, 151, 156, 157, 160
Mount Vernon Whiskey, 119
Multiculturalists, 4
Munsterberg, Hugo, 72–73
Murray, Philip, 18, 19
Music, 134

Nash, Gerald, 59 n.52
Nation, 3, 6, 19, 20, 43, 50, 55, 56, 64, 109, 123, 173; heritage, 126; organization, 119; racial, 119
National Association for the Advancement of Colored People (NAACP), 117
National Association of Manufacturers, 36
National Citizenship Education Program, 121, 135
National Committee for Mental Hygiene (NCMH), 79 n.53
National Council for the Social Studies, 116
National Defense Act of 1916, 51
National Distillers Products Corporation, 129 n.32
National identity, 5, 9
National industrial economy, 51
National Society for the Promotion of Industrial Education, 100
National War Fitness Conference, 137
Nationalism, 11, 30, 49, 89; culture, 134; education, 114, 117
Nauheim, Fred, 90, 95 n.36
Navajo code talkers, 171, 176 n.8, 176 n.10
Navy, 32, 35, 50, 73, 75, 140, 141
Nazis, 53, 54
Nelson, Daniel, 30; *Frederick Taylor and the Rise of Scientific Management*, 38 n.1, 39 n.13, 41 n.39

Nelson, O.L., 57 n.11
"New Nationalism," 158
New York Navy Yard, 33
Newberry, Truman (Secretary of War), 33
Newton, Isaac, 103
Nietzsche, Friedrich, 3, 9, 29, 162, 163, 170–75, 176 n.14, 177 n.19; *The Gay Science*, 43, 61, 81, 93 n.11, 99, 113, 131, 151, 166 n.54, 169, 173, 176 n.2, 177 n.16
Nippu Jiji, 171
Norfolk Navy Yard, 31
Norton, Charles D., 33

Obedience, 9, 73, 82, 84, 89, 152
O'Connoll, James, 37
Office of Agricultural Defense Regulations, 52
Office of Education, 121
Office of Price Administration, 52
Office of Production Management, 52
Operations Studies, 47
Oral Trade Test Manual, 71
Order: intellectual, 13; location, 19
Organized militia, 35
Organization, 12, 52, 87; control, 51; movement, 107; power, 52; skills, 13; society, 66; space, 107–8
Organization of Ground Combat Troops, 56 n.4
"Our School in Wartime and After," 145
Overholser, Winfred, 72, 73

Palmer, Robert "Mobilization of the Ground Army," 57 n.10
Partnership enterprises, 122
Patten, Simon, 100, 110 n.3
Patterson, Robert (Under Secretary of War), 46, 50; "Responsibility for Military Procurement," 59 n.41
Pearl Harbor, 90
Perkins, Harlow, 34, 166 n.48
Perry, Donald, 120, 129 n.36
Pershing, General John, 45, 46
Person, Harlow, 15, 16
Personality, 157

Philadelphia, Pennsylvania, 14, 33; Department of Public Works, 18; Director of Public Works, 17
Phillips Exeter Academy, 14
Philosophical Investigations, 161
Physical fitness, 137, 139
Physical Fitness Through Physical Education for the Victory Corps, 147 n.22
Physical movement, 161
Physicals, 67, 77 n.22
Planning Commission of the National Council of Teachers of English, 118, 128 n.27
Platoon Plan, 107
The Platoon School in America, 111 n.40
Pluralism, 10, 20, 44, 63, 75, 113, 117, 123
Pocock, J.G.A., 6–7
Polenberg, Richard, *War and Society*, 60 n.64
Political imagination, 5
Pollock, Horatio, 156, 165 n.26
Polls, 75
Posters, 55
"Postwar Educational Controversies," 149 n.85
Postwar objectives, 145, 146
Power, 4; industrial, 54; managerial, 30
Pragmatism, 152
Pre-Induction Training Courses, 144, 147 n.17
Prejudices, 87
Principles of Scientific Management, 31
"Principles of Scientific Management Applied to Teaching Music," 101
Private Pete Eats His Dinner, 86
Process Charts, 47, 48
Procurement, 49; system, 44
Production, 43, 50, 52, 66, 109; knowledge, 12; military, 52; studies, 31
Professional controls, 20
Professionalism, 35, 90
Progress and Educational Perspective, 132
Psychiatrists, 61, 72, 73, 76, 91

Psychiatry, 72, 73, 78 n.42
"Psychiatry at War," 79 n.59
"Psychiatry in the Navy," 79 n.45, 95 n.47
Psychological interview, 67–68
Psychology, 156
"Psychology and the Navy," 79 n.46
"Psychology for the Fighting Man," 158, 165 n.45
Puerto Rican Regiment, 86
Pyle, Ernie, 171, 176 n.9

Quigley, Thomas, 127 n.12

Rabinback, Anson, 14
Race, 6, 9, 12, 78 n.37, 117, 119, 120, 123, 124, 129 n.47, 170
Racial segregation, 86
Racism, 86, 104–5, 118, 119–25, 127 n.8, 138
Railey, Hilton, 90; "Morale in the U.S. Army," 93 n.1
Randolph, A. Philip, 170
Rational administration, 48, 49
Read, Cecil, 103, 111 n.21
Reagan, Ronald, 11, 87
Reception, 82
Recognition of value, 6, 11, 30, 36, 71, 119–20, 124, 125, 126, 173, 175, 176 n.15
Recruits, 61
Reform, 152
Regimentation, 19
Registration, 11, 62, 63, 64, 68, 133, 134; form, 65
Reinert, Paul, 146 n.5
Relativism, 11, 71, 119
Religion, 6
Relocation centers, 122, 123
Report of Mental Status, 69
Reports of the Chief of Ordnance, 39 n.22
Research Board, 85
Research Branch of the Information and Education Division of the United States Army, 74, 79 n.58, 90, 170
Resistance 91; to draft, 147 n.12; to training, 85

Revolution, mental, 16, 17
Rockwell, Norman, 143
Rogin, Michael, 128 n.30
Roosevelt, Franklin, 33, 35, 39 n.18, 46, 51, 54, 55, 65, 117, 136, 170
Roosevelt, Theodore, 33, 37, 158
Rosanoff, A.J., 156
Rose, Arnold, *The Social Structure of the Army*, 58 n.30
Rowntree, Leonard, 137
Ruch, Giles, 110 n.19
Rule of thumb, 48
Rules, Army, 48
Russell, James E., 101
Russell, William, 135
Russia, 50

Saipan, 4
Samuel, Lawrence, 176 n.7
San Diego, California, Board of Education, 145
San Francisco, California, 31
San Juan, Puerto Rico, 4
Sanka Coffee, 120, 129 n.33
Saturday Evening Post, 101
Savage, Howard, 105, 111 n.31
Scheduling, 52
Schibsby, Marian, 127 n.14
Schmidt (Henry Knolle), 31
School Administrators' Conference, 145
Schools, 4; military preparation, 135
Schultz, Frank, 109
Scientific knowledge, 65
Scientific management, 4, 10, 15, 16, 17, 18, 19, 29, 31, 32, 34, 35, 37, 38, 47, 58 n.35, 74, 91, 107; education, 100, 101, 102, 152, 156, 157, 160; unification of perspective, 159–60
Scientific Management in Action, 39 n.21, 40 n.24, 47 n.9
Sears, Jesse, 111 n.50, 132; *An Autobiography*, 146 n.3
The Second World War, Vol. 2, 56 n.3
Selective Service, 53, 54, 55, 56, 63, 66, 67, 68, 70, 73, 76 n.9, 77 n.25, 131, 137

Self-control, 146, 155
Senate, U.S., 35
Services of Supply (ASF), 46
Sexual desire, 68, 69
Sexual difference, 68
Sexual perversion, 69
Shaffer, L.F., 157
Shalloo, J.P., 128 n.15
Sherman, Mandel, 165 n.35
Skills, organization, 13
Skocpol, Theda, 8
Smith, Brig. Gen. Ben, 53
Smith, R. Eberton, *The Army and Economic Mobilization*, 58 n.25, 59 n.39
Smith-Connally bill, 54
Snedden, David, 102, 110 n.13
Social control, 11, 20, 36, 75, 155
Social knowledge, 4
Social roles, 20
Social science, 66, 74, 105
Society to Promote the Science of Management, 17
Soldier, 19, 55, 68, 83, 89, 91
"Soldiering" of labor, 14, 88
Somervell, Brig. Gen. Brehon B., 46, 52
Soul, 174
Spanish-American War, 30, 35, 38
Spaulding, Frank, 102, 104, 111 n.24
Special Training Units, 86
Standardization, 108; education, 106; physical, 62, 66, 67; physical movement, 160; Taylorite, 12
Stanford University School of Education Faculty, 109, 113, 114, 117, 127 n.1, 130 n.52, 142, 147 n.24; *Education in Wartime and After*, 111 n.48, 128 n.19, 129 n.48, 130 n.56, 148 nn.37, 47, 149 n.72, 166 n.47
"Stanford-Binet" test, 104
State, 3; institutions, 5, 18; Marxist descriptions of, 11; power, 4
State control, 52
Sterilization, 105
Stoddard, George, 110 n.19
Stonequist, Everett, 129 n.38
The Story of Private Pete, 86
Stouffer, Samuel et al., *The American Soldier*, 79 n.50, 94 n.13, 176 n.3

Strike breaking, 54
Strikers, 53, 54, 60 n.65
Studies: mental, 62; physical, 62; statistical, 105
Style, 174
Subjectivity, 6, 9, 11, 169, 172; political, 4
Sullivan, Harry Stack, 72, 73
Supplies, 46
Support staff, 44
Surveillance, 48, 93
"Surveys of the Office of the Under Secretary of War," 58 n.19
Suzzalo, Henry, 105
Swastika, 59 n.54
Symonds, Percival, 157, 165 n.33

Taft, William Howard, 33
Task management, 40 n.29
Task work, 30
Taylor, Charles, 176 n.15
Taylor, Frederick Winslow, 8, 12, 13, 16–19, 20, 29, 30, 32, 33, 35, 41 n.38, 46, 47, 62, 73, 74, 83, 101, 106, 107, 132, 151, 153, 159; theories, 37, 38; *The Principles of Scientific Management*, 38 n.4; *Shop Management*, 40 n.29, 57 n.9, 76 n.2, 88, 94 n.26, 111 n.35, 166 n.49
Taylor, Joseph, 104
Taylor Society's *Bulletin*, 17
"The Taylor System in Government Shops," 39 n.8
Taylorism, 4, 6, 10, 11, 13, 17, 19, 34, 37, 48, 63, 123; body discipline, 151; consciousness, 89, 91, 160; consultants, 12; education, 103, 106, 132; efficiency, 34; French adoption of, 57 n.13; information, 74; methods, 34, 37, 38, 88, 103; reorganization, 32, 172; resistance, 33; space, 108; standard tools, 104; subjectivity, 175; times, 107, 172
Terman, Lewis, 104, 111 n.27
Testing, 30, 61–76, 77 n.18, 103; education, 99, 126; mental, 81; military, 126; racism, 78 n.37; social scientific, 105; student efficiency, 104

Tests and Measurements in High School Instruction, 110 n.19
Textbooks, 104
Thomas, Lawrence, 148 n.46
Thompson, C. Bertrand, *The Theory and Practice of Scientific Management*, 39 n.20
Thorndike and Ayres Handwriting Scale, 103
Thorndike and Hillegas English Competency Test, 103
Time, 17, 107; schedule, 19, 93, 172; school day, 109; studies, 31, 32, 34, 35, 62
Todd Shipyards, 52
Tolerance, 117, 125
Total war, 49, 55, 56, 58 n.35, 117
Totalitarianism, 125
Towne, Henry, 40 n.30
Towne-Halsey Plan, 39–40 n.23
Training, 144, 147 n.19; manual, 71; specialized, 88
Tyack, David, 102, 110 n.14; *Managers of Virtue*, 146 n.6

Ueda, Reed, 116, 128 n.18
Understanding, 161
Uniforms, 55
Union busting, 54
Union for Democratic Action, 143
United Nations, 125
United States Office of Education, 135, 144
Unity: democratic, 118; musical, 115, 127 nn.8, 10
University: education, 140; utilization, 140
University studies, 106

V-12 program, 140–41
Van Nice, C.R., 138, 148 n.39, 149 n.75, 159, 166 n.46
Veterans Administration, 72
Victory Corps, 135, 138, 147 n.23
Virtue, 29, 30
Vocational Adjustment Bureau for Girls, 156
Vocations for Boys, 145, 149 n.84

Wald, Priscilla, 7
War, 9, 30, 36, 38, 51; agencies, 37
War and Society in North America, 41 n.40
War Department, 44, 45, 46, 47, 52, 90, 140
War Labor Policies Board, 33
War Manpower Commission, 53, 137, 139
"War Pattern for Teachers," 149 n.63
War production, 51
War Production Board (WPB), 49, 50, 52; General Administration Orders 2-23 and 2-33, 50
War program, 62
War Relocation Authority (WRA), 121, 122, 123
War Resource Administration, 52
War technology, 153
Wartime College Training Programs of the Armed Services, 148 n.49, 149 n.60
Wartime Production Controls, 59 n.37, 62, 76 n.3
"Wartime Program for Our Colleges," 148 n.54
Washington, D.C., 51, 65
Watertown Arsenal, 34, 35, 57 n.9
Watson, Elwood, 137
Weber, Max, 3, 5, 8, 9, 92; *Economy and Society*, 56 nn.1, 2
Weiss, Paul, 89
Western Defense Command, 121
Wheeler, C.B., "Questionnaire—Scientific Management," 39 n.23
Willard, Daniel, 15
Williams, Major C.C., 34
Wilson, Woodrow, 65
Wirt, William, 107
Wittgenstein, Ludwig, 161, 162, 163; *On Certainty*, 166 n.56; *Philosophical Investigations*, 166 n.51; *Tractatus Logico-Philosophicus*, 166 n.59
Women, 53
Wood, Gen. Leonard, 62
Work, 43; manual, 145; rationalization, 14
Work Simplification, 47
Work Simplification Officer, 47
"Work-or-fight" order, 53
Workplace, 133
Works Progress Administration, 55, 121
World War I, 9, 17, 34, 37, 38, 45, 63, 65, 69, 72, 73, 143; Americanization programs, 114, 118; Army, 86; Student Army Training Corps (SATC), 139
World War II, 4, 6, 9–13, 19–20, 30, 37–38, 43, 45, 50, 51, 56, 61, 62, 69, 73, 75, 76, 82, 86, 99, 108, 109, 118, 126, 144; Army, 86
WRA: A Story in Human Conservation, 129 n.46
Wrege, Charles, *Frederick W. Taylor*, 38 n.3
Wright, Gordon, 81; *Ordeal of Total War*, 93 n.2
Wright, J.C., *Efficiency in Education*, 146 n.8, 157, 165 n.34

Yale & Towne Manufacturing Company, 36
Yerkes, Robert, 104
Young, Donald, 128 n.15
Young, Kimball, 115
"Youth and War," 149 n.58

Zangwell, Israel, 116; *The Melting-Pot*, 128 n.17
Zipf, George Kingsley, 115, 127 n.8
Zizek, Slavoj, 129 n.35
Zook, George F., 127 n.2, 149 n.67

About the Author

CHAR ROONE MILLER is Assistant Professor of Government and Politics at George Mason University. Professor Miller's articles have appeared in edited collections and scholarly journals.

Printed in the USA
CPSIA information can be obtained
at www.ICGtesting.com
JSHW081739081124
73243JS00001B/9